A Brief History of Archaeology

Classical Times to the Twenty-First Century

Brian M. Fagan

University of California, Santa Barbara

PEARSON

Prentice
Hall

Upper Saddle River, New Jersey 07458

Library of Congress Cataloging-in-Publication Data

FAGAN, BRIAN M.
A brief history of archaeology : classical times to the twenty-first century / Brian Fagan.
p. cm.
Includes bibliographical references and index.
ISBN 0–13–177698–3 (pbk.)
1. Archaeology—History.   I. Title.

CC100.F335 2005
930.1'09—dc22   2003062312

AVP/Publisher: Nancy Roberts
Editorial Assistant: Lee Peterson
Senior Marketing Manager: Marissa Feliberty
Marketing Assistant: Adam Laitman
Production Editor: Joan Stone
Manufacturing Buyer: Ben Smith
Cover Art Director: Jayne Conte
Cover Design: Bruce Kenselaar
Director, Image Resource Center: Melinda Reo
Manager, Rights and Permissions: Zina Arabia
Interior Image Specialist: Beth Brenzel
Image Permission Coordinator: Carolyn Gauntt
Photo Researcher: Francelle Carapetyan
Composition: Interactive Composition Corporation
Printer/Binder: Courier Companies, Inc.
Cover Printer: Phoenix Color Corp.
Typeface: 10/12 Palatino
Cover Photo: John Egan, Irish-American, 1810–1882, © 1850. "Panorama of the
Monumental Grandeur of the Mississippi Valley." Tempera on lightweight fabric,
90 3 4176 in. (228.6 3 10607.1 cm). The Saint Louis Art Museum.

Acknowledgments for photographs from other sources and reproduced,
with permission, in this textbook appear on pages 254–55.

Pearson Education LTD.
Pearson Education Singapore, Pte. Ltd
Pearson Education, Canada, Ltd
Pearson Education–Japan
Pearson Education Australia PTY, Limited

Pearson Education North Asia Ltd
Pearson Educación de Mexico, S.A. de C.V.
Pearson Education Malaysia, Pte. Ltd
Pearson Education, Upper Saddle River, NJ

10 9 8 7 6 5 4 3
ISBN 0-13-177698-3

The stories scientists tell are not simply bedtime tales. They place us in the world, and they can force us to alter the way we think and what we do.

Thomas Levenson, *Ice Time*, 1989

Antiquarian Collecting

        └─> Archaeology as a
                Science
              -Obstacles - Church's
                       Religious Doctrine
                   - Earth Created
                         4004 BC
            - Findings/Cultural
               Material
               Dispute church's position

19th Cent.   - Search for The Earliest
                 Civilizations

contents

9 *Archaeology Coming of Age, 1920 to 1940* 139

10 *Culture History and Beyond* 156

11 *Radiocarbon Dating and World Prehistory* 175

preface

Lost civilizations, richly adorned royal burials, overgrown cities emerging miraculously from clinging rain forest: Archaeology has a long and romantic history of spectacular discovery. But there is much more to archaeology's history than the finding of palaces and ancient states. I would go so far as to say that you cannot understand today's archaeology without a thorough knowledge of its beginnings, and of the ideas that nurtured it.

Archaeology's achievements have been remarkable. Over the past century and a half, archaeologists have pushed back the story of human origins to a time more than 2.5 million years ago. They have traced the origins of modern humans—ourselves—to tropical Africa more than 150,000 years ago; chronicled the beginnings of agriculture; and reconstructed the minutest details of ancient life. The same 150 years have seen archaeology turn from an amateur pursuit into a sophisticated, multidisciplinary science in the hands of thousands of professional specialists. This history has unfolded against a background of changing intellectual and social environments: from the philosophical speculations of classical writers, and versions of human origins based on the Old Testament, to elaborate theories of multilinear evolution, cultural ecology, and the so-called "postprocessual archaeology" of the 1990s. This book is a brief introduction to the diverse strands of the history of archaeology, both intellectual and nonintellectual. It's a history that melds stories of compelling personalities and eminent archaeologists with accounts of spectacular and not-so-spectacular discoveries, and with ideas about the interpretation of our past.

A Brief History of Archaeology is a journey through the intriguing highways and byways of a discipline that has been a science for less than a century. Books like this are hard to write, because they combine people, discoveries, and ideas in ways that can easily become a confusing mélange of information. For this reason, I have chosen to write this book as a simple narrative, passing from archaeologists and their discoveries to changing ideas about the past in as seamless a way as possible.

Chapter 1 traces the beginnings of archaeology to the curiosity of Babylonian monarchs and the philosophical musings of classical writers. We show how theological beliefs limited archaeological inquiry until the nineteenth century, and describe early antiquarian researches, including the first excavations at the Roman cities of Herculaneum and Pompeii. Chapter 2 discusses the establishment of human antiquity in the mid-nineteenth century, tracing the roots of the ideas that led to the development of archaeology as we know it today. In Chapters 3 to 6, we describe the beginnings of archaeology in Egypt, Mesopotamia, and Central America. We also discuss the Three Age System for dividing prehistory and the simplistic ideas of linear human progress that dominated nineteenth-century thinking about the prehistoric past. We visit Heinrich Schliemann's excavations at Homeric Troy and describe the beginnings of biblical archaeology. Chapter 6 ends with the work of Flinders Petrie along the Nile and that of Arthur Evans on the Palace of Knossos on Crete after 1900. Their researches ushered in a new era, which saw a new emphasis on artifacts, dating, and science.

Chapter 7 traces the roots of such efforts in Europe and the Americas, combining a new emphasis on stratigraphic observation and dating with new discoveries in the Andes and Mesoamerica. Chapters 8 to 10 describe archaeology's coming of age. This was an era of spectacular discoveries like the tomb of Pharaoh Tutankhamun and Ur's royal cemetery, but also of much more sophisticated excavation methods and new ideas for explaining and understanding the remote past. Chapter 10 carries the story into the 1940s and 1950s, with the development of a sophisticated culture history in the Americas and the first efforts at ecological and settlement archaeology, as well as Julian Steward's development of cultural ecology. The story continues in Chapter 11, with the development of radiocarbon dating and increasingly pointed critiques of culture history. We also trace the beginnings of multidisciplinary research, and of salvage archaeology, and the development of world prehistory as a viable intellectual concept in the late 1950s.

Chapters 12 and 13 carry the story from the 1960s through the new millennium, beginning with the intellectual ferment of the 1960s, which saw the birth of the so-called "new archaeology," today called processual archaeology. We assess its significance and its legacy. Chapter 13 surveys the many new theoretical approaches that developed, and are still developing, as a reaction to processualism, as well as other developments such as cultural resource management and the study of an engendered past. Finally, Chapter 14 takes a look at the developing archaeology of the future.

Guides to Further Reading at the end of each chapter provide sources for additional research. A Glossary of Archaeological Sites and Cultural Terms at the end of the book gives additional information on the more important sites mentioned in the text.

This book is not a history of archaeological theory, nor is it a history of archaeology by personality or discovery. It's an attempt to provide a balanced, and, I hope, entertaining account of the history of a relative newcomer to the world of science. As these pages will testify, the discovery of the prehistory of humankind ranks among the greatest scientific achievements of the nineteenth and twentieth centuries. The perspective is international, for I believe that archaeology is a global enterprise, not just a narrowly focused view of the past based on, say, North America, Europe, or the eastern Mediterranean.

A Brief History is written in as jargon-free a style as possible and is aimed, in general terms, at readers with no experience of archaeology whatsoever. However, beginners might be advised to acquire a short introduction to archaeological method and theory if they are hazy on the basic principles of the subject.

Acknowledgments

This book has benefited greatly from the many generations of students who have taken courses on the history of archaeology from me. I am deeply grateful for their encouragement and interest. Several colleagues reviewed the draft of the manuscript. I appreciate their advice and criticisms: Elliot M. Abrams, Ohio University; I. Randolph Daniel, Jr., East Carolina University; Glen H. Doran, Florida State University; Christian E. Downum, Northern Arizona University; Randall McGuire, Binghamton University; Karen Muir, Columbus State Community College; and Edward Staski, New Mexico State University.

Lastly, my thanks to my editor, Nancy Roberts, and to her assistant, Lee Peterson, for their constant encouragement and many kindnesses. The production staff at Prentice Hall turned a complex manuscript into an attractive book and did all they could to minimize unexpected difficulties.

As always, I would be most grateful for criticisms, comments, or details of new work, e-mailed to me at **brian@brianfagan.com**

Brian Fagan
Santa Barbara, California

author's note

Glossaries

Key cultural terms and sites are highlighted in **bold** type in the text and defined in the Glossary at the end of the book.

Dates

The following conventions are used in the text:

- Dates before 10,000 years ago are expressed in years Before Present (B.P.).
- Dates after 10,000 years ago are expressed in years Before Christ (B.C.) or Anno Domini (A.D.).

Another common convention is B.C.E./C.E. (Before Common Era/Common Era), which is not employed in this book. By scientific convention, "present" is A.D. 1950.

Please note that all radiocarbon dates and potassium-argon dates should be understood to have a plus and minus factor that is omitted from this book in the interests of clarity. They are statistical estimates. Where possible, radiocarbon dates have been calibrated with coral and tree-ring chronologies, which add a substantial element of accuracy. For tree-ring calibration of radiocarbon dates, see *Radiocarbon*, 1998.

Measurements

In accordance with the publisher's house rules, all measurements are in metric values, with miles, yards, feet and inches, and pound equivalents added in parentheses.

maps

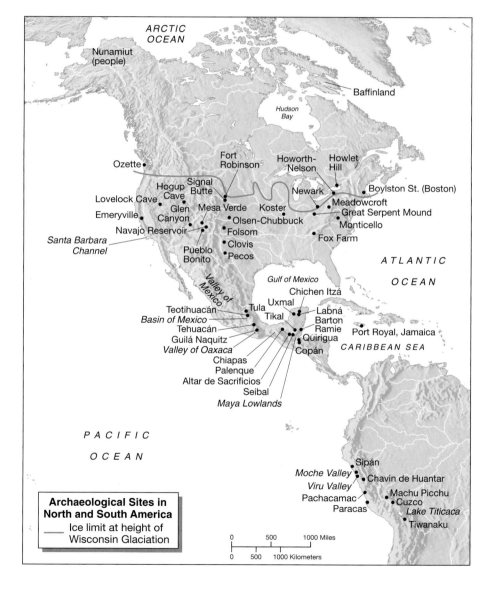

ARCTIC OCEAN

Nunamiut (people)

Baffinland

Hudson Bay

Ozette
Fort Robinson
Howorth-Nelson
Howlet Hill

Hogup Cave
Signal Butte
Newark
Boylston St. (Boston)

Lovelock Cave
Glen Canyon
Mesa Verde
Koster
Meadowcroft

Emeryville
Navajo Reservoir
Olsen-Chubbuck
Great Serpent Mound
Monticello

Santa Barbara Channel
Folsom
Fox Farm

Pueblo Bonito
Clovis
Pecos

ATLANTIC OCEAN

Valley of Mexico

Gulf of Mexico
Chichen Itzá

Teotihuacán
Tula
Uxmal

Basin of Mexico
Tikal
Labná
Barton Ramie

Tehuacán
Quirigua
Port Royal, Jamaica

Guilá Naquitz
Copán

Valley of Oaxaca

Chiapas

Palenque

Altar de Sacrificios

Seibal

Maya Lowlands

CARIBBEAN SEA

PACIFIC OCEAN

Sipán
Moche Valley
Chavin de Huantar
Viru Valley
Machu Picchu
Pachacamac
Cuzco
Paracas
Lake Titicaca
Tiwanaku

Archaeological Sites in North and South America
____ Ice limit at height of Wisconsin Glaciation

0   500   1000 Miles

0   500   1000 Kilometers

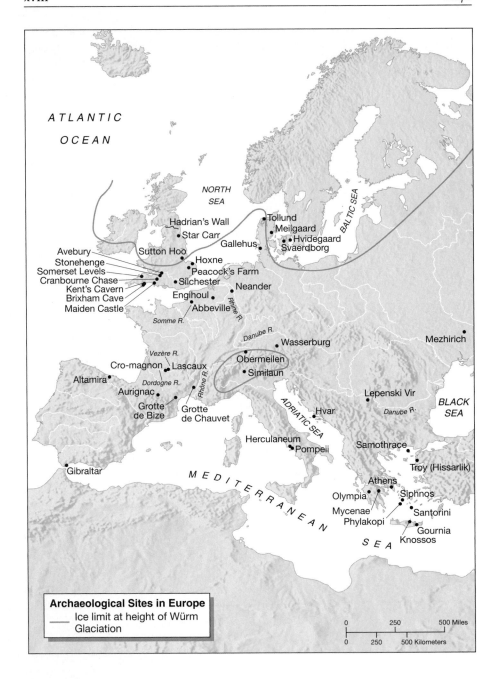

Archaeological Sites in Europe
Ice limit at height of Würm Glaciation

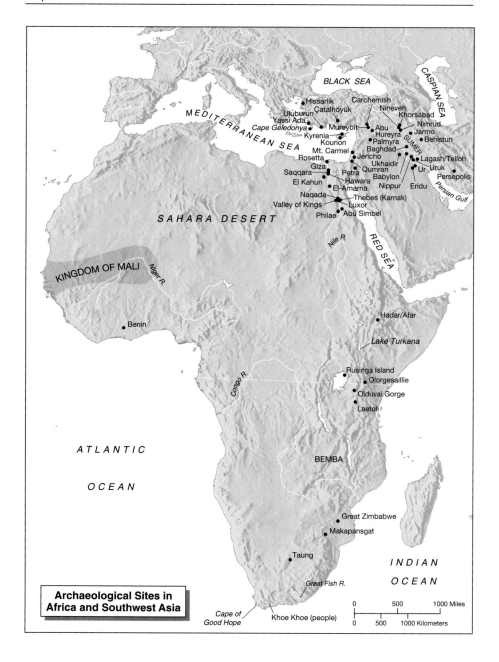

Archaeological Sites in Africa and Southwest Asia

BLACK SEA

CASPIAN SEA

MEDITERRANEAN SEA

Hissarlik
Carchemish
Nineveh
Khorsabad
Çatalhöyük
Nimrud
Uluburun
Jarmo
Yassi Ada
Behistun
Cape Geledonya
Mureybit
Abu Hureyra
Kyrenia
Palmyra
SUMER
Kourion
Baghdad
Mt. Carmel
Jericho
Lagash/Telloh
Rosetta
Ukhaidir
Uruk
Giza
Qumran
Ur
Persepolis
Saqqara
Petra
Babylon
El Kahun
Hawara
Nippur
Eridu
Naqada
El-Amarna
Thebes (Karnak)
Valley of Kings
Luxor
Philae
Abu Simbel

Persian Gulf

SAHARA DESERT

Nile R.

RED SEA

KINGDOM OF MALI

Niger R.

Benin

Hadar/Afar

Lake Turkana

Congo R.

Rusinga Island
Olorgesaillie
Olduvai Gorge
Laetoli

ATLANTIC

OCEAN

BEMBA

Great Zimbabwe
Makapansgat

Taung

INDIAN

OCEAN

Great Fish R.

Cape of Good Hope

Khoe Khoe (people)

0	500	1000 Miles
0	500	1000 Kilometers

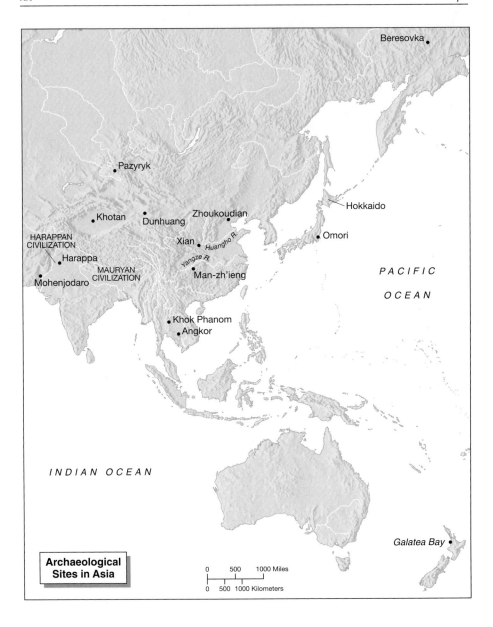

Beresovka •

Pazyryk •

• Khotan   • Dunhuang   Zhoukoudian •   — Hokkaido

HARAPPAN
CIVILIZATION   Xian •   • Omori
                                    Huangho R.
• Harappa   MAURYAN   *Yangze R.*   *PACIFIC*
              CIVILIZATION   • Man-zh'ieng
• Mohenjodaro   *OCEAN*

                        • Khok Phanom
                        • Angkor

INDIAN OCEAN

                                                    Galatea Bay •

**Archaeological
Sites in Asia**

```
0      500    1000 Miles
0   500  1000 Kilometers
```

major events

in the History of Archaeology from A.D. 1600

This summary of major discoveries and events makes no claim to be complete.

1615–26   Pietra della Valle visits Mesopotamia and brings back cuneiform tablets.

1642   James Lightfoot proclaims that the world was created at 9 A.M. on October 23 in 4004 B.C.

1649   John Aubrey gallops into Avebury.

1717   Michele Mercati's *Metallotheca* published more than a century after his death.

1718   Society of Antiquaries of London founded.

1723   William Stukeley at Stonehenge.

1738   First excavations at Herculaneum and Pompeii.

1764   Publication of Winklemann's *History of the Art of Antiquity.*

1765   Carsten Niebuhr at Persepolis.

1784   Thomas Jefferson excavates a mound in Virginia and makes stratigraphic observations.

1797   John Frere discovers a hand ax and bones of extinct animals at Hoxne, England.

1798   Napoleon's expedition to Egypt.

1799   Discovery of the Rosetta Stone.

1811   Claudius James Rich at Babylon.

1816   Three Age System introduced in the National Museum, Copenhagen.

1817   Giovanni Belzoni in Egypt.

1822   Champollion deciphers Egyptian hieroglyphs.

1825   Father MacEnery at Kent's Cavern, England.

1831–36   Voyage of the *Beagle.*

1837	Publication of John Gardiner Wilkinson's *Manners and Customs of the Ancient Egyptians.*
1839	Stephens and Catherwood's first expedition to the Maya ruins.
1840	Emile Botta appointed French consul in Mosul.
1843	Botta excavates Khorsabad.
1844	Austen Henry Layard at Nimrud and Nineveh.
1845	Ephraim Squier and Edwin Davis survey Ohio earthworks.
1854	Ferdinand Keller excavates Obermeilen, a Swiss lake dwelling.
1855	Smithsonian Institution opens to the public in Washington, D.C.
1856	Publication of Haven's *Archaeology of the United States.* Discovery of the Neanderthal skull, Germany.
1858	Excavations by Pengelly at Kent's Cavern, England.
1859	Establishment of the antiquity of humankind. Publication of Darwin's *Origin of Species.*
1863	Lartet and Christy begin their researches in French caves Le Moustier and La Madeleine.
1865	Charles Warren at Jerusalem. Publication of Lubbock's *Prehistoric Times.*
1868	Discovery of Cro-Magnon burials.
1871	Schliemann at Hissarlik (Troy). Carl Mauch at Great Zimbabwe.
1872	George Smith deciphers the Flood Tablets.
1875	German excavations at Olympia, Greece.
1876	Schliemann discovers shaft graves at Mycenae.
1879	Frank Cushing arrives at Zuñi pueblo, New Mexico. Discovery of Altamira cave paintings.
1880	Adolph Bandelier arrives in the American Southwest. General Pitt-Rivers starts excavations on Cranborne Chase, England.
1881	Flinders Petrie surveys the Pyramids of Giza, Egypt.
1888	Richard Wetherill visits the Cliff Palace at Mesa Verde, Colorado.
1892	Eugene Dubois discovers *Pithecanthropus* in Java.

1899	Robert Koldeway at Babylon.
1900	Arthur Evans excavates the Palace of Minos at Knossos, Crete.
1901	Palaeolithic art authenticated.
1905	Max Uhle at Emeryville shell mound, California.
1906	Aurel Stein at the Caves of a Thousand Buddhas, Dunhuang, China.
1911	Hiram Bingham at Machu Picchu, Peru.
1921	Discovery of *Homo erectus* at Zhoukoudian, China.
1922	Tomb of Tutankhamun found by Lord Carnarvon and Howard Carter. Leonard Woolley begins Ur excavations.
1924	Identification of the Harappan civilization, Pakistan. Raymond Dart discovers *Australopithecus africanus.* Alfred Kidder's *Introduction to Southwestern Archaeology* published.
1926	Folsom excavations document Paleo-Indians in North America.
1929	Gertrude Caton-Thompson establishes African origin of Great Zimbabwe.
1934	Mortimer Wheeler at Maiden Castle, England.
1938	Gerhard Bersu at Little Woodbury, England.
1939	Sutton Hoo ship burial discovered.
1940	Lascaux cave paintings discovered.
1944	Mortimer Wheeler becomes director general of antiquities in India.
1946	Gordon Willey begins Virú Valley survey, Peru.
1947	Discovery of the Dead Sea Scrolls, Jordan.
1948	Walter Taylor's *A Study of Archaeology* published.
1949	Star Carr excavations, England. Willard Libby announces radiocarbon dating.
1950	Tollund man discovered, Denmark.
1951	Kathleen Kenyon at Jericho, Jordan. Robert Braidwood at Jarmo, Iraq.

1953   Piltdown fake exposed.

1959   Mary Leakey discovers *Zinjanthropus boisei,* Olduvai Gorge, Tanzania.

1961   *Homo habilis* discovered at Olduvai Gorge.
            Grahame Clark's *World Prehistory* published.

1962   Lewis Binford espouses a "new archaeology."

1974   *Australopithecus afarensis* found in Hadar, Ethiopia.
            Discovery of Emperor Qin Shihuangdi's terra-cotta regiment, China.

1978   Mary Leakey unearths the Laetoli footprints, Tanzania.

1984   Excavation of the Uluburun ship, Turkey.

1989   Lords of Sipán discovered, Peru.

1991   Discovery of the Ice Man, Similaun, Italian Alps.

1994   Discovery of the Grotte de Chauvet art, France.
            Finding of *Ardipithecus ramidus,* Ethiopia.

2002   Discovery of *Sahelanthropus tchadensis,* Chad, Central Africa.
            Discovery of the Avebury Archer, England.

chapter 1

"The Backward Looking Curiosity"

Ole Worm's museum, complete with fossils, seashells, human artifacts, and natural history specimens.

He . . . loves all things . . . the better for being mouldy and worm eaten. . . .
A great admirer he is of the rust of old monuments, and reads only those
characters where time hath eaten the letters.

John Earle on antiquarians, *Microcosmographie*, 1628

The tomb robbers had struck gold in 1989—a magnificent funerary mask, fine ornaments, and beautifully fashioned clay vessels. For weeks, they had been digging surreptitiously into the adobe pyramid on the banks of the Lambayeque River near **Sipán** on Peru's North Coast, home of the ancient **Moche** civilization. Rumors of great wealth swept the community. Fortunately for archaeology, reports of the sensational finds reached the ears of local archaeologist Walter Alva. He rushed to the pyramid, posted armed guards, and saved the richly decorated burials of hitherto unknown Moche lords. For months, Alva and a team of conservators labored over not one but three royal burials, deposited in elaborate brick burial chambers, one above the other. The result was a triumph of fine-grained archaeological excavation, and of meticulous conservation of artifacts so fragile that they had to be lifted in blocks, then separated in the laboratory.

The Lords of Sipán lay in their full ceremonial regalia, glittering with gold and silver, carrying scepters, every part of their elaborate costumes reflecting a Moche world where the realms of the living and the dead flowed seamlessly one into the other. We know from painted scenes on Moche pots that these elaborately costumed lords presided over military campaigns and ceremonies involving the sacrifice of prisoners of war. On rare occasions, the Moche warrior-priests would appear in public dressed in all their glory. They would stand atop a pyramid, glittering brilliantly in the sun, the living personification of gods, showing themselves but rarely to the waiting crowds in the plaza far below (Figure 1.1).

The Lords of Sipán are one of the greatest archaeological discoveries of all time and represent a triumph of science over treasure hunting. They epitomize the romance of archaeology, which has captivated people for centuries.

To many people, archaeology is a world of grinning skeletons and gold-rich pharaohs, of soaring pyramids and lost civilizations. It's a realm of

Figure 1.1
A mannequin wearing a replica of a Lord of Sipán's ceremonial regalia.

pith-helmeted archaeologists, frenzied searches for mummies, and the kind of Indiana Jones–like adventures beloved of Hollywood. Nothing could be further from the truth. The early days of archaeology were indeed times when you could find a lost civilization in a week of searching or unearth that rarity of rarities, an undisturbed royal tomb. Today's archaeologist is no adventurer, but a highly skilled scientist. The development of archaeology as a serious science was one of the greatest scientific triumphs of the twentieth century. This book tells the remarkable, and often colorful, story of how archaeology changed from a pursuit based on curiosity about the human past into a pastime of high adventure, and then into a science.

Back in the eighteenth century, an anonymous antiquarian (a person who studies remains of the past) lightheartedly described archaeology as "the science of rubbish." Archaeologists are indeed concerned with ancient garbage heaps—with the discarded remains of human behavior; but it's perhaps more accurate to describe archaeology as "the backward looking curiosity." Whatever the methods used, most archaeology is, and has been, driven by a profound curiosity about the human past. This chapter traces the beginnings of archaeology in the curiosity of an obscure Babylonian monarch.

Beginnings

The past is always around us, offering encouragement, warning of danger, laying out precedents for the future. Material remains of ancient times surround us on every side—the Pyramids of **Giza** in Egypt, the stone circles of **Stonehenge** in southern England, the great city of **Teotihuacán** in highland Mexico (Figure 1.2). This is the realm of archaeology—the scientific study of ancient humanity in all its remarkable diversity from our origins in tropical Africa over 2.5 million years ago to the threshold of modern times.

I'm not talking about the past of mythic origins, chanted about by priests and tribal shamans, which defined a world of legendary creators and established the familiar order of things. I'm concerned here with a linear past, defined and described by archaeological research and Western science.

All societies have their own ways of explaining human existence and the world around them. Many Christians believe in the literal historical truth of Genesis 1, in which God created the world and all living things, including humans, in six days. To many societies, the cosmos was a series of layers, often fashioned by primordial waters. The Quiche Maya *Popol Vuh*, a book of

Figure 1.2   The Pyramids of Giza, Egypt.

prophecy and divination, describes the dark stillness at the beginning:

> There was not yet one person, one animal. . . . Only the sky alone is there; the face of the earth is not clear. Only the sea alone is pooled under all the sky; there is nothing whatever gathered together. It is at rest, not a single thing stirs. (Tedlock 1996:127)

Most societies have been content with their legendary origins. For example, we know that the biblical account of the Creation owes much to ancient Mesopotamian tribal lore passed from generation to generation for many centuries before being set down on clay tablets sometime after 3000 B.C. Babylonian kings of the sixth century B.C. were the first to dig in search of the past. King Nabonidus was an undistinguished ruler, remarkable only for his intense interest in ancient religious beliefs. He dug into, and restored, the great temple-pyramid (or ziggurat) of the **Sumerian** city of **Ur,** where he was delighted to unearth the inscriptions of long-forgotten monarchs. His daughter En-nigaldi-Nanna dug for years into another Sumerian shrine at the city of **Agade** without success. Then a heavy rainstorm cut a deep gully through the crumbling mound and revealed the foundations of the shrine. The discovery "made the king's heart glad and caused his countenance to brighten" (Oates 1979:162). En-nigaldi-Nanna's finds were displayed in a special room in the royal palace.

The Babylonians were well aware that history, and perhaps rich treasure, lay beneath their feet; but Nabonidus can hardly be called an archaeologist. Nor could the Greek traveler Herodotus, who visited Egypt in the fifth century B.C. He wrote a detailed and gossipy account of the Pyramids of Giza and the ancient Egyptians. He spent many hours talking to local priests, from whom he learned about mummification and how the embalmers drew the brain of the deceased through the nostrils with an iron hook. Herodotus was well aware of the importance of Egyptian civilization. Like other Greeks, and the Romans after them, he believed that the Nile Valley was the ultimate cradle of all civilization. Herodotus was no scholar and no archaeologist. He was a sucker for even the most outrageous tales, solemnly proclaiming that the pharaoh Khufu sold his daughter into prostitution to pay for the building of the Great Pyramid.

Neither the Greeks nor the Romans practiced archaeology as a way of studying the past. They were well aware of the existence of exotic peoples who lived outside the confines of the Mediterranean world. Many authors, among them Herodotus and Tacitus, wrote astute descriptions of people like the Scythians of the Russian plains and the fierce Celts who lived east of the Rhine River. They referred to them as "barbarians," describing peoples whom we only know of today through archaeological research.

Both Greek and Roman intellectuals were aware that earlier societies had preceded their own. Homer's *Iliad* and *Odyssey* described ancient Bronze Age societies and the **Minoan civilization** of Crete. The Greeks and Romans also knew of peoples living in much less sophisticated cultures than their own. In about 700 B.C., the Greek author Hesiod wrote of past ages of humanity, conceiving of them in technological terms. There had once been a Golden Age, he said, when humanity prospered and was content. More recently had come the Age of Iron, when people waged war constantly. No notions of human progress here, for Hesiod wrote in troubled times. But there was a perception of a philosophical past—a less stressful time often thought of as being superior to the present.

Another Greek author, Diodorus Siculus, who wrote a famous geography in the first century A.D., reflected the thinking of many scholars of the day when he proclaimed that all civilization had originally stemmed from Egypt. The ancient Egyptians, it was thought, were the foundation of all wisdom, of the institutions of civilization, and of medicine.

Then, as now, Egypt was a magnet for curious visitors. Roman tourists flocked to Alexandria near the mouth of the Nile, using a galley service that ran like clockwork from southern Italy. After a few days among the fleshpots of this cosmopolitan city, the visitor took a boat up the Nile, pausing to marvel at the Pyramids of Giza, then traveling upstream to admire the temples of the ancient sun god Amun at **Karnak** and **Luxor.** On the west bank of the river—the realm of the ancient Egyptian dead—they would wander among the empty royal sepulchers in the **Valley of the Kings.** Every sunrise, crowds of tourists would gather at the huge seated statues that had once adorned the funerary temple of King Amenhotep III (1386–1349 B.C.). As the sun rose, the stones forming the feet of one of the statues would creak and groan as they expanded in the warming sunlight. Emperor Septimus Severus abruptly terminated the strange noise when he ordered the stones patched in A.D. 202. The tourists' graffiti scribbled on the statues survive to this day.

Many of these tourists returned home with pendants, scarabs, and other Egyptian antiquities. None other than the Roman emperor Hadrian adorned his garden with Greek and Egyptian statuary.

On the other side of the world, Chinese philosophers also speculated about the remote past—about humanity before the legendary Xia and Shang dynasties founded civilization in northern China. In A.D. 52, a compilation of writings set out a Chinese past in which people had lived through three primordial ages—first an age of stone, then one of bronze, then one of iron. This prophetic scheme of three ages of the remote human past was not based on science; it was merely the product of intelligent minds thinking about ancient times, perhaps in the context of now forgotten and lost folklore.

A Past "Five Days Elder Than Ourselves"

The Chinese, Greeks, and Romans merely flirted with the past. Archaeology as we know it today did not exist. With the collapse of the classical world, casual speculations ceased, to be replaced gradually by a history that drew its inspiration from the Old Testament and from the surviving works of classical writers.

Medieval scholars in Europe created an invented past like the one proclaimed by Geoffrey of Monmouth in his *A History of the Kings of England*, published in 1508. He brought Brutus, the son of the classical hero Aeneas, to England in A.D. 1125 to start British history. Geoffrey's history was the sixteenth-century equivalent of space fiction, but one cannot blame him. He cast around in the only available biblical and classical sources for inspiration. There were few visible archaeological sites except the weathered stone circles of Stonehenge—"stones of wonderful size," as one twelfth-century text called them, set up "after the manner of doorways" (Figure 1.3).

In 1643, English physician Sir Thomas Browne set the stage for the past, which he thought to be framed by the six days of the biblical Creation. "Time we may comprehend," he wrote. "'Tis but five days elder than ourselves." His inspiration was Genesis 1, which defined the course of early archeological inquiry for many centuries.

Browne was steeped in the knowledge of the Renaissance, which had sparked a passion for Greek and Roman learning. The writings of Herodotus, of Diodorus Siculus, and of Tacitus were read anew, with their descriptions of exotic peoples living on the fringes of the ancient world, and of Egyptian civilizations. The Renaissance also stimulated an upsurge in the collecting of antiquities by cardinals and kings, and by wealthy nobility and gentlemen of leisure from throughout Europe, who traveled to Mediterranean lands in

Figure 1.3 Stonehenge, England.

search of learning and pleasure. They returned home laden with statuary and paintings, and with classical antiquities of all kinds. Their trophies adorned cabinets of curiosities at home, for then, as now, travelers sought souvenirs as pleasant reminders of their travels. Soon it became fashionable to be an antiquary—a collector of things ancient and exotic.

A Grand Tour to classical lands became an essential part of every affluent gentleman's education (many women also took the Tour). But only the wealthiest travelers could afford such an extravagance, so humbler collectors turned their attention to their own familiar countryside. This form of antiquarian inquiry had its roots not only in a lust for exotica, but in a natural curiosity about the landscape and the past.

British Antiquarians

The first homegrown European antiquaries were astute observers and inveterate travelers—men like John Leland (?1506–1552), who was appointed King's Antiquary by Henry VIII, and William Camden (1557–1623), a schoolmaster and heraldry expert. Camden traveled throughout Britain to compile his *Britannia* (1586), the first description of antiquities of all kinds—everything from Stonehenge to ruined monasteries. *Britannia* remained in print for more than two hundred years and went through several editions. Camden called the study of antiquities the "backward looking curiosity." In *Britannia*, he defended the study of the past as "sweet food for the mind," ideal for those of "sweet and honest disposition." He and his fellow antiquarians were skilled fieldworkers. Camden himself traced the streets of the ancient Roman town at **Silchester** by the stunted corn that grew in a crisscross pattern, revealing the invisible street plan below ground. Such crop marks did not become a standard part of the archaeologist's armory until the advent of aerial photography in the 1920s.

As these and many other antiquaries walked the countryside and searched newly plowed fields, they uncovered hoards of Roman coins and bundles of primitive-looking bronze axes, potsherds (pot fragments), and thousands of stone tools. The more scholarly among them circulated questionnaires to landowners, asking about earthworks and "ancient sepulchers." Many prominent antiquaries were polymaths, as interested in botany and geology as they were in ancient monuments. They lived at a time when science was in its infancy, and they traveled through a world teeming with mysteries and minor wonderments. Inevitably, they speculated about the ancient Britons, about the Celts, and about other peoples who had inhabited Europe before the Romans.

Inevitably, prominent earthworks and stone circles received much of the attention, among them **Hadrian's Wall,** the Roman fortification that protected Britain against the ferocious Scots (Figure 1.4). Even then, there were surprises. When a prosperous landowner named John Aubrey (1626–1697)

Figure 1.4   Hadrian's Wall, northern England.

galloped into the middle of the **Avebury** circles while fox hunting in 1649, he professed himself "wonderfully surprized" (Figure 1.5). The ambitious and self-serving Aubrey made Avebury something of a career and a way of currying favor with King Charles II. "It does as much exceed in greatness the so renowned Stonehenge, as a cathedral doeth a parish church," he wrote in his masterwork *Monumenta Britannica,* which remained unpublished until 1980. In this book, he described Avebury and speculated about the ancient Britons, whom he described as "almost as savage as the Beasts whose skins were their only raiment." They were, he supposed, "two or three degrees less savage than the Americans." By Americans, Avebury meant American Indians, whose artifacts and customs were the subject of lively interest in his day.

In his book, Aubrey relied heavily on classical sources, especially Julius Caesar's account of his brief campaign in England in 55 B.C., which mentioned Celtic priests known as Druids. He was also something of a romantic, as was another antiquary, William Stukeley (1687–1765), who was an excellent field observer. His surveys of Avebury and Stonehenge have priceless

Figure 1.5   An aerial view of the stone circles at Avebury, England.

value for modern researchers. Not that Stukeley was just a sober-minded fieldworker. He took ladders to Stonehenge and dined with friends atop the lintel of one of the famed trilithons (two uprights and a lintel), where he remarked that there was space to dance a minuet. In later life, Stukeley became a notoriously eccentric parish priest, obsessed with Druids, the ancient British priests who he thought had built Stonehenge. Stukeley's legacy lives on. Every midsummer's day, modern-day Druids hold a bizarre bacchanalia inside the stone circles.

Scandinavian Antiquarians

British antiquaries were not alone in their searches. In Scandinavia, Danish kings encouraged the study of antiquities and ancient runic inscriptions. (Runes were an ancient alphabetic script used in northern Europe before the adoption of Roman alphabet script in medieval times.) Ole Worm (1558–1654), a professor of various subjects at the University of Copenhagen, collected everything from antiquities to exotic animals and plants, then arranged them according to a system of his own devising and opened the world's first museum. This remarkable institution attracted visitors from all over Europe. In 1662, the University of Upsala in Sweden set up the first Professorship of Antiquities. Within a few years, royal proclamations protected both archaeological sites and portable antiquities in Sweden and Finland. Scandinavian antiquaries were far ahead of their colleagues in other countries in the eighteenth century.

The Danes dug into megalithic tombs, in some of the earliest archaeological excavations. (Megaliths are Stone Age sepulchers constructed with large stone slabs, then covered with an earthen mound; from the Greek *mega lithos*, "large stone.") So did French antiquarians as early as 1685; but, for the most part, antiquaries were collectors and observers rather than diggers. They assembled a massive jumble of stone axes, clay vessels, metal artifacts, and occasional spectacular finds such as the celebrated gold horn from **Gallehus** in Denmark, found in 1639 and described by Ole Worm, then placed in the royal collections. The horn, and a companion discovered a century later, were stolen in 1802 and destroyed. We have only Worm's drawings of the original find.

Antiquarian Societies

What could one make of this confusion of artifacts? Some people, like the redoubtable Dr. Samuel Johnson (1709–1784) of *Dictionary* fame, roundly declared that antiquities meant little. "All that is really known of the ancient state of Britain is contained in a few pages," he wrote. Others were of like mind; another writer, Horace Walpole, said of a volume of proceedings of the newly formed Society of Antiquaries of London that it was a "cartload of bricks and rubbish and Roman ruins." Despite their many critics, antiquarian societies came into being throughout Europe during the eighteenth century, among them the Society of Antiquaries of London (1718). Most of them were born of earlier clubs and gatherings of people with a common, and usually casual, interest in the past. The new societies came into being during an era of serious collectors, the most famous of whom was Sir Hans Sloane, a prominent London physician, who bequeathed his massive collections and library to the nation. They formed part of a "general repository" that became the British Museum in 1759. The British Museum, and other major museums founded over the next three-quarters of a century, were to become major players in the scramble for spectacular archaeological finds that developed in the nineteenth century (see Chapters 3 and 4).

All was chaos, even in the cozy world of antiquaries and collectors. The past was without order, a complex puzzle without apparent solution. Wrote Danish philosopher Professor Rasmus Nyerup in 1806: "Everything which has come down to us from heathendom is wrapped in a thick fog: it belongs to a time which we cannot measure" (Daniel 1981:65).

This confusion resulted from scholarly perspectives on the antiquity of humankind.

Stone Tools and Scriptures

As we have seen, seventeenth-century antiquaries like John Aubrey had only a limited number of sources for interpreting the remote past: the antiquities and sites they discovered or studied, classical writers, legends and folklore, and the Scriptures. Of these, the most pervasive was the story of the Creation in Genesis 1, which affirmed that God had created the world, and every living thing, including humans. The Old Testament was the only account of the past that had any chronological depth, and it was accepted as the literal historical truth. To suggest otherwise was heresy. To be branded a heretic was dangerous in seventeenth-century Europe.

From the early days of Christianity, the learned had used the genealogies of individuals mentioned in the Old Testament to calculate the date of the Creation. According to the Bible, many of these people lived to remarkable ages—in the case of Methuselah, a ripe 969 years! One is reminded of the mythic lives attributed to very early Egyptian kings, which also lasted several conventional lifetimes. But the scholars who pored over the biblical genealogies believed that they were studying actual history, recorded in calendar years. The Protestant Martin Luther accepted a date of 4000 B.C. as the date of the Creation, but there were numerous variations on this theme, ranging between 4032 and 3946 B.C. Then an astronomer named Johannes Kepler (1571–1630), who worked closely with Galileo, recalculated the chronology of the Christian era and came up with 4004 B.C., a figure that appeared in the margin of the Authorized King James Version of the Bible, published in 1611.

In 1642, Dr. James Lightfoot of Cambridge University went even further. His *New Observations on the Book of Genesis, the most of them certain, the rest probable, all harmless, strange, and rarely heard of before* (a lovely book title!) observed that "Man was created by the Trinitie about the thirde houre of the day, or nine of the clocke in the morning on 23 October 4004 B.C." By the time Archbishop James Ussher of Armagh in northern Ireland wrote his *Annals of the World Deduced from the Origins of Time* in 1658, the six-thousand-year chronology for human history had become ardent theological dogma. This was the dogma that caused Sir Thomas Browne to make his famous remark in 1642 about the world being "five days elder than ourselves." William Shakespeare had anticipated him in 1600 when he had Rosalind say in *As You Like It:* "The poor world is almost six thousand years old" (act IV, scene 1).

How, then, could one explain the crudely made stone axes and other flint tools that turned up in gravel pits and plowed fields? For centuries, they were explained away as natural phenomena, like thunderbolts. But the situation was confused by encounters with the Native Americans, many of whom still used stone arrowheads and spear points that often bore quite a close resemblance to Europe's "thunderbolts." Michele Mercati (1541–1593), an Italian physician, mineralogist, and geologist, was superintendent of the Vatican Gardens in Rome and an ardent collector of artifacts, fossils, and minerals. In his *Metallotheca*, a book that remained buried in church archives until 1771, he illustrated ancient stone tools and described them as weapons of war used before metal came into use. Mercati's book merely languished in the Vatican; but another author, the Frenchman Isaac de la Peyrère of Bordeaux, author of *A Theological System upon that Presupposition that Men were before Adam* (1655), was seized by the Inquisition and forced to recant statements to the effect that the "thunderbolts" were the work of primitive humans who had lived on earth long before Adam. The authorities burnt his allegedly subversive volume in public.

During the eighteenth century, many collectors and scholars quietly accepted the idea that the "thunderbolts" were, in fact, tools and weapons "once used in shooting here, as they are still in America." As for the suggestion that their specimens were arrows shot by fairies that descended to earth, one scholar, Edward Lhwyd (pronounced Th-lew-ud), remarked that "I must crave leave to suspend my faith until I see one of them descend." Most antiquaries had no difficulty in accepting the notion that the most ancient Europeans had used stone tools before metal became available. They were the first to draw on the example of living non-Western people, especially in the Americas, who used stone for their artifacts on a daily basis.

It was one thing to accept "thunderbolts" as humanly made artifacts, and quite another to argue that their makers had lived on earth long before the biblical Creation. But some puzzling finds began to raise that possibility. In 1715, antiquary John Bagford described a flint ax found in the heart of London by a Mr. Conyers, lying in the same level as the bones of an elephant. Bagford thought that the elephant was a Roman import. More finds of stone tools along with the bones of long-vanished large animals came from scattered locations throughout Europe throughout the century, some of them from deep caves where stone tools and animal bones abounded. But no one was prepared to say in public that the tools were used by "Antidiluvian man" (humans before the biblical flood) until 1797, when the secretary of the Society of Antiquaries of London received a short letter from John Frere (1740–1807), a country gentleman in eastern England. Frere enclosed some flint axes, known today to be at least 250,000 years old, from a gravel pit at the village of **Hoxne.** The axes came from 3.5 meters (11.5 feet) below ground level in what was once a lake bed, sealed in the same deep layer as the bones of long-extinct animals. Frere described the artifacts as "weapons of war, fabricated and used by people who had not the use of metals." So far, he had said nothing new. But he went on to say: "The situation in which these weapons were found may tempt us to refer them to a very remote period indeed, even beyond that of the present world" (Daniel 1981:27).

A letter from an obscure country landowner, however revolutionary its conclusions, caused not even a passing ripple in scientific circles. The secretary published Frere's prophetic communication in the Society's journal *Archaeologia* for 1800 without comment, and it was forgotten for sixty years.

Herculaneum and Pompeii

The Renaissance and the Grand Tour saw a boom in the collecting of classical antiquities. Generations of civilized collecting gave birth to the Italian word *dilettanti*—those who delighted in the arts. In 1709, a group of London gentlemen and scholars founded the Society of Dilettanti, a social club for those who had visited classical lands or gone on the Grand Tour. The members were "Some Gentlemen who had traveled in Italy, desirous of encouraging, at home, a taste for those objects which contributed so much to their entertainment abroad" (Daniel 1981:77). The Society ushered in a new era when gentlemen of leisure with superb artistic abilities traveled widely, collecting, sketching, and recording antiquities of every kind. The painter James Stuart (1712–1786) and the architect Nicholas Revett (1720–1804) spent three years in Athens between 1751 and 1753. Their great four-volume work *The Antiquities of Athens* appeared between 1762 and 1816. The Dilettanti supported another expedition in 1764, this time to western Greece. *The Antiquities of Ionia* appeared between 1769 and 1797. Other travelers wandered as far afield as **Palmyra** and **Baalbec** in Syria, again with lavish publication following.

Most of the collectors, scholars, and travelers now came from European countries other than Italy; there the acquisitive zeal of earlier centuries had dissipated. The German states had a long tradition of classical scholarship, based mainly on book learning. John Joachim Winckelmann (1717–1768) taught himself classical literature while working as a schoolmaster in Prussia. In 1748, he became librarian to Count Bunau of Saxony, then left for Rome in 1755, where he became librarian to Cardinal Albani, whose collection of classical art was famous throughout Europe. By this time, Winckelmann had developed a preoccupation with the Roman town of **Pompeii,** buried by an eruption of Mount Vesuvius in A.D. 79.

Rumors of spectacular finds from Pompeii and the nearby city of **Herculaneum** had swept through Europe. Pompeii had come to light during drainage work in the late sixteenth century. Excavations began in 1738, and were sufficiently promising for Italy's King Charles III to commission Spanish engineer Rocque Joaquin de Alcubierre to probe the depths of Herculaneum. Alcubierre used gunpowder to blast his way through many feet of lava to uncover intact buildings and magnificent statuary. The excavations were conducted in secrecy. Winckelmann was unable to gain access to them, only to the collections. Fortunately, he had learned how to sketch and was able to record many of the most important finds. By 1762, he had access to the excavations themselves and could review plans of the buildings. To Winckelmann, the statuary and artwork were far more than fine objects. He sought to study them in their original positions, to examine the social context of each object—a revolutionary idea for the day (Figure 1.6).

Winckelmann published his masterpiece, *History of the Art of Antiquity,* in 1764. The book contained the first systematic descriptions of Greek and

Figure 1.6 Excavations at Herculaneum during the late eighteenth century.

Roman art based in part on finds from the two buried cities. Unfortunately, he was murdered four years later; but his book remained a critical foundation for classical art and archaeology for generations. Not that his researches had any effect on the destructive excavations at Herculaneum and Pompeii, which saw the wholesale removal of friezes and of the entire contents of important buildings. The destruction continued unchecked until 1860, when King Victor Emanuel II began to encourage scientific excavations at Pompeii as a matter of national prestige.

Winckelmann's masterly researches and the flood of discoveries at Herculaneum and Pompeii had a profound effect on eighteenth-century European architecture, art, and popular taste. For example, Sir William Hamilton (1730–1803), the British ambassador at Naples, formed a superb collection of painted Greek vases that was acquired by the British Museum. His book *Antiquités Etrusques, Grecques et Romaines*, published in 1766–1767, inspired the English potter Josiah Wedgewood to fashion pieces based on Greek, Etruscan, and Pompeian vases. You can still purchase Wedgewood pottery based on these designs today.

Egypt and Mesopotamia

Beyond the familiar landscapes of Greece and Italy lay virtually unknown archaeological territory. Few travelers ventured into the Islamic world of the Ottoman Empire based in Constantinople. A handful of merchants and explorers visited Baghdad on the Tigris River, after a hazardous journey across the Syrian desert. Some of them gazed on dusty mounds south of the city, said to be the ruins of ancient Babylon. Far upstream, the desolate remains of another buried city, the biblical Nineveh, lay opposite the small town of Mosul. The occasional European visitor pondered the deserted tumuli (mounds) and the truth of the prophet Zephaniah's utterance to the effect that the Lord would stretch out his hand against the Assyrians. "He will make Nineveh a desolation, a dry waste like the desert" (Zephaniah 6:14). Divine vengeance seemed a reality.

All that remained beyond deserted city mounds were baked bricks, some of them covered with an exotic, wedgelike script (known to archaeologists as *cuneiform*, after the Greek word *cuneus*, wedge) that was unfamiliar. A few tablets reached Europe in the hands of Italian traveler Pietro della Valle in 1626 and caused considerable interest. In 1761, a five-man expedition sponsored by King Frederick V of Denmark set out from Copenhagen to explore Arabia. Two years later, only one member of the party was still alive—Carsten Niebuhr (1733–1815). Niebuhr was a remarkable scholar and a gifted surveyor. He managed to travel as far as the royal city of **Persepolis** in what is now Iran, where he copied the cuneiform inscriptions and surveyed the palace complex before returning overland via Babylon and Nineveh. Niebuhr was ignored on his return to Copenhagen, for the king had died. He spent the rest of his long life in happy obscurity. His *Description of Travels in Arabia* was ignored for years, but eventually formed the basis for new maps of eastern Mediterranean lands. It is said that General Napoleon Bonaparte carried a copy of the book on his Egyptian expedition in 1798 (see Chapter 3).

Once Niebuhr's achievements were recognized, a new scientific era of interest in Mesopotamia began, at the same time as an awakened concern with the mysterious civilization on the Nile. In the eighteenth century, Egypt was an obscure, little-known province of the Ottoman Empire—an Islamic country effectively off-limits to Christians. The few European visitors rarely traveled further upstream than Cairo and the Pyramids of Giza. Some of them flourished off a lively trade in pulverized ancient Egyptian mummies, which produced a substance named *mumiya*, after the Arabic word for "pitch." It was said that *mumiya* was a powerful aphrodisiac and general medicine. The commerce evaporated rapidly when enterprising Egyptian merchants started drying modern corpses in the sun, coating them with the same bitumen used by the ancients, then grinding them up and passing the resulting substance off as the real thing.

The greatest mystery surrounding Egypt was not the pyramids—widely thought to be the biblical Joseph's granaries or royal burial places—but the indecipherable hieroglyphs (Greek: *hieros, glyphos*, "holy writing"). Learned men pored over the script, even sent samples of what they thought were picture writings to Jesuit missionaries in China, in an attempt to compare the hieroglyphs to Chinese script; but to no avail. The hieroglyphs remained bafflingly unintelligible. Although a steady stream of travelers reached the Nile in the late eighteenth century, the ancient Egyptians remained a shadowy people, known only from the writings of Herodotus, Diodorus Siculus, and other classical writers, as well as from their pyramids. Any excavations or large-scale investigations were beyond the resources of any individual traveler and had to await the arrival of an ambitious general with a taste for science—Napoleon Bonaparte, who invaded Egypt in 1798.

During the eighteenth century, antiquaries and their studies became an integral part of the European intellectual tradition. For example, the Russian emperor Peter the Great issued a *rex scriptum* (royal proclamation) in 1722 ordering that meticulous records be kept of the circumstances of archaeological finds. A curiosity about the past was common to many scientifically inclined people. Unfortunately, in a scholarly world bound by the shackles of theological dogma, there was little incentive to do more than speculate about the origins of humanity or about the earlier chapters of a human history that had lasted no more than six thousand years. The same mentality generated a racism that made no attempt to understand and humanize non-Europeans. For antiquarianism to become archaeology required a much longer time frame for the human past, for the antiquity of humankind. As we shall see in Chapter 2, the establishment of human antiquity was one of the great scientific achievements of the nineteenth century.

Summary

Archaeology is the study of ancient humanity, a scientific discipline unique in its ability to study changes in human societies over very long periods of time. The earliest speculations about the past came from Greek and Roman philosophers and travelers, who theorized about golden ages of the past. Classical writers believed that all civilization had ultimately originated in Egypt. Serious archaeological inquiry began after a revival of interest in classical civilization during the Renaissance. The Grand Tour brought wealthy people to classical lands, while less affluent scholars investigated the antiquities of their home landscapes. These antiquaries were the founders of prehistoric archaeology, their work limited by a lack of historical sources except for the classics and the Bible. Their researches produced some valuable site surveys and unscientific excavations, which resulted in a jumble of artifacts from all time periods. The biblical story of the Creation limited the length of the human past to a mere six thousand years, despite the discovery of stone artifacts in the same geological layers as long-extinct animals. As the debate over humans and extinct animals continued, excavations at the Roman towns of Herculaneum and Pompeii in Italy produced the first studies of classical art based on archaeological excavation at the hands of German scholar John Joachim Winckelmann. Meanwhile, a few travelers visited the sites of biblical Babylon and Nineveh in Mesopotamia, while others puzzled over the decipherment of ancient Egyptian hieroglyphs.

Guide to Further Reading

General Books on the History of Archaeology

Bahn, Paul, ed. 1996. *The Cambridge Illustrated History of Archaeology.* Cambridge: Cambridge University Press.

A lavishly illustrated history on a regional basis, written by a team of specialists. Aimed at a general audience.

Ceram, C. W. 1951. *Gods, Graves, and Scholars.* New York: Alfred Knopf.

A classic account of the discovery of early civilizations for the general reader. Outdated, but vivid.

Daniel, Glyn. 1981. *A Short History of Archaeology.* London: Thames and Hudson.

Daniel's short summary is cursory, but covers the main points. A good starting point.

Fagan, Brian. 1985. *The Adventure of Archaeology.* Washington, DC: National Geographic Society.

Heavily illustrated and aimed at a *National Geographic* audience, *The Adventure* emphasizes Society-sponsored researches but offers a general summary.

Trigger, Bruce. 1989. *A History of Archaeological Thought.* Cambridge: Cambridge University Press.

Trigger has written the definitive survey of the subject. Aimed at a more specialized audience.

Reading for Chapter 1

These references are in addition to the general accounts listed above.

Klindt-Jensen, O. 1975. *A History of Scandinavian Archaeology.* London: Thames and Hudson.

This is the authoritative history of the subject. Excellent on antiquarians.

Leppman, Wolfgang. 1970. *Winckelmann.* New York: Alfred Knopf.

Leppman's biography covers the ground admirably.

Marsden, Barry M. 1983. *Pioneers of Prehistory: Leaders and Landmarks in English Archaeology (1500–1900).* Ormskirk, UK: G. W. & A. Hesketh.

A general account of English antiquarians written for a general audience.

Piggott, Stuart. 1976. *Ruins in a Landscape: Essays in Antiquarianism.* Edinburgh: Edinburgh University Press.

_____. 1985. *William Stukeley: An Eighteenth-Century Antiquarian.* Rev. ed. London: Thames and Hudson.

Two books on antiquaries by an acknowledged master of the subject.

chapter 2

The Antiquity of Humankind

French antiquarian Boucher de Perthes points to a flint ax in the Ice Age gravels at Abbeville, France, 1959.

Am I satyr or man?
Pray tell me who can
And settle my place in the scale.

A man in ape's shape,
An Anthropoid ape,
Or monkey deprived of his tail?

"Monkeyana" by "Gorilla." *Punch*, 1861

chapter outline

The great Victorian biologist Thomas Henry Huxley called it the "question of questions"—the relationship between humans and their closest living relatives, the chimpanzee and the gorilla. Charles Darwin skirted the question in his essay on evolution and natural selection, *Origin of Species*, published in 1859; but Huxley faced it head on. It has remained one of the fundamental questions of science ever since.

As early as medieval times, scholars had puzzled over the anatomical relationships between humans and other animals, and had debated the place of humanity in the vast Chain of Being. This ladderlike scheme placed humans on the top rung of the ladder, with other animals in serried order below them. The Chain of Being seemed a logical way of ordering the animal world in a scholarly environment in which the world was believed to be the result of the Divine Act of Creation, assembled by God in six days.

I have already quoted the Elizabethan philosopher Sir Thomas Browne, who proclaimed that the world was but "five days elder than ourselves." The debilitating theological dogma of Divine Creation shackled any serious inquiry into human origins for centuries. But was humanity older than the mere six thousand years of the biblical chronology? This chapter describes the events that led to the establishment of a much greater antiquity for humankind—an open-ended history with endless potential for scientific inquiry and for archaeology.

Stratigraphic Geology

In a scholarly world where the Bible was considered the literal historical truth, scientists also assumed that the geological layers of the earth were formed by divine acts. However, during the eighteenth century there was a

20

growing awareness that the geological layers of the earth represented the passage of long periods of time. The French scholar Georges Cuvier (1769–1832) was a brilliant paleontologist (a student of fossil animals), who identified long-extinct animals in different rock strata, among them dinosaurs and the pterodactyl. Cuvier enjoyed a high profile, so much so that he was called the "Prophet of Bones," but he was convinced that the earth's history was marked by a series of great catastrophes initiated by God. The latest of these was Noah's flood in Genesis. He flatly stated that it was impossible for humans to have lived before the biblical flood. Many scholars agreed with him. French geologists in particular erected elaborate schemes of successive creations—as many as 27 of them!

Other creationists were more modest in their calculations, among them the Reverend W. D. Conybeare (1787–1857), dean of Llandaff Cathedral in Wales. He settled for three "universal deluges" before Noah's inundation. The most famous scientist of this persuasion was Dean William Buckland (1784–1857), an eccentric professor of mineralogy at Oxford University, who later became dean of Westminster Cathedral. Buckland was an eloquent speaker whose Oxford courses attracted large crowds. But he was an ardent creationist who argued that the strata of the earth proved the existence of a Universal Deluge—after which humans had peopled the world.

Buckland, famous for serving his guests such exotic foods as insects and rats, was a scientific anachronism even in his own day, his reputation perpetuated by his religious prestige. His *Reliquiae Diluvianae* (1823) and *Geology and Mineralogy Considered in Relation to Natural Theology* (1836) spelled out his position in no uncertain terms. Both the religious and geological creationists used these books as intellectual ammunition. Buckland resolutely denied any suggestion that humans had lived at the same time as extinct animals. When Buckland excavated a red-ocher–covered human skeleton buried in a cave at Paviland in southwestern Wales, which lay in the same layer as elephant, rhinoceros, and bear bones, he proclaimed the burial "Romano-British." As for the ivory ornaments found with the skeleton, they had been fabricated of the "antidiluvian" (preflood) bones that happened to be lying in the cavern at the time. Today, thanks to radiocarbon dating, we know that the Paviland skeleton is 26,000 years old.

The idea of geological layers—of stratification—was already present in the seventeenth century. Professor John Michell (1724–1793) held the chair of geology at Cambridge University from 1762 on. Long before Cuvier became famous, Michell was proclaiming that "the earth is not composed of heaps of matter casually thrown together." He himself traced geological layers over long distances across the countryside. Another scientist, James Hutton (1726–1797), published his *Theory of the Earth* in 1785. Hutton flatly stated that the earth's geological layers resulted from entirely natural processes that were still operating, not from divine intervention.

A humble field geologist, an expert on canals and farm drainage, was the true father of stratigraphic geology. William Smith (1769–1839) was the epitome of the hardworking fieldworker, more at home tramping across geological exposures with a hammer than in the intellectual salons of London. He first observed geological strata while surveying the route of a canal in southwestern England, then devoted his life to mapping the geology of the entire country with such enthusiasm that he became known as "Strata Smith." Smith was an ardent fossil collector, for he realized that the fossil contents of natural layers served as a way of linking widely separated geological deposits. He produced not only the first geological map of England in 1814, but a table of 32 different strata and the fossils in them. William Smith was no creationist. He knew full well that natural processes formed geological layers over immensely long periods of time.

The researches of Hutton, Smith, and others permeated geological circles in the early nineteenth century, at a time of frenzied canal- and railroad-building activity. A new doctrine, that of uniformitarianism (the notion that natural geological processes formed the earth's layers and surface) came to the fore. Uniformitarianism came into the public eye with the writings of the celebrated geologist Sir Charles Lyell (1797–1875), who was a master synthesizer of geological fieldwork and stratigraphic sequences over much of western Europe. In 1830–1833, Lyell published a classic work of nineteenth-century science: *The Principles of Geology, being an attempt to explain the former changes of the Earth's Surface by reference to causes now in action.* The lengthy title says it all. Even some ardent creationists hailed Lyell's book as a breakthrough in geology, for he was careful not to discuss the tricky question of the antiquity of humankind in his book. More than 60 years later, Lyell's sister-in-law described him as the man who freed science from Moses. There is some truth in this characterization. Lyell exercised a profound influence on the young Charles Darwin, who read *The Principles* during his epochal voyage around the world aboard HMS *Beagle* from 1830 to 1836.

Humans and Extinct Animals

In Chapter 1, we recounted how the eighteenth century saw isolated finds of humanly manufactured stone tools in the same layers as fossils of long-extinct animals, culminating in John Frere's Hoxne finds, reported to the Society of Antiquaries of London in 1797. During the early years of the nineteenth century, reports of such finds became ever more frequent, to the point that they garnered serious scientific attention.

Early Excavations

The French were especially active. Pierre Tournal, a pharmacist and the curator of the Narbonne Museum, excavated the Grotte de Bize in the

Aude in southern France, finding human bones and pottery associated with numerous animal bones, many of them of extinct species. Tournal is commonly credited with being the first person to use the term *prehistory* to refer to the earliest periods of the human past. He published his Bize excavations in an antiquarian journal in 1828, by which time he was referring to two periods of the human past—a prehistoric and a historic era. A year later, he published extinct animal bones that bore marks left by human cutting tools.

A Belgian physician named P. C. Schmerling was sufficiently excited by Tournal's researches to start excavations in several caves at Engihoul near Liège. His finds included no fewer than seven human skulls and numerous stone artifacts, some of them from the same levels as mammoth and rhinoceros bones. Schmerling published his finds in a monograph in 1833, in which he wrote that "there can be no doubt that the human bones were buried at the same time and by the same cause as the other extinct species." His work was ignored by the scientific establishment, who were then, as now, arbiters of the cutting edge in science. A quarter century was to pass before his contemporaries accepted Schmerling's ideas.

Across the English Channel, a Catholic priest, Father J. MacEnery, between 1824 and 1829 excavated Kent's Cavern, a large cave near the town of Torquay in southwestern England. As a priest, MacEnery was, of course, a devout Catholic, but when he found stone artifacts in the same earth layers as rhinoceros sealed *under* an undisturbed stalagmite floor, he was convinced that he had evidence for the contemporaneity of humans and extinct animals long before six thousand years ago. He consulted the redoubtable Dean Buckland, a creationist if ever there was one. Buckland refused to come down from Oxford to see the site and blithely proclaimed that ancient Britons, who had dug ovens through the stalagmite, had introduced the artifacts into the earthen layers. MacEnery pointed out that there were no such ovens. Buckland simply told him to go on looking for them, as he would find them eventually. Discouraged, MacEnery continued to dig sporadically at Kent's Cavern, but he abandoned plans to publish his work, which attracted little attention at the time.

Slowly the evidence was accumulating—from Belgium and France, from Austria, and even from the Rock of Gibraltar, where a beetle-browed Neanderthal skull was found in 1848, though the discovery was ignored and was not reported until 1907. Despite all these important finds, the sheer weight of theological dogma prevented any public discussion of a great antiquity for humankind—of the possibility that humans existed much earlier than 4004 B.C. In a devout world, where the church was all-powerful and preached that the biblical Creation was the true story of human beginnings, there was little room for maneuver, despite the writings of Strata Smith, James Hutton, and Charles Lyell.

The Scientific Establishment Takes Notice

By the 1830s and 1840s, the tide was turning, slowly and imperceptibly, in considerable part because of Lyell's book, and in part because of new thinking about the processes by which humans had come into being. Those who dared to challenge conventional thinking were still dismissed out of hand, but, increasingly, the scientific establishment, especially in England, was taking the many associations of human artifacts and extinct animals more seriously.

In part, they were influenced by the discoveries of Jacques Boucher de Crèvecoeur de Perthes (1788–1868), a minor customs official at Abbeville in northern France who was also an ardent collector of prehistoric artifacts. Abbeville lies in the Somme River valley, whose gravels abound in antiquities of all kinds. De Perthes took to visiting the quarries and dumps left by dredgers cleaning out the Somme canal. He soon became interested in the often finely made stone axes that the workers dug out of the river gravels, from the same layers that contained the bones of elephants and other extinct animals. He called his axes "Pre-Celtic" and said they were the work of people who had lived before the flood. De Perthes was a garrulous individual, given to obsessive lectures about his finds. In short, he was a bore. He exhibited his finds in Abbeville and in Paris in 1838–1839, when he published a verbose five-volume book entitled *De la Création: essai sur l'origine et la progression des êtres*. The scientists of the day labeled him a crank. He wrote despairingly: "At the very mention of the words 'axe' and 'diluvium,' I observe a smile on the face of those to whom I speak." But he was undeterred and kept on collecting, publishing the first volume of a three-volume work entitled *Antiquités Celtiques and Antédiluviennes* in 1847. By this time, he was convinced that his Somme axes were very old indeed, and that they dated to an era older than the biblical flood.

Most French geologists were still catastrophists; but a few of them visited the gravel pits, conducted their own excavations, and became convinced that de Perthes was correct. Their influential voices were heard both in Paris and across the Channel. Had de Perthes not been such a bore, recognition might have come earlier.

From Skepticism to Acceptance

Just as de Perthes was finishing his *Antiquités* book, the Torquay Natural History Society set up a committee in 1846 to explore Kent's Cavern anew. A local schoolmaster, William Pengelly, who was a gifted geologist, led the excavations, which confirmed everything that Father MacEnery had said a quarter-century earlier. In 1858, quarrying across Tor Bay above the town of Brixham revealed another cave. Geologist William Pengelly excavated there in 1858–1859, this time with a formal committee of the Royal Society in

London supervising and observing the work. With the scientific establishment looking over his shoulder, Pengelly unearthed a sheet of stalagmite up to 20 centimeters (8 inches) thick, with below it "the relics of lion, hyena, mammoth, rhinoceros and reindeer," as well as humanly made flint artifacts.

Many of the high-powered scientists on the Royal Society committee were convinced by Brixham Cave. Charles Lyell wrote that skepticism about the antiquity of humankind "had previously been pushed to an extreme."

A handful of geologists had crossed to France and looked at Boucher de Perthes's Abbeville excavations. They were sufficiently convinced that the eminent geologist Joseph Prestwich, along with John Evans, at the time the world's leading expert on stone tools, made a special trip to visit de Perthes in 1859. Their visit was a fleeting one, but it lasted long enough for Evans himself to dig out a stone ax from the same layer as an elephant bone. The two men proclaimed their acceptance of a high antiquity for humankind in papers read to the Royal Society and the Society of Antiquaries of London, two organizations that at the time exercised a profound influence over the scientific world. Wrote a leading antiquary, John Evans (1823–1908), geologist, archaeologist, and prosperous papermaker: "Think of their finding flint axes and arrowheads at Abbeville in conjunction with bones of elephants and rhinoceroses. . . . It will make my ancient Britons quite modern if man is carried back . . . to the days when elephants, rhinoceroses, hippopotamuses, and tigers were also inhabitants of the country" (John Evans, diary entry for April 30, 1859). More geologists crossed to Abbeville and found axes and extinct animals in the same gravel layers. Skepticism remained for two or three years afterward, but eventually the association of extinct animals and humans was accepted as scientific reality.

The contemporaneity of humans and extinct animals was disturbing to the religious, but they could live with it, since the association begged the question of the age of humanity. Inevitably, however, the Brixham and Somme discoveries raised fundamental questions about the age of humans. Had modern people come into being as the result of divine acts some six thousand years ago, or had they originated twenty thousand years B.P., or even as long ago as 100,000 years before the present, as Charles Lyell now argued? After 1863, the tide of scientific opinion had swung so far that only staunch religious traditionalists defended the biblical chronology. For the first time, scientists contemplated a human past that seemed open-ended, of unknown duration.

Another scientific question also engaged the antiquaries and geologists of the day. Who had made the Somme axes, or hatchets, as the Victorians called them? In 1856, the skull and limb bones of a heavily built individual came to light in a cave in the **Neander Valley** in Prussia. The skull was large, with a low forehead and enormous bony ridges over the eye sockets. The anatomist Hermann Schaafhausen identified the remains as those of a man from a "barbarous and savage race," an ancient inhabitant of Europe. His colleague

Rudolf Virchow dismissed the bones as those of a pathological idiot. The brilliant British biologist Thomas Henry Huxley (1825–1895) made the most detailed study of the Neanderthal remains and compared them to the skeleton of a chimpanzee, noting surprisingly close anatomical similarities. In his classic *Man's Place in Nature,* published in 1863, Huxley concluded that the Neanderthal skull was the most apelike human found so far, "most nearly allied to the higher apes." In doing so, Huxley was profoundly influenced not by the findings of stratigraphic geology or archaeology, but by the publication of the most influential scientific work of the nineteenth century, Charles Darwin's *Origin of Species.*

Evolution and Natural Selection: Human Progress

The *Origin of Species* appeared in 1859, only a few months after Evans and Prestwich had described their finds to London's most prominent learned societies. Charles Darwin's essay on the theory of evolution and natural selection burst on a society where there were now serious challenges to the Christian faith. The great expansion of scientific knowledge in the first half of the nineteenth century had seriously depleted the number of phenomena that could not be attributed to natural causes. Theological dogma had shifted as a result. Instead of preaching God's direct intervention, theologians and scientists of traditional persuasion had tended to look for signs of his provident design instead. Under this argument, the special creation of new animal species, each adapted to its specific environment, was the last arena for God's continued, and intimate, involvement with the natural world. Darwin's *Origin of Species* evicted the Lord from the process of speciation in favor of natural forces. The new theory threatened to eliminate God from any involvement in the design or creation of nature. Not only that, but the *Origin* raised the horrifying possibility that humans, God's supreme creation, were also simply a product of natural forces.

Darwin's theory of evolution and natural selection arose from a complex social and political milieu—from times of revolution and major socioeconomic change, from unprecedented international warfare and a burgeoning industrial revolution. The ideas of Jean Baptiste Lamarck and others about the biological transformation of animals and humans were also part of the intellectual equation. But Lamarck had worked within the shackles of biblical chronology and could never achieve what Darwin did, believing as the latter did in a vast age for the earth.

Darwin Develops His Theory

Charles Darwin (1809–1882) had not intended to become a biologist until he became an undergraduate at Cambridge, fell under the influence of some prominent biologists, and went off on the five-year voyage of HMS *Beagle* in 1830–1836. Darwin took Lyell's *Principles of Geology* with him, a book that stressed that the introduction of new species was a primary cause of the extinction of older forms. The young scientist was fascinated by the doctrine of uniformitarianism, and he had many opportunities to observe geological layers that demonstrated it on his global voyage. (The same book had a profound influence on the social evolutionist Herbert Spencer [1820–1903], who was a passionate advocate of progress in human societies.) Darwin observed a myriad of plants and animals on the *Beagle* voyage. Soon he began compiling notebooks on what he called the "species question." But it was not until he read economist Thomas Malthus's *An Essay on the Principle of Population* in 1838 that he was convinced that selection was the principle that drove evolution. Malthus had published his classic work in 1798, proposing a theory that is now considered a foundation of modern demography—the study of populations. Malthus took a pessimistic view of growing populations. He argued that they expanded to the limits of the available food supply. Darwin took this argument further. He believed that human progress came from unremitting struggle, the product of "nature, red in tooth and claw."

Charles Darwin sat on his theory for years, while he worked away on other fundamental biological problems. He was well aware of the furor that would erupt around his head if he published his revolutionary theories. For a start, Captain Robert FitzRoy, his mentor aboard the *Beagle*, was a devout Christian and bitterly opposed to Darwin's ideas. FitzRoy had a troubled career, serving as a member of Parliament, then as governor-general of New Zealand. His creationist views caused him considerable mental anguish and he eventually committed suicide.

Darwin Publishes *Origin of Species*

Darwin's hand was forced in 1858, when another biologist, Alfred Russell Wallace (1823–1913), sent him a paper on the species question that mirrored his own ideas. Wallace is one of the forgotten heroes of nineteenth-century biology. He began his career as a teacher, then went on an expedition to South America from 1848 to 1852 to collect animals and plants along the Amazon River. In 1854, he set off on an eight-year journey through southeast Asia, where he explored the Spice Islands. He acquired huge numbers of specimens and identified the so-called Wallace Line, which separated Asian and Australian animal life. During a bout of fever in 1858, he pondered the issue of why some animals survived and others did not, and concluded that the "strongest and most cunning" would survive—the survival of the fittest. Excited by his ideas, Wallace wrote to Darwin, unaware that Darwin had been pondering the same question for years.

Darwin received Wallace's letter with consternation, but arranged for its publication. He also bestirred himself and wrote what he called a short

essay: *Origin of Species*. This was the most detailed argument for the evolution of species ever written. It stood on the shoulders of Lamarck, Lyell, and
others and was unprecedented in its accuracy and sheer scope. *Origin* used
evidence and marshaled complex arguments for evolution with a brilliance
seldom exceeded since.

Origin of Species is a book that one would expect to appeal to only a small
circle of technically minded people capable of appreciating the full force
of its arguments. But *Origin* was far more than a scientific treatise. Within the
compass of what he modestly called "a brief essay," Darwin brought
together diverse themes and legitimized quiet thinking about the species
question that had been in the backs of many peoples' minds for a generation
or more. The author had no theological or intellectual baggage to bring to his
tour de force. The book had a fairly sharp philosophical message about the in-
evitability of progress and about the justice of a system of struggle without
which progress could not be achieved. Darwin wrote of each organic being
constantly striving, of an incessant war of nature where "the vigorous, the
healthy, and the happy survive and multiply."

As early as 1842, when he wrote a first sketch of his theory of evolution,
Darwin was convinced that the struggle applied to all mammals, including
humans. But he did not take up the issue of human evolution in *Origin*,
largely because he felt it would prevent his book from getting a fair hearing.
Twelve years were to pass before he published *The Descent of Man*, in which
he explored the relationship between natural selection and human evolution.
By then, Herbert Spencer and others had already blended biological and social evolution, and the notion of the survival of the fittest was commonplace.

Reactions to the Theory

The first printing of *Origin of Species* sold out in a few days. Within weeks,
the book was the subject of vigorous debate in scholarly circles, for it hit at
the very heart of the debate over science as opposed to theology. Until *Origin*
appeared, scientists, the religious, and laypeople shared a series of interrelated ideas. First, they believed in natural theology, the notion that the earth
and the history of life provided evidence of God's existence and of his benev-
olence. Second, most people believed in organic progression—the idea that
life on earth had grown ever more complex, culminating in humanity. Lastly,
they assumed that humans had arrived on earth after its landscape, climate,
plants, and animals had achieved their modern forms. These three general
ideas interlocked to form a relatively coherent context for the recent findings
of geology, paleontology, and archaeology.

Origin of Species robbed this coherent vision of all its explanatory power.
The theory of evolution and natural selection, and the scientific acceptance of
the antiquity of humankind, provided a common foundation of new ideas on
which scientists from different disciplines could erect separate but linked

explanations of the past. The coexistence of humans and extinct animals, an open-ended chronology for human prehistory, and notions of steady but slow progress over the long millennia of prehistoric times destroyed the long-standing boundaries between the modern world and that of former worlds peopled by extinct animals. Nothing—no great floods, cataclysms, or great extinctions—separated Darwin and his scientific contemporaries from the immensely old toolmakers of the Somme Valley. There was now a new question to be asked. Not "Did humans live alongside extinct animals?" but "How long ago and in what geological epoch did humans first appear?"

The events of the year 1859 created a vast span of human history without shape or form, known to be inhabited, but with the inhabitants unknown. In the decades that followed, archaeologists and anthropologists worked hand in hand with geologists, peopling this vast landscape with hitherto unknown human forms and with both simple and elaborate societies revealed by the archaeologist's spade.

The furor over the *Origin of Species* revolved principally around the possibility that humans had descended from apes. Victorian matrons drew their children to their ample skirts and whispered to one another that they hoped the rumors were not true (Figure 2.1). Biologist Thomas Huxley became such an ardent advocate of evolution that he was nicknamed "Darwin's Bulldog," while Darwin himself remained quietly in the shadows. But gradually the opposition dwindled, except among the most extreme devotees of the

Figure 2.1   A period cartoon by Thomas Nast lampooning Darwin's linking apes to humans.

Scriptures. Archaeology and human paleontology—the study of early humans and human origins—became a serious academic discipline, much of whose work went forward out of the public eye. We return to the subject of human origins and theories about human ancestry in Chapter 4, where we also examine the first efforts to classify and order the tens of thousands of artifacts that littered the landscape of ancient times.

Before delving further into prehistory, we must retrace our steps. In Chapter 3, we discuss the discovery of Ancient Egypt and of early Mesopotamian civilization.

Summary

Chapter 2 summarizes the controversies over the antiquity of humankind, which reached a head in the mid-nineteenth century. Medieval scholars believed in a Chain of Being, a ladderlike hierarchy of animal life, with humans on the top rung. During the eighteenth and early nineteenth century, repeated finds of humanly made artifacts in the same geological levels as the bones of extinct animals put science on a direct collision course with religious teachings. At the time, almost everyone believed in the historical truth of the Scriptures—that God had created the world in six days in 4004 B.C. The discoveries of stratigraphic geologists and the doctrine of uniformitarianism, which assumed that the earth's layers were formed by natural processes, undermined the biblical chronology. In 1859, British scientists accepted the contemporaneity of humans and extinct animals long before the biblical flood as a result of de Perthes's discoveries of hand axes and extinct animal bones in northern France's Somme Valley. In the same year, Charles Darwin's *Origin of Species*, with its theories of evolution and natural selection, provided the theoretical framework for human evolution. Biologist Thomas Huxley championed Darwin's theories in the context of the Neanderthal skull, found in 1856. Within a few years, the antiquity of humankind was widely accepted, opening the way for the study of human prehistory on a long time scale, far longer than the mere six thousand years of the biblical chronology.

Guide to Further Reading

Browne, Janet. 1995. *Charles Darwin: Voyaging*. New York: Alfred Knopf.

———. 2002. *Charles Darwin: The Power of Place*. New York: Alfred Knopf.

   Browne's biography of Darwin comes in two parts and represents the definitive source on his life and work.

Grayson, Donald. 1983. *The Establishment of Human Antiquity*. Orlando, FL: Academic Press.

A thorough academic study of the antiquity-of-humankind controversies that delves into primary sources. Strongly recommended for the serious student.

Trigger, Bruce D. 1989. *A History of Archaeological Thought*. Cambridge: Cambridge University Press.

Trigger's discussion adds a wider perspective.

Van Riper, A. Bowdoin. 1993. *Men among the Mammoths*. Chicago: University of Chicago Press.

Van Riper's splendid and well-written introduction is an excellent summary of a complex subject. He is especially good on the impact of Darwin's theories. An excellent bibliography.

Winchester, Simon. 2001. *The Map That Changed the World*. New York: HarperCollins.

A lovely biography of William Smith and his geological map for a broad audience.

Young, Robert M. 1985. *Darwin's Metaphor*. Cambridge: Cambridge University Press.

A fundamental source on Darwin for students of archaeological history.

chapter 3

Pharaohs and Assyrians

Austen Henry Layard's finds being transported down the Tigris River on a raft supported by inflated goatskins. Assyrian boatmen used the same kinds of rafts three thousand years earlier.

Between them Sennacherib and his hosts had gone forth in all their might and glory to the conquest of distant lands, and had returned rich with spoil and captives. . . . Through them, too, the Assyrian monarch had entered his capital in shame, after his last and fatal defeat.

Austen Henry Layard, *Nineveh and Babylon*, 1853 (p. 221)

chapter outline

"Every step I took I crushed a mummy in some part or other. . . . When my weight bore down on the body of an Egyptian it crushed like a band-box. I sank altogether among the broken mummies with a crash of bones, rags, and wooden cases. . . . I could not avoid being covered with bones, legs, arms and heads rolling from above" (Belzoni 1822:81). Thus did circus strongman turned tomb robber Giovanni Belzoni describe his adventures exploring narrow rock fissures in the steep cliffs opposite Luxor on the west bank of the Nile in 1818. He was in the heart of the city of the dead—the arid valleys, gullies, and precipitous rock faces where thousands of ancient Egyptians lay buried. The common people lay in narrow fissures, stacked vertically by the dozen. Belzoni, who stood well over 2 meters (6 feet 6 inches) tall, squeezed his way through the crowded passageways in the company of local tomb robbers. He was searching for papyrus inscriptions and jewelry wrapped in the bandages of the dead, spending his evenings around village fires fueled by broken-up wooden mummy cases. These were the days of high adventure in archaeology. Along the Nile, you sometimes chased your competitors with guns. After three years of often brazen looting, Giovanni Belzoni left Egypt in 1819 in fear of his life.

The beginnings of archaeology lie not only in a quest to satisfy curiosity about the past through cultured collecting and leisured antiquarianism, but also in a search for the world's earliest civilizations, which continued throughout the nineteenth century. In this chapter, we describe how this search began, along the Nile and in Mesopotamia (Greek: "the land between the rivers"), the legendary site of the biblical Garden of Eden.

Napoleon in Egypt

In the late eighteenth century, Egypt was still a remote province of the Ottoman Empire, ruled by the sultan of Constantinople. The Nile Valley was part of the Islamic world, off limits to all but the boldest Christian travelers. Occasional travelers ventured there and brought back samples of a mysterious hieroglyphic script and descriptions of tombs and pyramids. The English traveler Richard Pococke published *Travels in Egypt* in 1755, after traveling extensively around Cairo. He described not only the Giza pyramids, but the earliest account of King Djoser's Step Pyramid at **Saqqara.**

With the onset of the Napoleonic Wars, Egypt's strategic importance increased rapidly. The Nile Valley and the Red Sea lay astride a major route to India, Britain's most prized possession. In 1798, General Napoleon Bonaparte invaded Egypt. Napoleon fancied himself a scientist, so he took with him a team of experts, who were charged with describing and mapping Egypt ancient and modern. His soldiers called them "Napoleon's donkeys." After the French defeated the Egyptian army at the Battle of the Pyramids, the scientists fanned out over the Nile Valley, sketching, mapping, and collecting. On occasion, they accompanied military expeditions and sketched under fire. They were intoxicated with the exotic civilization that unfolded before them. The pyramids of Giza, the temples of Luxor and Karnak with their columns covered with hieroglyphs, the Valley of the Kings with its rock-cut royal tombs, and the magnificent Temple of Isis at **Philae** in Aswan at ancient Egypt's southern frontier—all these monuments and many others were quite unlike the familiar architecture of Greece and Rome. The scientists collected crate after crate of artifacts, mummies, and sculpture, and also Egypt's most famous artifact—the Rosetta Stone.

In 1799, an artillery officer was supervising the construction of a fortification at the town of Rosetta in the low-lying Delta, downstream of Cairo. One of the stone slabs collected for a wall bore an inscription in Greek and Egyptian hieroglyphs. The army sent the stone to the experts in Cairo. The scientists realized at once that the Rosetta Stone had the potential to unlock the secrets of ancient Egyptian script. It is an interesting reflection on the warfare of the day that Napoleon immediately ordered that accurate plaster casts of the stone be made, to be sent to scientists all over Europe, including those in enemy nations.

Napoleon's expedition ended in failure in 1804. By then, he had slipped out of the country, leaving his army and his scientists behind. The "donkeys" were given safe passage to France, with all their crates. Only the Rosetta Stone was handed over to the British, which is why it can be seen in the British Museum in London, and not in the Louvre in Paris. They claimed it knowing it was the most important find of all.

Between 1809 and 1821, the scientists compiled a lavish compendium of their discoveries, the nine-volume *Description de l'Egypte.* This beautifully illustrated monograph burst like a thunderbolt on Europe. For the first time, the glories of ancient Egypt were revealed to an astonished public, through accurate, beautifully executed engravings that went so far as to reconstruct the original appearance of some of the temples. A fashion for things Egyptian developed almost at once, with the inevitable lust to own mummies and other exotica from this hitherto forgotten civilization.

The Decipherment of Hieroglyphs

Long before the discovery of the Rosetta Stone, epigraphers (ancient script experts) in many lands had puzzled over ancient Egyptian script, usually without success. It soon became apparent that hieroglyphs were not picture writing. The Greek inscription on the Rosetta Stone proved to be a proclamation of 196 B.C. by the priests at the temple of Memphis in Lower Egypt praising King Ptolemy Epiphanes for his many benefactions and granting him divine honors. A routine inscription, but for the fact that it was also in two versions of hieroglyphs—a cursive form called *demotic,* and the formal script. Using the Rosetta Stone and other inscriptions, including one from the temple at Philae, the great French scholar Sylvestre de Sacy was able to decipher several names in the demotic passage, including that of King Ptolemy; but he declared decipherment impossible. Other workers succeeded in deciphering some of the proper names, among them Dr. Thomas Young (1773–1829), a physicist and physician, who made considerable progress with the demotic script. Young's work helped a handful of scholars already working in Egypt to partially decipher some inscriptions.

In contrast to the decoding of other ancient scripts, a solitary scholar succeeded in deciphering hieroglyphs. Frenchman Jean François Champollion (1790–1832) was a linguistic genius. By age 13 he was fluent in Arabic, Syriac, and Coptic. While still in his teens, he devoted himself seriously to the study of hieroglyphs. In 1808, he turned his attention to the Rosetta Stone, but it was not until 1822 that he completed decipherment. Success came when he turned to a cartouche—a royal title—from the temple of **Abu Simbel** in what was once Nubia, the land upstream from ancient Egypt. Champollion deciphered the king's name—Rameses II—and finally realized that the hieroglyphs were phonetic signs. He is said to have rushed out into the street crying "I've got it," before collapsing in a dead faint. On September 27, 1822, Champollion's famous letter to the Académie Royale des Inscriptions was published, in which he announced decipherment.

Champollion was a man of powerful ego, with a low tolerance for disagreement; he was very much a loner. As a result, his decipherment was considered controversial, even after he published a book on the subject in 1824. By now a curator at the Louvre, he led a triumphant expedition to the Nile in 1828–1829, where he and his companions took delight in translating the

Figure 3.1   Jean François Champollion (left foreground) and friends and members of his 1828–1829 expedition pose against a suitably romantic background. The expedition was co-led by a Tuscan scholar, Ippolito Rosellini (standing to the right of Champollion) and included 12 architects and draftsmen.

inscriptions on temple walls (Figure 3.1). Unfortunately, Champollion died prematurely of a stroke in 1832. By then his decipherment was accepted, having been validated by scholars laboriously copying tomb inscriptions along the Nile.

Looters and Archaeologists

The publication of *Description de l'Egypte* unleashed a passion for Egyptian antiquities in Europe. After the Napoleonic Wars, the British and French governments each appointed a consul in Egypt. Both were charged with acquiring antiquities for their national collections, a task they assumed with glee. The French consul was Bernardino Drovetti (1776–1852), a ruthless looter who surrounded himself with a band of ruffians. He bribed local officials, dug recklessly into tombs and temples, and was not above using force to achieve his ends. The British consul was the austere Henry Salt, who was a more genteel collector and left much of the dirty work to others. The most successful of his agents was a colorful circus strongman turned tomb robber—Giovanni Battista Belzoni (1778–1823).

Giovanni Belzoni was born in Padua, Italy, and came to England in 1804 to escape being drafted into Napoleon's armies. He soon became a well-known theatrical performer, famous as the "Patagonian Sampson" for his weight-lifting acts and feats of strength. Over the next 12 years, he acquired an expertise in levers, weights, and "hydraulics," through countless hours in circuses and theaters. Tiring of England, he ended up trying to sell a mechanical irrigation device to the Pasha of Egypt. The enterprise failed, but Henry Salt soon hired Belzoni to move an enormous statue of Rameses II from the king's mortuary temple at Luxor to Alexandria, a task that had defeated Napoleon's soldiers. Equipped with only some palm logs and rope, Belzoni hired 150 men and used his weight-lifting expertise to haul the statue 2.4 kilometers (1.5 miles) to a waiting Nile boat. The statue can be seen in the British Museum to this day (Figure 3.2).

From 1817 to 1820, Giovanni Belzoni embarked on a remarkable career as a tomb robber. He recovered mummies, papyri, and statues from temples and tombs in Luxor, was the first person to enter Rameses II's temple at Abu Simbel, and discovered the lavishly decorated tomb of the New Kingdom pharaoh Seti I in the Valley of the Kings. At Giza, he blasted his way with gunpowder into the Pyramid of Khafre, where you can still see his name painted in soot on the wall of the burial chamber.

Belzoni was so successful that Drovetti went after him. He fled Egypt in fear of his life, taking his loot with him. In 1821, he mounted a spectacular

Figure 3.2   Giovanni Belzoni transports the head of Rameses II to the Nile.

exhibition of his finds in London, including a plaster replica of Seti I's tomb, complete with the magnificent alabaster sarcophagus of the king. Belzoni was above all a showman. Just before the opening of the exhibition, he invited some leading doctors to assist in the unwrapping of the mummy of a young man "perfect in every part." He also published a stirring account of his adventures, complete with heroes, villains, and "difficulties encountered with the natives."

Giovanni Belzoni was one of the most colorful of the early archaeological adventurers, a man hungry for fame and public acclamation. In 1822, he tired of Egypt and set sail for West Africa on an expedition to find the source of the Niger River. He died of dysentery within a few weeks of landing.

The early days of Egyptology were little more than a glorified treasure hunt. But alongside the Belzonis and Drovettis were a small band of quieter travelers who lived in Egypt for years, often dwelling comfortably in empty sepulchers. They were artists, as interested in modern Egypt as in ancient times. Principal among them was John Gardiner Wilkinson (1797–1875), who worked with both Thomas Young and Jean François Champollion's decipherments and recorded countless tomb paintings and inscriptions. In 1837, Wilkinson published one of the classic works of Egyptology. *Manners and Customs of the Ancient Egyptians* was an account of a hitherto little-known civilization, written with the aid not only of archaeology, but of inscriptions and tomb paintings. For the first time, the general reader learned of the Egyptians as once living, colorful, and busy people—as a vibrant civilization. *Manners and Customs* was a landmark in the understanding of early civilizations, at a time when Egypt was considered to be the oldest civilization in the world.

Slowly, serious archaeology triumphed over treasure hunting along the Nile. But the struggle endured throughout the nineteenth century. In 1842, the king of Prussia sent Egyptologist Richard Lepsius (1810–1884) and a large expedition to Egypt. For the next three years Lepsius explored sites the length and breadth of Egypt, and ventured as far south as Khartoum in the Sudan, even recording inscriptions written by Egyptian copper miners in the Sinai. He returned to Germany in triumph with thousands of finds and comprehensive records of the sites he had explored. The massive report of the expedition is still of use to Egyptologists today.

Meanwhile, blatant looting continued almost unchecked, until the tide slowly began to turn in the late nineteenth century. To a considerable degree, this was the result of the efforts of Frenchman Auguste Mariette (1821–1881), a teacher who developed a passion for ancient Egypt at an early age. In 1849, he assumed a minor post at the Louvre, and the following year he was sent to Egypt to collect manuscripts. He turned to excavation instead and excavated a series of spectacular bull burials honoring the god Apis at Saqqara, subsequently becoming Egypt's first director of antiquities and founder of the Cairo Museum. Mariette's way of saving sites was to dig them one step ahead of the looters—a questionable and brutal strategy that did at least do something to stem the tidal wave of destruction.

Discovering the Assyrians

In the early nineteenth century, the lands east of the Euphrates River in what is now Syria were virtually inaccessible to European travelers, lying as they did in the heart of the Ottoman Empire. As we saw in Chapter 1, a few travelers visited the dusty mounds of Nineveh and Babylon, bringing back some inscribed bricks with them. Between 1811 and 1820, Claudius James Rich (1787–1821), the British Resident in Baghdad, visited the two ancient biblical cities, did some mapping, and collected examples of exotic cuneiform (wedge-shaped) script. He was unable to excavate either site, as diplomatic affairs absorbed most of his time.

In 1840, the French government appointed Paul Emile Botta their consul in the small town of Mosul in the northern part of what is now Iraq. Botta (1822–1870) was an experienced diplomat, but no archaeologist. He was instructed to excavate ancient Nineveh. The consul dug into the mounds of Kuyunjik across the river from the town, but to no avail, for his trenches were too shallow. When one of his workers reported finding strange sculptures in the foundations of his house at **Khorsabad** 23 kilometers (14 miles) upstream, Botta transferred his excavations there. Within a few days, his workers exposed a palace adorned with friezes of kings, gods, and wild beasts. In triumph, Botta reported to Paris that he had discovered Nineveh. In fact, he had unearthed the palace of the Assyrian monarch Sargon (721–705 B.C.). The French authorities responded magnificently in the spirit of Napoleon's Nile expedition, with ample funding and the services of an artist to record the excavations.

Botta continued to dig under difficult political conditions. It was a solitary life, except when he entertained occasional European travelers who passed through Mosul, among them a young Englishman named Austen Henry Layard (1817–1894), who enjoyed the shortest but most spectacular archaeological career of all time.

Austen Henry Layard was born to impoverished but genteel parents who enjoyed living in Italy. His family could not afford university fees, so he was apprenticed to a London law firm. For five years, he led a miserable existence, relieved only by periodic vacation travels abroad. Then fate intervened. In 1839, he leapt at a chance to travel overland to Ceylon (now Sri Lanka) with Edward Mitford, a 32-year-old businessman, with a view to setting up a law practice on the island. Such a journey is no easy undertaking even today, let alone in the 1840s. Because Mitford was chronically seasick, he elected to travel overland; had this not happened, Layard would most likely have lived a life of dull respectability and would never have found a lost civilization.

By the time the two men arrived in Constantinople, Layard had fallen in love with the East. They lived off beans, bread, and fish roe for about 39 cents a day in today's U.S. currency. At Jerusalem, Layard set off on his own with two camels to visit **Petra,** then a remote and difficult destination. He was robbed of all his possessions, then held hostage, but he used his charm to bluff his way to safety. By April 1841, Layard and Mitford reached Mosul, where they rode over the desolate ruins of what was said to be biblical Nineveh on the eastern bank of the Tigris River. Layard was ecstatic. "Desolation meets desolation. A feeling of awe succeeds to wonder," he wrote (1849:210) as he became obsessed with the idea of digging into the city. Downstream in Baghdad, he spent two months with Colonel James Taylor, the British consul, poring over wedge-shaped cuneiform inscriptions on the clay tablets in the diplomat's library.

Layard Excavates Nimrud and Kuyunjik

Layard was now seriously addicted to adventure. He parted company with Mitford and spent a year among the Bakhtiari nomads of what is now Iran, wandering with a chief whose son he cured of fever with quinine and "Dr. Dover's Powder," a well-known (but probably ineffective) medicine of the day. He took part in local skirmishes and barely escaped with his life, dressed from the skin out as a nomad. He next served as a confidential assistant to the British ambassador in Constantinople, where his knowledge of local affairs made him highly effective as a secret agent. But he never forgot his ambition to dig into the mysterious cities along the Tigris River. In 1845, he managed to persuade the ambassador to sponsor two months of excavations at the biblical city of Calah (Nimrud) downstream of Mosul.

At the time, no one had any idea that **Nimrud** was a biblical city. The site comprised a long line of narrow mounds covering 364 hectares (900 acres), dominated by the remains of a mudbrick temple mound. Layard selected a spot at random and promptly—within two days—found a couple of royal palaces. The first cuttings entered the palace of King Ashurbanipal (883–859 B.C.). Another imposing structure, known as the Southwestern Palace, belonged to King Esarhaddon (680–669 B.C.) and lay atop the ruins of yet a third royal residence, constructed by King Tiglath-Pileser (774–727 B.C.). At the time of his first excavations, Layard could not identify the owners of the palaces, for cuneiform remained undeciphered. He concentrated on spectacular finds, trenching and tunneling along the walls of the palace, where he found magnificent bas-reliefs of military campaigns. Like the bas-reliefs from Khorsabad upstream, the art style was quite unlike any Egyptian or classical art.

Layard soon realized that he had found an entirely unknown civilization, the same society Botta had uncovered at Khorsabad. Working in temperatures as high as 47 degrees centigrade (117 degrees Fahrenheit), Layard and his workers found walls decorated with figures of kings and their servants, horsemen and gods, along with scenes of the chase. Great human-headed lions guarded the gates of the palace of King Ashurbanipal. Working almost alone, Layard sketched each bas-relief, then sawed them from the walls, transported them to the Tigris, and floated them downstream to the port of Basra on the Persian Gulf on crude rafts supported by inflated goatskins identical to those depicted on some of the palace walls.

From Nimrud, Layard moved to **Kuyunjik** opposite Mosul, where Botta had found nothing. The young Englishman used different excavation methods, tunneling deep into the heart of the dusty mounds. After a month of hectic digging, he uncovered nine rooms of a magnificent palace adorned with scenes of a city siege. In a series of scenes, heavily armed men attacked the walls with ladders and ramps as the defenders threw stones and boiling oil on their heads, to no avail; the attackers overran the city, then killed and enslaved the inhabitants in the presence of the king. Layard suspected that he had found Nineveh, but proof could only come from still undeciphered cuneiform tablets.

Exhausted and suffering from malaria, Layard returned to London to find himself the hero of the hour. His spectacular finds had arrived at the British Museum and caused a sensation. In the intervals of a hectic social life, he wrote what he called a "slight sketch" of his excavations. *Nineveh and Its Remains* appeared in early 1849 and became an instant best-seller. Like his near-contemporary, the New Yorker John Lloyd Stephens, who wrote of ancient Maya civilization (see Chapter 5), Layard was a fluent, entertaining writer, so much so that his book is still in print today. He made his excavations come alive on the printed page. No one challenged his claim that he had revealed "the most convincing and lasting evidence of the magnificence, and power, which made Nineveh the wonder of the ancient world."

The Decipherment of Cuneiform

By this time, serious progress had been made in the decipherment of cuneiform script, thanks to the work of three men: Henry Creswicke Rawlinson; Edward Hincks, an Irish priest; and Jules Oppert, a French epigrapher. Unlike the decipherment of Egyptian hieroglyphs, which was, in the final analysis, the work of a single scholar, Jean François Champollion, cuneiform yielded its secrets to a loosely knit team of three, who corresponded regularly with one another. The most flamboyant of the three epigraphers was Henry Rawlinson, the only member of the team who spent many years in Mesopotamia.

Henry Creswicke Rawlinson (1810–1895) was a brilliant horseman, an energetic Indian army officer, and a gifted linguist who rose from an ordinary background to international prominence. He became an expert rider practically from birth and demonstrated exceptional ability at languages while still at school. In 1827, at age 17, he sailed for India, destined for a career in a cavalry regiment of the Indian army. He led two lives, one as a carefree cavalry officer, the other as a serious student of Asian languages. The latter pursuit soon qualified him for work as an interpreter at remote stations. Rawlinson rapidly became a legend for his horsemanship. On one occasion, he rode 1,200 kilometers (750 miles) in 150 hours to warn the officer in charge of an isolated outpost of the presence of a Russian agent. For years, British sporting magazines hailed this as the ride of the century.

In 1835, Rawlinson was posted to a military mission in Persia (present-day Iran), where he explored Kurdistan and visited the Great Rock at **Behistun.** He gazed upward at a sheer, polished surface bearing an inscription commemorating Persian King Darius's victory over rebels in 522 B.C. The trilingual inscription was in Old Persian and two versions of cuneiform, which we now know to be Elamite and Babylonian. Rawlinson could read the Old Persian and realized at once that Behistun was the Rosetta Stone of cuneiform. For the next 12 years, Rawlinson devoted most of his spare time to copying the inscriptions, climbing high above the ground and employing a nimble Kurdish boy with nerves of steel to complete the task, "hanging on with his toes and fingers."

Rawlinson was appointed British consul in Baghdad in 1843, an ideal post for a man with his linguistic passions. By 1847, he had deciphered the Behistun inscription in tandem with Edward Hincks, who was the first scholar to identify syllables in cuneiform script. Once Rawlinson understood that cuneiform characters represented more than one syllable, he made rapid progress. Soon he could read more than 150 characters and the meaning of some 200 words in Akkadian, the language behind the script.

Henry Rawlinson's consular duties kept him in regular touch with both Botta and Layard. He corresponded with the latter, visited his excavations, and used inscriptions to identify the excavated cities as Calah and Nineveh. His conclusions surprised Botta and the French, who had announced that Khorsabad was Nineveh.

Layard Excavates a Palace

Meanwhile, in 1849 Layard returned to Nineveh, where he resumed excavations in the Kuyunjik mounds. He soon uncovered the Assyrian King Sennacherib's "Palace without Rival," dating to 700 B.C.—a vast complex with a huge ceremonial hall guarded by human-headed bulls and adorned with bas-reliefs depicting prisoners quarrying and transporting the vast statues. The façade of the palace was 55 meters (180 feet) long, guarded by huge bulls and gigantic human figures, adorned with scenes of the king's conquests. The limestone slabs of the palace entrances still bore the ruts of Assyrian chariot wheels. Another large chamber bore scenes of a vicious siege of a city identified as Lachish in Israel, a battle mentioned in the Old Testament (2 Kings 18:13). The find caused a sensation among the devout, for it proved the historical veracity of the Old Testament.

In 1850, the excavations uncovered a room complex packed with piles of clay tablets. Perennially in a hurry, Layard simply shoveled the tablets into baskets, packed them in six crates, and shipped them off to London. Rawlinson picked through the baskets and realized their great historical value. He wrote in high excitement that Layard had found the Royal Library of King Assurbanipal, whose tablets contained "the system of Assyrian writing, the distinction between phonetic and ideographic signs . . . the grammar of the language, classification and explanation of technical terms. . . . A thorough examination of the fragments would lead to the most curious results" (Fagan 1979:119). Sitting in a tent lashed with rain, atop the Kuyunjik mounds, he wrote an outline of the history of Assyrian civilization "in great haste, amidst torrents of rain, in a little tent, upon the mound of Nineveh, without any aids beside a tolerably retentive memory, a pocket bible, and a notebook of inscriptions" (Fagan 1979:120).

Layard's excavations were rough and ready at best, based on crude tunneling and designed to find as many bas-reliefs and other spectacular artifacts as possible. He was well aware that the success of his excavations depended on a steady stream of new exhibits for the British Museum. After an abortive attempt to excavate at the ancient site of Babylon south of Baghdad, where his methods were too rudimentary to identify unbaked mud brick, Layard returned to London in 1851 to renewed popular acclaim. Two years later, he published *Nineveh and Babylon,* a longer and more mature work than his earlier best-seller. This time, he had the benefit of cuneiform inscriptions, enabling him to write the first historical account of Assyrian civilization, which he called "a kind of confederation formed by many tributary states."

Austen Henry Layard gave up archaeology after the publication of his second book at the tender age of 36. He became a member of Parliament, a much-respected diplomat, and a fine-art collector. By the time of his death in 1894, Layard had become one of the archaeological immortals, an archaeological adventurer of legendary energy with an unrivaled nose for spectacular finds that served him well. Unfortunately, scientifically trained excavators did not follow in his footsteps for another half-century, by which time incalculable damage had been done to ancient cities in both northern and southern Mesopotamia.

Summary

Chapter 3 describes the first archaeological investigations in Egypt and Mesopotamia. Egyptology began with the invasion of Egypt by Napoleon Bonaparte in 1798. The expedition's scientists compiled the first description of ancient Egyptian civilization and recovered the Rosetta Stone. The Stone's inscriptions helped Jean François Champollion decipher hieroglyphs in 1822. While a few scholars worked on ancient Egyptian inscriptions, looters descended on the Nile in the name of diplomacy, among them Bernardino

Drovetti and Giovanni Belzoni. The wave of looting did not subside until the late-nineteenth century, after the appointment of Auguste Mariette as Egypt's director of antiquities.

Serious Mesopotamian archaeology began with the appointment of Paul Emile Botta as French consul in Mosul, northern Iraq, in the 1840s. He claimed that his discovery of an Assyrian palace at Khorsabad was the biblical city of Nineveh. Subsequently, Englishman Austen Henry Layard excavated at Nimrud (biblical Calah), and subsequently at Kuyunjik, which proved to be ancient Nineveh. Layard was helped in his researches by the decipherment of cuneiform script by Henry Rawlinson, Edward Hincks, and Jules Oppert. Layard's excavations were rough and ready, and were mainly aimed at finding spectacular artifacts and sculpture. However, he did write the first account of Assyrian history from his excavations and cuneiform inscriptions.

Guide to Further Reading

Fagan, Brian. 1979. *Return to Babylon.* Boston: Little, Brown.

A popular account of early Mesopotamian archaeology from its beginnings to the Ur excavations of the 1930s.

———. 2004. *The Rape of the Nile.* 3rd ed. Boulder, CO: Westview Press.

This general account of early Egyptology focuses on the deeds of Giovanni Belzoni and other nineteenth-century pioneers.

Lloyd, Seton. 1980. *Foundations in the Dust.* Rev. ed. London: Thames and Hudson.

Lloyd's history of Mesopotamian archaeology is a classic.

Reeves, Nicholas. 2000. *Ancient Egypt: The Great Discoveries.* London and New York: Thames and Hudson.

This beautifully illustrated account of early Egyptology covers discoveries on a year-by-year basis. A wonderful browsing and reference book.

chapter 4

Human Progress and the Three Ages

A nineteenth-century British burial mound excavation as described in Gentleman's Magazine, 1840.

Eight barrows were examined. . . . They are generally of slight elevation above the natural chalky soil, the graves . . . being from two to four feet deep. Most of them contain skeletons, more or less entire, with the remains of weapons in iron, bosses of shields, urns, beads, fibulae, armlets, bones of small animals, and occasionally glass vessels.

Thomas Wright, account of a Victorian excavation,
Archaeological Journals, 1845 (p. 6)

chapter outline

By the late seventeenth and early eighteenth century, northern Europe had become the hub of a slowly developing world economy. The scientific advances of the Italian astronomer Galileo and the Englishman Isaac Newton encouraged a growing belief that humanity had progressed through time. This viewpoint did not lead to evolutionary theories of human history; these came into being as part of the Enlightenment philosophy of the eighteenth century, headed by French scholars such as Voltaire, and through the thinking of Scottish thinkers like John Locke and the notorious Lord Monboddo, who boldly declared that humans and orangutans belonged to the same species. This chapter examines ideas of human progress and how they affected thinking about the prehistoric past.

The Enlightenment and Human Progress

Enlightenment philosophers brought together a series of important principles based on a general assumption of human progress. They believed that all humans had similar levels of intelligence. Thus, all humans could aspire to progress—to the most technologically sophisticated civilization. Differences among human societies could be attributed to differences in climate and environment, or could simply be the result of historical accident. It followed that cultural progress was the dominant theme of human history from the earliest times, caused by natural factors. Such progress occurred continuously, because all humans wanted to improve their condition. Progress was not confined to technology, but extended to all aspects of human society, including social institutions and religious beliefs. Ignorance and superstition vanished as progress unfolded. All this progress resulted from humanity's ability to think rationally, a quality that distinguished humans from all other animals. Rational thought enabled human societies everywhere to exercise ever greater control over their environments. None of this was seen as contradicting Christian belief that a wise deity planned human existence. There were benevolent laws that controlled human destiny.

The scholars of the Enlightenment had much more information about human diversity to work with than their predecessors. Apart from an increasing knowledge of Native American societies, the voyages of the Comte de Bougainville, Captain James Cook, and others brought such peoples as the Pacific Islanders, the Maori of New Zealand, and the Australian Aborigines to scholarly notice. By the early nineteenth century, scholars believed that human societies had progressed from the simple to the more complex; but it took little account of archaeology, which remained a confusion of jumbled artifacts, badly excavated burial mounds, and unintelligible stone tools and earthworks.

The notion that humans had progressed from primitive beginnings became an important underpinning for understanding the remote past. Enlightenment philosophers took a renewed interest in the writings of the Roman philosopher Titus Lucretius Carus (98–55 B.C.), whose poem *De Rerum Natura* ("On the Nature of Things") argued that the earliest human artifacts were stone and wood fragments, which amplified hands, nails, and teeth. Later on, people manufactured tools of bronze and iron. Lucretius merely speculated about the past, as had others such as the Greek writer Hesiod of the eighth century B.C., who saw a degeneration of human existence from a fabled age of gold to the chaotic, violent times of an age of iron. By the eighteenth century, French scholars often wrote of three ages—of stone, bronze, and iron—as did Danish antiquarians, culminating in a book on Danish history by L. S. Vedel Simonsen in 1813. None of these writings were anything more than intelligent speculations based on a general notion of human progress with no foundation in archaeological observation, even if many scholars believed that ancient Europeans had made stone tools at some point in the remote past. The six-thousand-year chronology of theological dogma still constrained thinking about human prehistory.

The Barrow Diggers

Antiquarianism flourished in Europe during the seventeenth and eighteenth centuries, with the observations of John Aubrey at Avebury and the eccentric William Stukeley at Stonehenge, both in southern England, to mention only two examples. Stukeley in particular fostered romantic notions of an ancient Britain populated by flamboyant Druids. The discovery of the Tahitians in the South Pacific by Bougainville and Cook unleashed a torrent of interest in "noble savages," fueled by the writings of the French philosopher Jean-Jacques Rousseau, who wrote of the natural, carefree nature of savagery. The noble savage did not stand the test of time; but a strong sense of romanticism permeated antiquarian studies for generations.

Survey gave way to casual digging, then to serious digging, prompted both by curiosity and by the sensational excavations at Herculaneum and Pompeii. During the late eighteenth century, burial mound excavation became a popular pursuit among country ministers and landowners. The Reverend Bryan Faussett (1720–1776) excavated no fewer than 750 Anglo-Saxon mounds in southeastern England. John Douglas (1713–1819) published several volumes of *Nenia Britannica, or a Sepulchral History of Great Britain*, in which he compiled information on burial mound (barrow) excavations throughout the country. He went so far as to assume that barrows with only stone tools were earlier than those with metals.

Perhaps the most assiduous excavators of all were the wealthy landowner Sir Richard Colt Hoare and the wool merchant William Cunnington, who excavated no fewer than 465 burial mounds in the Wiltshire area of southern England from 1801 onward. This was barrow excavation on a grand scale—rapid trenching to the core of a mound to locate the burial and grave furniture, then a move to another location nearby. Colt Hoare located the sites, while Cunnington and two workers dug them. He often trenched two or three burial mounds in a day, boasting that he could tell what a mound contained just by looking at it! In the evening, the two friends would toast the ancient Britons, drinking port as "the rude relicks of 2000 years" sat among the fruit and wine glasses. These dedicated barrow diggers destroyed as much as they recovered. All too often, a pick would shatter an urn or a skeleton, or a delicate find would crumble to dust when exposed to the air.

Colt Hoare and Cunnington were little more than collectors of curiosities, but they did record the layers of burial mounds, recognized original and later interments, and used coins to date some barrows that belonged to historic, Roman times. However, they were unable to subdivide any of the prehistoric burial mounds into chronological periods. Everything was a jumble. There was no sense of order in the random collections of clay urns, bronze tools, gold ornaments, and iron swords.

The two barrow diggers were not alone in their confusion. Danish philosopher and antiquary Rasmus Nyerup started a small museum in Copenhagen, but he despaired of putting anything in chronological order. "Everything which has come down to us from heathendom is wrapped in a thick fog," he complained (Daniel 1981:56). He was certain that his artifacts were older than Christianity, but whether by a millennium or a few centuries remained a mystery. Nyerup's collections were to form the nucleus of the National Museum of Denmark, founded in 1807.

The antiquarians of the day relied on historical records, on the Scriptures, and on conjectural medieval histories. But, as antiquarian Richard Wise commented, "where history is silent and the monuments cannot speak for themselves, demonstration cannot be expected; but the utmost is conjecture supported by probability (Lynch and Lynch 1968:17). Some excavators were already observing stratigraphic layers in archaeological sites; others assumed that there had been an era when stone tools were universal before the use of metals. Almost everyone thought that the artifacts of the past and monuments like Stonehenge merely illustrated recorded history. That history could only come from historical documents or reliable oral traditions. Until antiquarians liberated themselves from this assumption, they had no chance of understanding human prehistory.

The Native Americans

Nowhere did this pervasive notion exercise a stronger influence than in the debates over the origins of the Native Americans. Speculations about their origins began soon after Christopher Columbus landed in the Bahamas and Hernán Cortés overthrew the Aztecs. Inevitably, scholars turned to written sources—to classical literature and the Scriptures. Since the Catholic Church had proclaimed the Indians human beings capable of conversion to the Christian faith, they were assumed to have descended from Adam and Eve and to have spread from the Garden of Eden. Were the inhabitants of the Americas descendants of the mysterious Ten Lost Tribes of Israel? Were they descended from ancient Canaanites, Carthaginians, or Egyptians, or even from survivors of the lost continent of Atlantis? Such speculations continued unchecked until the nineteenth century.

Only a few soberer voices were raised. As long ago as 1589, Jesuit missionary José de Acosta, who had served among the Indians of Mexico and Peru, argued in his *Historia Natural y Moral de las Indias* that the Indians had reached the New World in the same manner as wild beasts, by land from Asia, with "only short stretches of navigation." Acosta calculated that only a few people arrived at first, at least two thousand years in the past. Their descendants developed not only agriculture but elaborate states like those of the Aztecs and Incas. He wrote all this a century and a half before Russian explorer Vitus Bering sailed through the strait that now bears his name in 1728.

Acosta also theorized that the first Native Americans were hunters, not farmers, which some saw as evidence of a divine wrath that had made them inferior to Europeans and Asians. At the same time, more dispassionate observers thought that living Native Americans like the Virginia Indians mirrored what life had been like for the ancient Britons and other early Europeans. The antiquarian John Aubrey drew on such arguments when he developed his famous description of prehistoric life in southern Britain in his *Monumenta Britannica*, already mentioned in Chapter 1.

Few people paid any attention to the spectacular ruins of ancient Mesoamerican or Andean civilizations such as the city of **Teotihuacán** in

Figure 4.1   Teotihuacán, Mexico. The view is taken from the Pyramid of the Moon and looks down the main artery of the city—The Avenue of the Dead (a modern name). The Pyramid of the Sun is at the left.

highland Mexico (Figure 4.1). Only a handful of European travelers penetrated the dense rain forest of the Maya lowlands or visited the adobe pyramids of Peru's North Coast.

The late eighteenth century saw the first stirrings of more serious archaeological inquiry. In 1789, the botanist William Bartram (1739–1823), who traveled widely through what is now the southeastern United States, found numerous deserted mound sites, which he compared to ceremonial structures used by living Creek Indian communities. This is one of the first instances of the use of ethnographic data to interpret archaeological data.

Five years earlier, Thomas Jefferson excavated an Indian burial mound on his country estate at Monticello, Virginia. Unlike Colt Hoare and Cunnington, he set about his task with deliberate care, undertaking an excavation to answer a specific question: Was the mound a village burial place, a communal sepulcher for numerous surrounding communities, or a "funerary pyre" for battlefield dead? Jefferson dug trial trenches at first and uncovered "collections of human bones at different depths." He then excavated on a larger scale, cutting a profile through the mound "so that I could examine its internal structure." Jefferson observed at least five layers of human skeletons, but no signs of traumatic wounds or weapons, so he concluded that the tumulus was no battlefield cemetery. He estimated that at least a thousand skeletons lay in the mound, which had accumulated as a result of "the customary collection of bones and the deposition of them together" (Jefferson 1788:26).

Jefferson's archaeological endeavor is one of the earliest examples of scientific inquiry into an archaeological site, which did not rely on written records. He posed specific questions, then tried to answer them with careful excavations that included stratigraphic observations. His approach was a scientific one, and it convinced him that the mound, and many others like it, were of Indian manufacture and origin.

As Jefferson carried out his remarkable work, dozens of other such mounds and earthworks disappeared during forest clearance and plowing as settlers swarmed westward into the Ohio Valley. "It is too early to form theories on these antiquities," wrote Jefferson in a letter to a friend in 1787. "We must wait with patience till more facts are collected." In the meantime, popular writers speculated about the remarkable mounds that were to be seen everywhere in what were then known as "the western territories." In these writers' specious tales, Canaanites, Homer's warriors, and other ancient peoples from the Mediterranean world had fought epic battles across North American soil. A myth of a magnificent race of moundbuilders rapidly took hold in American antiquarian literature, ignoring the few careful observations of earthworks and their artifacts amid racist speculations to the effect that a superior race, a people of foreign and higher civilization, had once lived in this remote land. Just as in Europe, archaeology was a slave to classical writings and the Scriptures, and was shackled by a seeming chaos of artifacts and archaeological sites that made no historical sense at all.

The Three Ages

The first attempts to create order out of archaeological chaos came in Denmark, where there was a strong patriotic interest in pre-Christian artifacts and archaeological sites of all kinds. Like their British and French counterparts, the Danes wrestled with an apparent confusion of archaeological finds. We have seen how the philosopher Rasmus Nyerup started his own museum and complained of a "fog" of confusion about "Heathendom." Nyerup was influential in the setting up of the Danish Commission on Ancient Monuments in 1806, which was charged with protecting archaeological sites and establishing a national museum. He was also responsible for the appointment of Christian Jurgensen Thomsen to place the collections of the new museum in order and display them to the public.

Christian Jurgensen Thomsen (1768–1865) was the son of a wealthy merchant and was a coin enthusiast. His experience with coin classification made him the ideal person to set the museum in order. At the time, the museum's collections were stacked in a church loft with no one to look after them. Thomsen organized the collections like a business, entering new acquisitions in a ledger, cataloging them, and assigning them numbers. More than five hundred specimens passed through his hands in a few months, so he soon became familiar with a wide range of prehistoric artifacts.

Once cataloged, the collections had to be made intelligible to the general public. Thomsen considered various options and decided to concentrate on the materials from which the tools were manufactured as a scientific basis for classification. In 1816, he divided Danish history into three phases, the earliest being the "Heathen Period," which corresponded to prehistoric times. He then subdivided this period into three ages: the Stone Age, a time when stone tools and weapons were used, followed by a Bronze Age with bronze and copper artifacts, and finally an Iron Age marked by the use of iron objects. Thomsen based his new "Three Age" scheme entirely on the museum collections. He drew on Nyerup and other earlier writings about archaeology, and especially on grave furniture, where, typically, several objects of different type lay in the same sepulcher, and thus were of the same age.

Christian Jurgensen Thomsen was a lively conversationalist and a prolific letter writer, although only one book, the museum catalog, came from his pen. The only popular exposition of Thomsen's Three Age System was in the new National Museum's galleries, where the visitor found separate cases devoted to each of the Three Ages. Nevertheless, Thomsen's ideas spread widely, largely because he spent a great deal of time showing visitors around the museum, which opened at first for just two hours a week, then for longer periods. Every Thursday between eleven and one o'clock he would show visitors through the galleries, enchanting young people with his stories and his down-to-earth enthusiasm (Figure 4.2). He would take the trouble to place a prehistoric gold necklet around a young girl's neck as a way of making the past come alive for her.

To Thomsen, the past was not just legend, but was made up of material evidence. "A tumulus, a stone circle in the countryside, a stone tool, or a metal ornament unearthed from the sequestered burial chamber—all these afford us a more vivid picture of the prehistoric age," he wrote in his classic museum catalog, *Guidebook to Nordic Antiquity (Ledestrad til Nordisk Oldekyndighed)*, published in 1836. This obscure Scandinavian work soon drew the attention of archaeologists elsewhere. In 1848, the noted British archaeologist Sir John Lubbock translated Thomsen's slim volume into English, ensuring its circulation throughout Europe and in North America. Within a few years, the Three Age System had become the foundation of all attempts to subdivide and classify the prehistoric past in Europe.

Thomsen was a museum man above all else; he had little time for archaeological excavation. When he did dig, it was with meticulous care by the standards of the day. In 1845, he and four colleagues, one an anatomist, excavated a Bronze Age burial at **Hvidegaard** north of Copenhagen. The stone-lined tomb contained cremated bones and a fine array of textiles, along with a leather pouch containing seashells, a snake's tail, and other unusual, perhaps sacred, objects. The grave goods, which lay on an ox-skin, included a sheathed sword, a fine brooch, and a pair of simple pliers. Thomsen's excavation was unusual for its careful recording methods, and for the presence of an anatomist, who proclaimed the cremated bones those of a man. The grave goods were typical for a Bronze Age warrior.

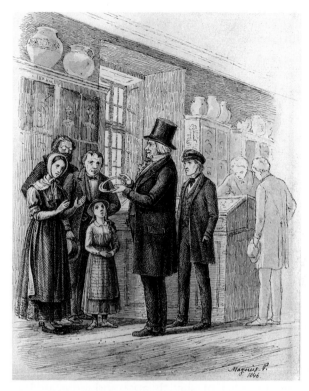

Figure 4.2 Christian Jurgensen Thomsen showing artifacts to museum visitors, 1846.

During Thomsen's directorship, the National Museum collections expanded to more than 27,000 items. Today it is one of the finest museums in Europe. Thomsen had one of the essential gifts of an archaeologist—a sharp eye for form and ornamentation, for the small details of individual artifacts. The Three Age System was the result. With this simple, and now much elaborated, framework, the modern science of archaeology and archaeological classification was born.

Three Ages Proven

In 1838, a university student named Jacob Jens Worsaae (1821–1885) introduced himself to Christian Jurgensen Thomsen. He had developed an interest in archaeology while still a young man and had acquired a large collection of antiquities. Worsaae became a museum volunteer, but Thomsen was suspicious of the highly intelligent young man, who was not afraid to express his opinions and was a fluent writer, unlike his mentor. When Thomsen refused to pay him a salary, Worsaae found a new patron in King Christian VIII, who supported his research and the writing of Worsaae's first book, *The Primeval Antiquities of Denmark,* published in 1843 and translated into English in 1849. This short book was a brilliant discourse on the Three Age System, as well as a reminder that "our fathers, a free independent people, have dwelt from time immemorial in this country." In 1847 the king sent Worsaae on a tour of Viking sites in Britain and Ireland, which resulted in another important synthesis a year later—*Remains of the Danes and the Norsemen in England, Scotland, and Ireland.*

Worsaae now was given the post of Inspector for the Conservation of Antiquarian Monuments, a job that kept him traveling constantly, inventorying sites, conserving them, and saving them from destruction. He also excavated numerous prehistoric sites, many of them spectacular Stone Age and Bronze Age sepulchers where the dead lay with their finest possessions, including swords and shields, fine clay vessels, and skin clothing. Worsaae's many excavations showed the stratigraphic validity of Christian Jurgensen Thomsen's Three Age System, which, until then, had been based on museum collections alone.

As inspector, Worsaae also served as a member of a three-scientist commission responsible for investigating prehistoric shell-mounds—piles of empty mollusk shells accumulated by ancient shellfish collectors along Danish coasts. Working with a geologist and a zoologist, Worsaae examined many such middens (ancient shell heaps) and excavated a large mound found during road-making near **Meilgaard** in east Jutland. He removed a large section of the midden, observing thick layers of oyster shells and mussels, and also finding antler spearheads, stone tools, hearths, and other traces of human occupation. Worsaae described the mounds as "some kind of eating place." These sites soon became "kitchen-middens" in contemporary scientific literature.

The simple antler and stone tools from the shell mounds were cruder than those from later Stone Age burial mounds, allowing Worsaae to divide the Danish Stone Age into two stages. The earlier period was a culture of simple hunters and fisherfolk; the later stage was marked by farming. Worsaae's geological and zoological colleagues studied ancient climatic change using layers of peat bogs and the vegetable remains in them, animal bones, and shells. Zoologist Japetus Steenstrup was even able to use the bones of migratory birds to establish in which seasons of the year the mounds had been occupied. This research made Worsaae acutely aware of the importance of studying ancient environments, a century before such approaches became commonplace in archaeology.

In 1855, Worsaae began teaching at the University in Copenhagen, the first professional teacher of prehistory in Scandinavia. He resigned in 1866, when he became director of the National Museum of Denmark, a post he held until his death in 1885.

Jacob Jens Worsaae proved the scientific validity of the Three Age System and laid the foundations for much more detailed studies of prehistoric European artifacts that followed in the late nineteenth century.

The Swiss Lake Dwellings

Neither Thomsen nor Worsaae thought of the Three Ages as showing human progress in Scandinavia. Rather, they argued that bronze and ironworking were introduced into the north by waves of immigrants from the south or as a result of contact with "other nations." Their Three Age scheme provided a model for expanding archaeological research elsewhere in Europe, especially in Scotland and Switzerland.

Across the North Sea, the Scottish antiquarian Daniel Wilson (1816–1892) used the Three Age System to organize the large collections of the Society of Antiquaries of Scotland in Edinburgh; this became the basis for his *Archaeology and Prehistoric Annals of Scotland,* published in 1851. Wilson was ahead of his time. Not only did he demonstrate differences between Scandinavian and Scottish prehistory, but he also pointed out that the kind of reconstruction of the past derived from artifacts was very different from that obtained from historical records. In due course, he wrote, archaeologists would be able to learn about the social life and religious beliefs of ancient societies. Wilson's approach was far more evolutionary than that of the Scandinavians. It fell on deaf ears in England, where he failed to persuade the British Museum to reorganize its displays with the Three Age System.

Discoveries at the edge of Swiss lakes added new credibility to evolutionary theories. For years, fishermen working these lakes had told stories of submerged forests lurking beneath the surface. Then a drought in the 1850s caused lake levels to fall sharply, exposing some of the "forests" as hundreds of wooden pilings set into the mud. In 1854, Ferdinand Keller (1800–1881), a professor of English and president of the Zurich Antiquarian Society, dug into one of these pile complexes near the village of **Obermeilen** on Lake Zurich. He found all manner of perishable objects, among them animal bones, wooden ax handles, even hazelnuts—finds that gave a much more detailed picture of ancient society by the lake than stone implements alone. Keller's methods were rough at best, but they led to the discovery of more than two hundred such sites by 1869, and to more excavations (Figure 4.3)

Originally, Keller and his successors interpreted the piles as the remains of "lake dwellings" set on piles driven into shallow water, just like modern-day New Guinea settlements reported by French travelers. But later excavators in the 1920s used more sophisticated methods to show that the lakeside settlements were originally built on swampy ground—dry land that was flooded by rising lake waters during a time of higher rainfall.

Some of the Swiss lake villages yielded Roman artifacts, but most of them clearly predated the Roman era and could be classified within the Three Age

Figure 4.3 A reconstruction of the Obermeilen lake village painted by artist Rodolphe Auguste Bachelin in 1867. This is the classic nineteenth-century depiction of a lake dwelling. Rudolphe-Auguste Bachelin, "Gemalde, Idealbild einer Pfahlbauersiedlung," 1867. Swiss National Museum, Zurich, LM-44602, COL-5332.

System. Keller's researches caused considerable interest throughout Europe and in the United States, where people searched without success for similar settlements. The anthropologist Frank Cushing located one such site at Key Marco, Florida, in 1895–1896, with disastrous results (see Chapter 5).

Hand Axes and Lake Dwellers

By the 1870s, the broad outlines of European prehistory were coming into focus. The earliest known societies were those of the hand ax makers, whose artifacts came from the gravels of the Somme and Thames Rivers, in association with the bones of long-extinct animals like elephants. Then there was apparently a long chronological gap before the beginning of the Scandinavian Stone Age and the rest of the Three Age sequence so well known from Danish graves and the Swiss lake villages. Prehistoric times ended with the Roman conquest of barbarian Europe. The apparently near-ubiquitous stone, bronze, and iron sequence was a powerful argument for human progress over the long millennia of prehistoric times. But what lay between the crude hand axes of the Somme, the Neanderthal skull, and later societies?

Keller's excavations and collections, like those of the museum in Copenhagen, were soon part of a much-followed itinerary that antiquarians took through western Europe. Increasingly, from the mid-1860s on, these travelers also visited the lush Dordogne region of southwestern France, where a French lawyer and an English banker were making remarkable finds in enormous rock shelters carved by water out of high limestone cliffs.

Edouard Lartet (1801–1871) was a country lawyer with a passion for fossil collecting. In 1852, he developed an interest in archaeology when a road worker near Aurignac in the Pyrenees foothills of southern France uncovered a long-buried cave containing the remains of 17 people buried with perforated shell disks and mammoth teeth. The skeletons were promptly reburied in the local cemetery, but Lartet subsequently dug into the cave and discovered a hearth and flint artifacts that he believed dated to "the remotest antiquity."

Ten years later, Lartet came across a box of animal bones and flint tools from the village of Les Eyzies in southwestern France's Vezère Valley lying forgotten in the store of a Paris fossil collector. Visiting Les Eyzies, he was astounded to find dozens of undisturbed caves and rock shelters near the then-tiny rural village, and he devoted the rest of his life to their excavation.

Lartet joined forces with a wealthy British banking friend, Henry Christy (1810–1865), who loved travel and antiquities. Christy bankrolled the research; Lartet supervised the excavations. Apart from recovering thousands of antler, bone, and flint artifacts, Lartet identified different levels of human occupation, using both animal bones and tools. His excavators shoveled their way through dense occupation levels, recovering not only hearths and artifacts, but also bones of reindeer, mammoth (arctic elephants), bison, and arctic fox, among other extinct European animals. The finest antler and bone artifacts came from a rock shelter named **La Madeleine**, right at water's edge; they included reindeer antler harpoons with curved barbs and superb decorated bone fragments, some of them so beautifully executed that one could even identify the tear ducts in bison and reindeer eyes (Figure 4.4).

Figure 4.4   Cro-Magnon artistry. A bison licking its flank—a rendering so precise that the tear duct of the eye can be seen. La Madeleine rock shelter, southwestern France, 10.5 centimeters (4.1 inches) long.

In 1868, workers excavating a railroad cutting uncovered a buried rock shelter near a rock named **Cro-Magnon** on the outskirts of Les Eyzies. At the back of the shelter, Lartet's son Louis uncovered the remains of a human fetus and the skeletons of several adults, including that of a woman apparently killed by a blow to the head. These round-headed people were entirely modern in appearance, in sharp contrast to the Neanderthals, whose artifacts and remains lay at the base of some of the Les Eyzies caves and rock shelters. They had flourished in a time of extreme cold, during the Great Ice Age—the last of the geological epochs, recently identified by Swiss geologist Louis Agassiz—long before the Scandinavian shellfish collectors and the Swiss lake dwellers.

The discoveries of Lartet and Christy completed the first cultural sequence for prehistoric Europe—an incomplete one by modern standards, but a chronicle of human progress, from very simple beginnings right up to the Romans. The sequence was based on the Three Age System, and above all, on careful stratigraphic observations that led to sequences of different ancient societies, some working with stone, others with metals. Such stratigraphic observations were based on the principles of superposition—the first relative chronology for prehistoric archaeology anywhere.

Inevitable Human Progress?

Contrary to what many scientists believe, prehistoric archaeology developed not just from theories of stratigraphic geology and biological evolution. The study of prehistory also stemmed from notions of human progress espoused during the Enlightenment and from experience with artifact classification, derived, in Thomsen's case, from numismatics—the study of coins. These developments unfolded against a social climate in which an expanding middle class was enthralled with technological development, and was also imbued with a strong moral sense of the importance of progress harnessed for the general good of society. Danish archaeology was strongly nationalistic; the emerging prehistoric archaeology everywhere reinforced ideas of human progress, of social evolution.

Thomsen, Worsaae, and others originally developed the Three Age System within the context of the biblical chronology of six thousand years. This gave them enough time to account for what was known of prehistoric times before the establishment of the antiquity of humankind in 1859 (see Chapter 2). Worsaae dated the first settlement of Denmark to about 3000 B.C., an estimate that is remarkably close to much of what is known of later Danish prehistory today. The development of **Palaeolithic** ("Old Stone Age"—Greek: *paleos*, old, *lithos*, stone) archaeology added thousands of years to the short Three Age chronology—not only the hand axes of the Somme, but the Les Eyzies rock shelters with their lengthy Cro-Magnon occupations dating to a time when Europe was much colder than today.

In 1865, the English banker and naturalist John Lubbock published his *Prehistoric Times,* in which he divided the Stone Age into an earlier Palaeolithic or Old Stone Age and a more recent **Neolithic,** or New Stone Age (Greek—*neos,* new), to which the Swiss lake villages and the earliest Scandinavian tombs belonged. Lubbock was a strong advocate of human progress through time; but the French archaeologist Gabriel de Mortillet (1821–1898) carried this approach to extremes. De Mortillet was a geologist and paleontologist who developed an interest in prehistoric archaeology and became professor of prehistoric anthropology at the School of Anthropology in Paris in 1876. Like many of his geological contemporaries, De Mortillet was caught up in a profound enthusiasm for evolution. He regarded early prehistory as a bridge between paleontology, the study of fossil animals, and later prehistoric cultures.

Whereas Lartet and Christy had distinguished between different stages of human occupation in their Dordogne rock shelters by using the frequency of different animals, de Mortillet focused on distinctive artifacts. He used a few "typical" artifacts to define ancient cultures, treating them just like paleontological fossils and naming the layers from which they came after the site where they were first found. We owe to de Mortillet such cultural labels for Upper Palaeolithic cultures as **Aurignacian** (named after the Aurignac cave) and **Magdalenian** (after La Madeleine rock shelter near Les Eyzies). The trouble was that de Mortillet treated archaeological sequences and cultures like geological epochs, each with its distinctive "type fossils." In time, he developed a sequence of cultural stages spanning all of prehistoric times— based on French sites, but considered applicable to the entire world.

De Mortillet's approach implied that one could read the entire chronicle of human progress in one sequence or series of sequences, just like geological strata. While Scandinavian archaeologists like Thomsen and Worsaae were interested in what ancient peoples ate and in how they behaved, many French scholars thought of the past in terms of type fossils, a dogmatic approach that made little allowance for cultural variations between neighboring sites and areas—for the idiosyncrasies of human behavior. At the Paris International Exposition of 1867, de Mortillet's handbook to the prehistoric exhibit boldly proclaimed human progress as a universal law of humanity. His approach was to persist, especially in French circles, well into the twentieth century.

Cultural Evolution and Human Progress

While de Mortillet and his contemporaries wrestled with type fossils and human progress in the past, the new discipline of anthropology was coming into being—especially the branch called *ethnology*, the comparative study of non-Western societies. By the 1860s, there was strong interest in theoretical models as to how human societies had developed into the complex industrial civilizations of the Victorian world. The rapid expansion of Western civilization and a stepped-up pace of exploration in Africa and the Pacific revealed many hitherto unknown living societies. By studying societies at all stages of complexity, it might be possible to develop scientific, as opposed to philosophical, theories about how ancient European societies developed.

Much of this research stemmed from the travels of the German ethnologist Adolf Bastian (1826–1905), who journeyed around the world collecting specimens for the Royal Museum of Ethnology in Berlin. Bastian was a strong believer in the psychic unity of humankind, under which all humans at different stages of development shared certain "elementary ideas," which enabled their societies to develop in broadly similar ways, within the constraints imposed by their environments.

The sociologist Herbert Spencer (1820–1903) was another pioneer. During the 1850s, he championed a general evolutionary approach to all manner of philosophical and scientific problems. He argued that human societies had developed from the simple and homogeneous into the complex and highly diverse. Spencer considered individualism and free enterprise key elements in cultural progress, a popular doctrine in nineteenth-century societies that placed a high value on progress with a capital P.

Two pioneering anthropologists in particular rode the crest of evolutionary theorizing about human progress. Both took account of exploding knowledge about non-Western societies, which gave them a rich comparative archive. The American scholar Lewis Henry Morgan (1818–1881) believed that human progress was inherent in the human condition. In his *Ancient Society* (1877), Morgan placed European society at the pinnacle of human achievement, then worked back into the past in a series of cultural stages, starting with Lower Savagery, where people subsisted on "fruits and nuts," through various grades of Savagery and Barbarism to Civilization, marked by a phonetic alphabet and writing. Morgan's research contained some valuable insights into the evolution of kinship, but was far too all-embracing and simplistic to accommodate an increasingly complex record of the past.

The British anthropologist Sir Edward Tylor (1832–1917) in his *Researches into the Early History of Mankind* (1865) conceived of human societies, ancient and modern, in three broad stages: Savagery, referring to hunter-gatherer societies; Barbarism, for subsistence farming societies; and Civilization. This unilinear, single track of human progress sat well both with general Victorian notions of human progress and with what little was known about prehistoric humanity. Tylor, Morgan, and their contemporaries had confidence in their evolutionary schemes, living as they did in an age when technological innovation was assumed to be the solution to everything and a driving force of human progress, ancient and modern.

Inevitably, late-nineteenth-century archaeologists tended to interpret the prehistoric past in unilinear terms, confronted as they were with De Mortillet's "laws of humanity" and with an archaeological record comprising, for the most part, rows and rows of stone artifacts.

Belief in human progress was a popular theme for a technological age, and for the new discipline of prehistoric archaeology—a discipline that enjoyed great prestige, linked as it was to paleontology and geology, and providing as it did an exciting new perspective on ancient Europe. That this progress had proceeded in a linear fashion did not faze the scholars of the day. Nor should one entirely blame them for theories that, in retrospect, seem ethnocentric and racist. At the time, nothing was known about the prehistory of other continents—of regions outside the narrow confines of Europe. As we shall see in Chapters 5 and 6, new archaeological discoveries in Africa, the Americas, and Asia soon showed that Morgan and Tylor's formulations were far too simplistic to reflect even a semblance of prehistoric reality.

Summary

Chapter 4 discusses ideas of human progress and some of the nineteenth-century archaeological discoveries and theories that fostered such thinking. Assumptions of human progress date back to the Enlightenment movement of the eighteenth century, which assumed that all humans had similar intelligence levels. Progress resulted from people's ability to think rationally and control their environment. These notions of human progress unfolded in a world where excavation was in its infancy and burial mounds only crudely excavated, yielding a jumble of artifacts from all periods of the past. Intense speculation also surrounded the origins of the Native Americans and the so-called moundbuilders of North America. In 1816, Christian Jurgensen Thomsen arranged the displays of the National Museum of Denmark in Copenhagen according to a Three Age System, which was widely adopted across Europe. Subsequently, another Danish archaeologist, Jacob Jens Worsaae, proved the stratigraphic validity of the system. The discovery of the Swiss lake dwellings and of the late Ice Age Cro-Magnon cultures of southwestern France filled in gaps between the early hand axes of the Somme River and the first Stone Age inhabitants of Scandinavia.

Doctrines of inevitable human progress developed from archaeology's close associations with stratigraphic geology, and from new theories of cultural, as opposed to biological, evolution. French prehistorian Gabriel de Mortillet developed a geologically rigid scheme for the development of Stone Age cultures, which came into wide use after 1867. Meanwhile, early anthropologists like the American scholar Lewis Henry Morgan and the Englishman Edward Tylor espoused theories of a unilinear evolution of humankind, from simple hunter-gatherer societies to the pinnacle of technology, Victorian civilization. Such schemes were attractive in an era when archaeology enjoyed high prestige and technological progress was the fashion of the day.

Guide to Further Reading

Daniel, Glyn. 1963. *The Idea of Prehistory.* Cleveland, OH: World Publications.

This short essay is still a fundamental source on the Three Ages.

Gräslund, Bo. 1987. *The Birth of Prehistoric Chronology.* Cambridge: Cambridge University Press.

Gräslund offers an excellent essay on how order came from chaos.

Harris, Marvin. 1968. *The Rise of Anthropological Theory.* New York: Thomas Y. Crowell.

Although outdated, this book offers superb critiques of early anthropology, with some archaeology thrown in.

Marsden, B. M. 1974. *The Early Barrow-Diggers.* Princes Risborough: Shire Publications.

A useful narrative account of early excavators in Britain.

Willey, Gordon R., and Jeremy Sabloff. 1993. *A History of American Archaeology.* 3rd ed. New York: W. H. Freeman.

A widely quoted summary of early American archaeology, including the moundbuilders.

chapter 5

Early American Archaeology

Pueblo Bonito, Chaco Canyon, New Mexico.

All was mystery, dark impenetrable mystery, and every circumstance increased it. . . . Here an immense forest shrouds the ruins, hiding them from sight, heightening the impression and moral effect, and giving an intensity and almost wildness to the interest . . .

John Lloyd Stephens on the Maya city of Copán, *Incidents of Travel in Central America, Chiapas, and Yucatán,* 1841 (p. 56)

chapter outline

This chapter describes the early days of American archaeology, starting with the sensational descriptions of Maya ruins in Central America by John Lloyd Stephens and Frederick Catherwood from 1839 to 1842. These discoveries came at a time of intense controversy over the North American mound-builders and the date of the first Americans. Southwestern archaeology developed in the late nineteenth century, emerging out of pioneering ethnological field researches by Adolph Bandelier and Frank Cushing.

Many of these developments were the result of complicated interactions between early archaeologists, increasingly powerful academic institutions, and those who sought to exploit the past for profit.

The Discovery of Ancient Maya Civilization

After the Spanish Conquest of 1519, the Maya civilization of lowland Mesoamerica with its great centers went into rapid decline. The people survived, dispersed in rural villages and small towns; but their temples, pyramids, and plazas were soon overgrown and were rapidly forgotten. When Dominican friar Diego de Landa (1524–1579) arrived in Yucatán in 1549, he and his missionary colleagues persecuted the Maya and forced them with fanatical zeal to convert to the Catholic faith. They beat and tortured back-sliders, destroyed thousands of "idols," and burned numerous bark codices with their mysterious writings—all of this much to the horror of the Maya. De Landa himself was a contradiction. On the one hand, he pursued back-sliders and idolaters with unrelenting vigor. On the other, he developed an interest in ancient Maya culture, rationalizing it as a way of better converting them to the One True Faith. In his book *Relación de las Cosas de Yucatán,* written partly to defend himself against allegations that he treated Indians cruelly, de Landa described several Maya ruins, among them the city of Uxmal. He also puzzled over the elaborate Maya glyphs and over their indigenous calendar, and he even succeeded in deciphering some of the script centuries before any scholar achieved such a feat. De Landa's *Cosas* languished in church archives until the nineteenth century, presumably because it was considered too controversial to publish, while the zealous friar himself went on to become bishop of Chiapas and Yucatán.

Between the sixteenth and nineteenth centuries, Maya civilization languished in historical obscurity. Dense rain forest mantled pyramids and plazas, as the great Maya cities vanished, known only to local villagers living as far away from colonial tax collectors as possible. A handful of travelers heard rumors of great cities and ventured into the clinging forest, but their reports aroused little interest in the outside world. Among the travelers was the French artist Jean Frédéric Waldeck, who visited **Palenque** and other centers in 1832 and depicted them in romantic, even fanciful terms. Some army officers also visited the ruins, but, again, their reports had little impact on the scholarly world.

Nevertheless, rumors of lost cities in the Central American rain forest did circulate in New York and in European capitals. In 1839, they attracted the attention of two experienced and gifted travelers—John Lloyd Stephens and Frederick Catherwood.

John Lloyd Stephens (1805–1852) was the son of a wealthy New York merchant. He trained for the law, but instead of graduating in 1824, he traveled westward to Illinois—at the time an ambitious journey to the expanding frontier. His trip whetted his appetite for travel, and this appetite never abated. After ten years as a New York attorney, during which time he became active in several political campaigns, the eloquent Stephens developed a throat infection. His physician recommended a long European trip as a cure. Stephens never returned to the law.

Between 1835 and 1837, Stephens traveled widely in Europe. He ventured east to Russia as far as Moscow and St. Petersburg, bouncing along for hundreds of miles in creaky wagons. In Paris, he came across an account of the little-known rock-cut city of Petra in modern-day Jordan and promptly decided to go there. First he traveled up the Nile enjoying ancient Egyptian ruins, wearing Arab dress. Then he crossed the desert to Petra, nearly dying of thirst in the process. Stephens was so entranced by Petra that he developed a serious interest in archaeology almost overnight.

Throughout his travels, Stephens had written long, entertaining letters home. Returning to New York, he found himself famous; his friends had published the best of the letters in local newspapers. These epistles became the basis for his first book, *Incidents of Travel in Arabia Petraea,* published in 1837. The book became an immediate best-seller, for its author had a vivid and easy style and an engaging sense of humor. He promptly wrote a second book, about his travels in Greece and Russia, which enjoyed equal success at a time when travel and adventure books were hot properties.

While writing his first two books, Stephens met the Scottish artist Frederick Catherwood (1799–1854), who shared his passion for ancient civilizations. Catherwood had traveled widely in Egypt and the Holy Land and enjoyed a considerable reputation for his accurate and evocative drawings of ancient ruins, some of which were almost as accurate as photographs. It was Catherwood who drew Stephens's attention to some little-known publications that described mysterious ruins in the forests of Central America. Sensing a unique opportunity, Stephens wangled an appointment as American chargé d'affaires in Central America to give legitimacy to an expedition to the rain forests of Guatemala and Mexico.

Catherwood and Stephens sailed for Belize and Izabal in Guatemala in October 1839. After a difficult journey through rough, forested country, their five mules arrived at the remote village of **Copán,** where they saw well-preserved stone walls across a small river. The next day, they explored a vast overgrown Maya city, silent except for "monkeys moving along the tops of the trees." Stephens was moved to profound eloquence in one of the finest descriptions of an archaeological site ever written: "The city was desolate. No remnant of this race hangs around the ruins. . . . It lay before us like a shattered bark in the midst of the ocean" (Stephens 1841:65). Meanwhile, Catherwood sketched, ankle-deep in mud, trying to copy the intricate carvings on the weathered stelae (columns) set in Copán's great plaza (Figure 5.1). Stephens wanted to ship the finest parts of the forgotten city back to New York piece by piece. However, the river was unsuitable for rafts, so he contented himself with buying the site for fifty dollars—the bargain of a century.

While Catherwood sketched, Stephens embarked on a 1,930-kilometer (1,200-mile) diplomatic journey to San Salvador and Costa Rica; then the two men traveled a further 1,600 kilometers (1,000 miles) northeastward to another great Maya city, Palenque. Practically indistinguishable from the local people, they traveled through thick forest in the heart of rebel-infested country. The journey was worth it. Stephens admired the Temple of the Inscriptions with its "spirited figures in bas-relief" (Figure 5.2). While examining Palenque's artwork, he realized that it was the work not of ancient Egyptians or other immigrants, but of "a people originating and growing up here . . . having a distinct, separate, and indigenous existence" (Stephens 1841:251). His carefully reasoned observations set the stage for much future Maya archaeology.

The explorers returned to New York in July 1840, after a ten-month journey. Nine months later, *Incidents of Travel in Central America, Chiapas, and Yucatán* appeared to rapturous acclaim. More than twenty thousand copies were sold in a few months, a stupendous sale for the time. *Incidents* is still in

Figure 5.1   Frederick Catherwood's rendering of a stela at Copán, Mexico. The picture is somewhat romantic, but almost as accurate as a photograph.

Figure 5.2   Temple of the Inscriptions, Palenque.

print to this day. In this most famous of archaeological books, Stephens was strongly influenced by the researches of the Boston historian William Prescott (1796–1859). Nearly blinded as a result of an accident while a student at Harvard, Prescott devoted his life to historical research. He employed local researchers to comb hitherto little-known archives in Spain, Mexico City, and Lima, Peru. His first book was an acclaimed biography of King Ferdinand and Queen Isabella of Spain. He followed this with his greatest work, *The Conquest of Mexico,* which appeared in 1843. Prescott's account of the Spanish Conquest read like a romantic, swashbuckling adventure, but was also remarkable for its general accounts of earlier Central American civilizations, among them that of the Maya. Prescott and Stephens exchanged ideas and information to their mutual benefit.

In September 1841, Catherwood and Stephens, accompanied by a young physician, Samuel Cabot, returned to Yucatán. They mapped the spectacular ruins of **Uxmal,** arguably the most magnificent of all Maya cities. From Uxmal, they traveled to other sites, spending 18 days at **Chichén Itzá,** where Stephens admired the ball court. He studied historical records of ancient ball games collected by a local historian, which gave him yet another link with the ancient Maya. He learned that in these arenas teams of players tried to shoot a rubber ball through a hoop in the court wall. The losers were sacrificed.

In 1843, Stephens published his second best-seller on the Maya. *Incidents of Travel in Yucatán* reaffirmed his belief that the ancient Maya were the ancestors of the present inhabitants of the region. "I leave them with all their mystery around them," he wrote, setting the stage for the Maya research of today.

Stephens himself never returned to the Maya lowlands. He became involved in a project to build a trans-Panama railroad in 1849 and died in New York of complications from tropical fevers in 1852. This remarkable traveler brought ancient Maya civilization to the consciousness of scholars and the general public alike. Frederick Catherwood's intricate drawings and photographs of the ruins gave as vivid impression of this exotic civilization as the *Description de L'Egypt* had done for the ancient Egyptians two generations earlier.

The Moundbuilders of North America

Settlers in the Ohio Valley chose to build their townships on the fine locations chosen by ancient Native Americans for their mounds and earthworks. From 1787 through 1788, retired brigadier Rufus Putnam laid out the township of Marietta, Ohio, with great care, situating it close to a complex of large mounds, which he regarded as a potential asset for the town. Putnam himself drew a plan of the mounds. The Reverend Manasseh Cutler counted the con-centric rings in the trunks of felled trees on one of the earthworks. One tree yielded no fewer than 463 rings, allowing Cutler to speculate that the mound under it had been built before A.D. 1300, perhaps earlier. Cutler anticipated the science of dendrochronology—tree-ring dating—by at least a century; the technique was first used scientifically in the Southwest in the early years of the twentieth century. In the 1830s, the enlightened citizens of Marietta raised money to fence off the earthworks against erosion caused by grazing cattle. Other city fathers were less careful. Within a few years the mounds in the center of Cincinnati were flattened under urban development after only hasty excavations.

Except for Thomas Jefferson and the botanist William Bartram, few travel-ers or scholars had a serious interest in the mounds other than in the poten-tial treasure buried within them. Inevitably, popular writers started telling of a magnificent race of moundbuilders, overshadowing the more sober obser-vations of Jefferson and Bartram. These were foreigners, the writers said, who had settled these fertile lands long before the Native Americans. The same speculations led to a rash of treasure hunting, which yielded copper objects, clay pipes, earthenware pots, and numerous human skeletons, but not the gold and royal graves so coveted by the looters. Soon, farmers routinely plowed under mounds that stood in the midst of their newly cleared fields.

In those racist days, everyone assumed that the ancestors of the few Native Americans still living in the region were incapable of constructing such elaborate earthworks. Speculation centered on the Ten Lost Tribes of Israel, the Old Testament idolaters documented in 2 Kings, who "set them up images in all the high places, as did all the heathen." Divine punishment ensued, culminating in the Assyrian conquest, and the Ten Tribes vanished from history. Now they reappeared suddenly and conveniently in the Midwest—mainly in the imaginations of eager clergymen with theological points to make and little to occupy their minds.

These were rough and rowdy days on the frontier, days of vicious, unde-clared war on Indians that was sometimes justified by claims that the moundbuilders, not Native Americans, were the original owners of the land. Only a few antiquaries lived out west, most of them community leaders who were members of the American Philosophical Society or the American Antiquarian Society, the latter an organization founded in Boston in 1812. The first volume of this society's proceedings, entitled *Archaeologia Americana,* appeared in 1820 and contained a lengthy essay by Caleb Atwater (1778–1867), postmaster of Circleville, Ohio. "Description of the Antiquities Discovered in the State of Ohio and Other Western States" surveyed mounds and earthworks throughout the Ohio Valley, many of them in danger of imminent destruction. Atwater classified Ohio earthworks into three groups. Those of the Indians "are neither numerous nor very interesting," he

remarked. Others were of European construction or were those of "that people who raised our ancient forts and tumuli." He concluded that "people far
more civilized than our Indians, but far less so than Europeans," had built
the mounds. His was a form of simple unilinealism like that described in
Chapter 4.

Atwater's observations were more useful than his conclusions. He speculated that a "population as numerous as that which once animated the bor-
ders of the Nile, or of the Euphrates, or of Mexico" had once lived along the
Mississippi River, where many other earthworks were coming to light.

Atwater's conclusions were seized on by writers of lively imagination,
perhaps the best known of them being Josiah Priest, whose *American
Antiquities and Discoveries in the West* appeared in 1833 and sold well over
twenty thousand copies in two and a half years, mainly through door-to-
door salesmen. Priest's moundbuilders were interred in vast cemeteries,
relics of wars between armies as large as those of Alexander the Great. The
mound dwellers were "white people of great intelligence and skill," who
"perished amid the yells of their enemies." This was splendid, heroic stuff
that appealed to the patriotic spirit of the times. Priest told a rattling good
story, which was scientific nonsense yet appealed to a wide audience. His
book was the nineteenth-century equivalent of Indiana Jones and of today's
archaeological fantasies about the quest for Noah's Ark.

The Book of Mormon, compiled by Joseph Smith and Oliver Coudery in
1830, was another consequence of the moundbuilder controversies, said to
be based on a set of golden plates found in a mound in New York State. Smith
said that the plates were lent to him by a messenger of God named Moroni.
The Church of Jesus Christ of Latter-Day Saints originated in Smith's revela-
tions and the epic teachings of the book, which have the status of scriptures
for millions.

By the 1840s, the myth of the moundbuilders was well entrenched in the
popular mind, while the earthworks themselves were ravaged by collectors
and treasure hunters, or simply plowed under. One notorious collector, a
physician named Montroville Dickenson, claimed that he had excavated
over a thousand Indian sites and collected more than forty thousand
artifacts. Dickenson was a showman, too, traveling the length and breadth of
the United States with a huge painted panorama designed to be unrolled
in small village halls. The vast panorama, *Monumental Grandeur of the
Mississippi Valley,* depicted scenes of the death of conquistador Hernando de
Soto in 1542, the effects of a tornado, and the mysterious earthworks of the
Mississippi Valley.

There were more serious scholars as well, among them geologist-turned-
ethnologist Henry Rowe Schoolcraft, who became an expert on Native
American culture and was much concerned with the mounds. His *History
and Statistical Information Respecting the . . . Indian Tribes of the United States,*
published in 1865, is a burdensome work, but is remarkable for ascribing the

mounds to Native Americans, not to "an expatriated type of civilization of either an ASIATIC or EUROPEAN origin."

Between 1845 and 1847, two Ohio antiquarians, journalist Ephraim George Squier (1821–1888) and physician Edwin H. Davis (very much the lesser partner in the enterprise) excavated more than two hundred mounds, surveyed many earthworks and enclosures, and assembled a huge collection of artifacts. Squier's surveys are so accurate that they are of value to this day, and are displayed at the sites of many of the earthworks that are open to the public (Figure 5.3). The newly founded Smithsonian Institution published the resulting monograph, *Ancient Monuments of the Mississippi Valley*, in 1848. It was the first scientific publication of that famous organization and was the first of many Smithsonian contributions on moundbuilders.

Most of the monograph is pure description, often of sites that have vanished today. Squier and Davis distinguished between sacred enclosures and what they called "forts," set on higher ground. They puzzled over the chronology of the earthworks, allocating them a "total antiquity" of about a thousand years; observed stratified layers in their excavations; and noted that many burials lay with clay vessels "such as we know to have been in use among the Indians at the period of the earliest European intercourse." The report ended with six pages of conclusions, which spoke of lines of fortifications

Figure 5.3 Squier and Davis's plan of the **Hopewell** circles and earthworks at **Newark,** Ohio. Much of the earthworks have now vanished under the modern city of Newark. The largest circle is under a golf course.

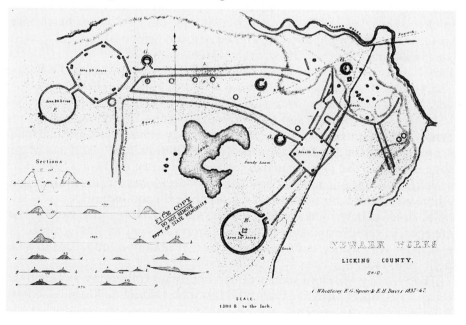

designed to protect the builders from "hostile savage hordes," which eventually destroyed the moundbuilders and their sites. All of this reads in sharp contrast to the sober tone of the remainder of the monograph and reflects the racist prejudices of the day. *Ancient Monuments* was recognized as a classic from the moment of its publication and is still a useful source of information on Ohio Valley earthworks today.

Science, Moundbuilders, and the First Americans

Squier and Davis's report did little to stem the torrent of fantasy and speculation that surrounded the moundbuilders. This controversy, and that over the date of the first Americans, were to preoccupy archaeologists for the rest of the nineteenth century.

The First Americans

But there were by now many more sober voices, among them that of a measured scholar, Samuel Haven (1806–1881), librarian of the American Antiquarian Society. In 1856, the Smithsonian Institution published his carefully reasoned essay *The Archaeology of the United States*, in which Haven summarized what was known about ancient North America. His elegant essay cut through the speculations and surveyed current researches that threw light on the origins of Native Americans. "We desire to stop where the evidence ends," he wrote—a comment that some modern-day archaeologists would do well to remember. He argued that the Native Americans were of great antiquity, that their physical characteristics linked them with "Asiatic races," and that they had come from northeastern Asia across the Bering Strait. Modern-day research into ancient North America effectively began with Haven's wise and sober essay.

In 1866, businessman and philanthropist George Peabody endowed the Peabody Museum of Archaeology and Ethnology at Harvard University and a professorship of American archaeology and ethnology. His letter of gift suggested that the new museum conduct fieldwork on Native American societies both ancient and modern. The Peabody Museum came into being at a time when the controversy over the origin of the moundbuilders was still no abstract debate. It was the reflection of the feelings of a new nation engaged in rapid expansion and colonization as well as thinly disguised genocide. This reality gave research into the moundbuilders considerable political relevance.

The Peabody Museum soon acquired important collections, among them the private collection of the French prehistorian Gabriel de Mortillet, whose theories of human progress we described in Chapter 4. Frederick Ward

Putnam (1839–1915) became curator. He was interested both in Ohio mound sites and in the antiquity of humankind in the Americas. He investigated numerous rumors of humanly manufactured artifacts associated with bones of extinct animals and was unable to verify any of them. Putnam himself was convinced that human settlement in the Americas had come much later than in Europe, but the debate continued to rage until the closing years of the nineteenth century. Then biological anthropologist Ales Hrdlicka examined every report of human remains in North America and dismissed all of them. At the same time, geologist Henry Jackson examined stone artifacts from gravels at Trenton, New Jersey, and other locations. Like Hrdlicka, he roundly declared that none of them were anything more than more recent tools, many of them by-products of quarrying by ancient stone workers looking for good raw material. Both these powerful scientists believed that the first human settlement of the Americas had occurred within the past four thousand years, no earlier—a dogmatic viewpoint that was to hamper the study of the subject for a generation.

Cyrus Thomas and the Moundbuilders

Meanwhile, the major controversy still surrounded the moundbuilders. Institutions now replaced individuals as the major researchers on the question, notably the Bureau of Ethnology at the Smithsonian Institution, set up in 1879 as a special agency to study rapidly vanishing North American Indian cultures and languages under the directorship of John Wesley Powell (1834–1902), famous for his descent of the Grand Canyon by boat a decade earlier. The bureau flourished for 85 years, before it was merged with the Smithsonian's Office of Anthropology in 1964, by which time its researchers had contributed volume after volume of invaluable reports on anthropological topics of every kind, especially on North American Indians.

Powell found himself in continual conflict with Congress, which had little interest in languages but a great deal in the acquisition of fine artifacts. Powell's primary interest was in ethnology, not archaeology, but in 1881, a group of archaeologists persuaded Congress to add a rider to the bureau's appropriation, allocating 20 percent of the funds to moundbuilder research. The following year, Powell recruited Professor Cyrus Thomas (1825–1910) to head the bureau's Division of Mound Exploration. Thomas, an entomologist and botanist, came to his task with the firm belief that the moundbuilders were a distinct people, quite separate from Native Americans. He and eight assistants fanned out all over mound country, and especially in the Mississippi Valley, where frenzied destruction of earthworks by looters was under way.

Having been forced into the mound business, Thomas now sounded a clarion cry against such destruction and against mythmaking "by the gambling and perversion of the lower class of writers supplemented by the phantasies of those better intentioned" (Thomas 1894:10). Thomas carried out fieldwork over a huge area between Ohio and Wisconsin, exploring more than two thousand mounds over seven years. He collected as many as 38,000 artifacts of all kinds, classified the earthworks into eight cultural districts, and concluded that all "which have been examined and carefully studied are to be attributed to the indigenous tribes found inhabiting this region and their ancestors" (1894:222). His *Report on the Mound Explorations of the Bureau of Ethnology* appeared in 1894, a massive 730-page work that stands as one of the great monographs of nineteenth-century American archaeology. Thomas documented the indigenous origin of the earthworks and mounds beyond question and showed that the builders were as diverse in their cultures as living Native American societies. He laid the foundations for one of the great achievements of twentieth-century American archaeologists—chronicling the great diversity of ancient American societies through their artifacts, architecture, and, later, food remains.

There were other mound explorers, too, notable among them Clarence B. Moore, who traveled the rivers of the southeastern United States in his private houseboat in the 1890s and early 1900s. He excavated dozens of sites, then wrote descriptive reports with lavish illustrations that masked his destructive methods.

Unfortunately, many of the sites recorded by Thomas and his contemporaries no longer exist, so *Mound Explorations* remains the only definitive account of them. This great monograph was the final nail in the mythmakers' coffin, even if writers like Congressman Ignatius Donnelly continued to propagate exotic stories. Donnelly believed that Atlanteans from the lost continent had settled in North America and had fled to Mexico when attacked by "savages from the north." His *Atlantis: The Antediluvian World* appeared in 1882, just as Thomas was getting into his stride. The book went through fifty printings and is still in print. The Thomas monograph circulated through a much more limited audience, but ranks as one of the fundamental works of North American archaeology.

The Beginnings of Southwestern Archaeology

Cyrus Thomas studied the mounds from the perspective of the artifacts in them, which he linked to modern-day Native American material culture. He even went so far as to employ a biologist to identify the animals depicted on ceremonial pipes and other artifacts, to establish that they were not exotic species. His researches worked from the present back into the remoter past. The same method, albeit more refined, was to pay rich dividends in the Southwest.

The American settlement of the West accelerated dramatically with the completion of the transcontinental railroad in 1869. Meanwhile, the main preoccupation of the government was a grand reconnaissance of the vast lands that lay west of the Mississippi. The Corps of Topographical Engineers sent out a series of expeditions instructed to pay as much attention to flora and fauna and to details of Indian life as they did to surveying. The West became a vast natural laboratory to be explored; the popular stereotypes of the West and of Native Americans that sprang from these expeditions, and the stories about them that appeared in popular literature, have been with us ever since.

Spaniards from New Spain (Mexico) had settled in New Mexico as early as 1598, after earlier abortive colonization attempts and a fruitless quest for the legendary Seven Lost Cities of Cibola, alleged to be awash in gold. By the nineteenth century, these legends were long forgotten, and the pueblos that formed the subject of the legends had fallen into slow decay under Spanish control. But the government expeditions of the 1840s and 1850s penetrated deep into pueblo country and visited the ruins of Pecos Pueblo and Casa Grande in Arizona. In 1849, Colonel John Washington led a punitive expedition into Navajo country, during which the party marched up the Chama River and entered **Chaco Canyon,** with its spectacular great houses. Lieutenant James Henry Simpson and artist Richard Kern spent much time there sketching and mapping, and also collected artifacts in the ten major pueblos they found there. Simpson's report described not only Chaco Canyon but also **Canyon de Chelly,** giving the first precise description of such famous sites as **Pueblo Bonito** at Chaco.

Civilian expeditions gradually replaced the military surveys of earlier decades. These were conducted through such agencies as the United States Survey of the Territories, a section of the Interior Department set up in 1869. The Survey was the catalyst for many important geological and surveying expeditions led by notable scientists, among them the geologist Ferdinand Vandiveer Hayden, who worked over enormous areas of the West. He hired William Henry Jackson, the greatest of all early western photographers, and another geologist, William Henry Holmes, who was to achieve fame as an archaeologist concerned with the first Americans. In 1874, Jackson visited **Mesa Verde,** where he photographed pueblo structures perched under narrow cliff overhangs above the deep canyons. But his party missed the Cliff Palace, the largest of all Mesa Verde's pueblos (Figure 5.4). Hayden suddenly developed an interest in archaeology and sent Jackson on a wide-ranging survey of the pueblos. The photographer also constructed models of the major sites for the Philadelphia Centennial Exposition of 1876, which were subsequently donated to leading educational institutions throughout North America.

Bandelier and Cushing: The Ethnologists

By the 1880s, the West was familiar territory, even if archaeology, geology, and native peoples were still little known. The time was ripe for more

Figure 5.4   The Cliff Palace, Mesa Verde, Colorado.

focused research, which first came at the hands of Adolph Francis Alphonse Bandelier (1840–1914), a Swiss-born banker and coal mine administrator from a small town in Illinois. Bandelier somehow acquired a passion for the history of the Spanish Conquest of the New World and became a mine of information on New Spain's indigenous inhabitants. His researches brought him in contact with anthropologist Lewis Henry Morgan of *Ancient Society* fame. Morgan became Bandelier's patron, as the younger man steeped himself in Spanish records of Mexico and the Southwest. Fortunately, he was an adept linguist who spoke four languages on a daily basis. This linguistic virtuosity gave him an unparalleled knowledge of sources that were little consulted by his contemporaries. By 1880, Bandelier had already published several important monographs on Mexican culture for Harvard University's Peabody Museum.

In that year, Morgan arranged a small grant of $1,200 from the Archaeological Institute of America, which enabled Bandelier to study the social organization of the Indians of the Southwest and pueblo architecture. Bandelier acquired a mule and traveled, blissfully happy, from pueblo to pueblo between 1880 and 1892. "I am dirty, ragged, and sunburnt, but of good cheer," he wrote.

He started at **Pecos Pueblo,** site of a Spanish mission, surveying and describing the ruins. Unlike his few predecessors, he stepped outside the ruins and recorded both the historical and traditional history of the pueblo. He interviewed elderly people who had lived there until its abandonment in the

1830s. His report was a model of detail but received little academic attention. More than 30 years were to pass before his conclusions were confirmed by archaeological excavation (see Chapter **7**).

Bandelier moved from pueblo to pueblo in Arizona and New Mexico, helped at every turn by the Catholic clergy, who were his constant companions. He had converted to Catholicism, which opened many otherwise inaccessible doors and archives. Over the years, he supported himself by writing a Catholic history, contributing articles to popular journals, and even by writing *The Delight Makers*, a novel that conveyed vivid insights into Indian life but was not a commercial success. Bandelier was an omnivorous collector of information. His copious notes were gleaned from church records, traditional histories, and the architecture of ruins. He was one of the first scholars to interpret the past on the basis of modern ethnographic data—to work, as he put it, "from the known to the unknown, step by step." To Bandelier, archaeology was a means of extending anthropology and recorded history into the more distant past. It was not the objects that were important, but the history and information they supplied.

Adolph Bandelier left the Southwest in 1892 and worked mainly in Mexico, South America, and Spain until his death in 1914. He never published his Southwestern notes, which were finally rescued from oblivion and published in the 1960s and 1970s. This remarkable fieldworker was the first scholar to study the native peoples of the Southwest in the context of their past. In so doing, he established a fundamental archaeological methodology, working from the present into the past, now called the "Direct Historical Method."

The Direct Historical Method is based on the principle that artifacts change over long and short periods of time. Thus, the historic artifacts found in layers of known age are descendants of those found in earlier levels. In theory, and indeed in practice, one can trace changes in, say, pot decoration or form back into ever-earlier levels. This method is very effective when there is cultural continuity over time, as was the case in the Southwest and in much of eastern North America.

Ethnographic analogy, in which the archaeologist uses historic artifacts to interpret objects made by much earlier societies, is an extension of the Direct Historical Method. It came into use early in Europe, where Stone Age archaeologists made bold comparisons between such historic societies as those of the Inuit of the Arctic with the later Ice Age Cro-Magnon cultures of southwestern France. Such wholesale comparisons soon fell out of favor because the time gap between the Inuit and the Cro-Magnons was too large. Nevertheless, ethnographic analogy continued to be much used to compare individual artifacts, house styles, and other culture traits under carefully controlled conditions, and is now a powerful tool for archaeologists.

The Southwest attracted curiosity seekers, collectors, and private expeditions like a magnet. In 1886, a Massachusetts philanthropist, Mary Hemenway, financed the Hemenway Southwestern Archaeological Expedition. The expedition, which Bandelier joined, became a reality through the smooth talking of Frank Hamilton Cushing (1857–1900), a traveler and ethnologist with a flair for the visionary and the dramatic, as well as for judicious publicity.

Cushing was the son of a physician and became an assistant in ethnology at the Smithsonian Institution in 1875, at age 18. In 1879, he accompanied Colonel James Stevenson on a Smithsonian-sponsored expedition to the Southwest. He arrived at Zuñi pueblo in September 1879, intending to stay there for only a few weeks. He remained for four and a half years. After a difficult start, when the people thought about killing him, Cushing learned the language and was allowed to stay, developing a close trust with the Zuñi— so much so that they initiated him into the secret Priesthood of the Bow. Cushing dressed in Indian clothes and spent many hours recording creation myths and folk tales. So great was the trust that the Zuñi placed in him that they made him a war chief. Cushing duly recorded his title—"First War Chief of Zuñi, U.S. Assistant Ethnologist."

Frank Cushing was a pioneer of participant observation, in which an anthropologist lives for a prolonged period among his subjects. He developed great rapport with the Zuñi, even accompanying a group of their leaders to the East Coast in 1882. President Chester A. Arthur received the visitors in Washington. There is no question that the Zuñi befriended Cushing because they perceived him as a valuable bridge to an alien culture, but the mutual respect between him and the people was a genuine one. He was indeed a powerful advocate for the Zuñi. His departure from Zuñi came about because he fought efforts to grab pueblo land and alienated powerful political figures in the Senate.

Back in Washington, Cushing became a public figure to people attracted by the romance of his life far out on the frontier. He never published his work except in the popular arena, where it won many readers. Like Bandelier, Cushing considered archaeology "ethnology pushed back into prehistoric times." His descriptions of Zuñi life, and the many legends, myths, and songs he recorded, have proved invaluable to later researchers. Many pueblos closed in on themselves when they learned how much Cushing had revealed of their secret societies and beliefs. No anthropologist in later years has ever enjoyed such free access to pueblo life.

Cushing himself joined the Hemenway Expedition and proved an ineffectual leader. Plagued by ill health, he excavated a pueblo cemetery in the Salt River Valley, Arizona, full of elaborately decorated burials.

In 1895–1896, Cushing led an expedition to **Key Marco,** Florida, where he discovered a remarkably well-preserved Calusa Indian settlement— spectacular evidence of a vanished Native American society in southwestern Florida. The Calusa had constructed their settlements over the water on mounds built up of mollusk shells. The waterlogged site yielded well-preserved wooden sculptures, painted masks, carved bone and shell ornaments, even netting and cordage. Despite painstaking efforts, Cushing's conservation methods were inadequate to preserve artifacts that were so wet that they had turned to spongy mush. Nevertheless, he collected a rich and unique collection of Calusa material culture, which is of priceless scientific value today. Sadly, his health deteriorated before he could finish a full report on this remarkable site. He died in Florida in 1900 at the early age of 43.

Collectors, Patrons, and Institutions

Unfortunately, the pot hunters and the dealers read Cushing's articles and books. They followed in the footsteps of the scientists in searching for desiccated mummies, painted pots, and buried treasure in the form of antiquities that would command a high price on the East Coast. Local ranchers turned to looting archaeological sites as a profitable sideline. Among them was Richard Wetherill, who collected antiquities from sites throughout the Southwest in the intervals of cattle ranching. In 1888, Wetherill and his cousin Charlie Mason came across the Cliff Palace at Mesa Verde, and they spent a winter ransacking its rooms and sacred kivas (subterranean ceremonial chambers). They sold their Mesa Verde collection to the Denver Historical Society in 1890 for the then colossal figure of $3,000, but only after Mason sent the city a desiccated mummy that attracted frenzied attention.

In the following years, the two Wetherill brothers surveyed and mapped the pueblos in the Mesa Verde region and assembled three more collections, the last of them for the Swedish archaeologist Gustav Nordenskjöld, who published the first descriptions of the cliff dwellings for a scientific audience in 1803. Meanwhile, Richard Wetherill sold antiquities to tourists, but after 1895 he collected almost exclusively for the American Museum of Natural History. He spent his last years working at Pueblo Bonito in Chaco Canyon, on excavations sponsored by the wealthy Hyde family from the East Coast. Frederick Putnam of the Peabody Museum was consulted (the small archaeologist's settlement at Chaco Canyon was even named Putnam in his honor), hundreds of rooms were cleared, large collections made. Wetherill opened a store near Pueblo Bonito, for both Hyde and Wetherill were worried about new legislation designed to protect the pueblos from collectors and vandals. Wetherill gambled that squatter's rights would give him ownership of the site—and what an investment that would be! The huge excavations ended in 1900, after the clearance of over 190 rooms. More than half the site had been dug out at a cost of over $25,000, a huge sum.

A number of archaeologists, among them Edgar Hewitt, director of the School of American Research in Santa Fe, became concerned about the wholesale ransacking of pueblos, and about the large collections of antiquities heading east. He alerted federal authorities, and the federal government ordered the excavations closed down. An investigation by the secretary of the interior revealed many abuses. In 1906, the first Antiquities Act was signed into law, offering the first measure of protection to the pueblos and other Southwestern sites. Wetherill reluctantly signed over the title of his land to the government. He was murdered by a Navajo gunman while rounding up cattle three years later.

From the 1880s to the 1920s, Southwestern archaeology witnessed a growing rivalry between patrons of lavish collecting expeditions and the growing ranks of professional archaeologists, whose aims conflicted with those of collectors, museums, and others. Edgar Hewitt in particular had a vision of a Southwestern archaeology that created heritage and studied the relationships between people, landscape, and history. It was from the interplay of these many cross-currents that modern Southwestern archaeology was born, with the development of tree-ring chronology and the first stratigraphic excavations in the pueblos, described in Chapter 7.

Southwestern archaeology was a product of ethnology—of the imaginations of a small number of scientists who pursued knowledge rather than artifacts. Their vision of the Southwestern past stemmed from complicated interactions between individuals and powerful museums, each with their patrons, from petty rivalries and politics, and from a new generation of archaeological discoveries, which turned the Southwest into American archaeology's greatest archaeological laboratory.

Summary

Chapter 5 summarizes the early history of North American and Maya archaeology, beginning with the expeditions of John Lloyd Stephens and Frederick Catherwood to the Maya lowlands of Central America between 1839 and 1842. Stephens's lyrical descriptions of Maya ruins, and Catherwood's magnificent drawings, caused a sensation and brought ancient Maya civilization into public consciousness. All subsequent Maya research is based on Stephens's conclusion that Maya civilization developed from indigenous roots without any influence from outside.

In North America, controversy over the mounds and earthworks of the Midwest and Southeast continued throughout the nineteenth century, beginning with the researches of Caleb Atwater, and continuing with the more thorough fieldwork of Ephraim Squier and Edwin Davis, published by the Smithsonian Institution in 1848. Squier and Davis's researches and surveys were a major step forward, some of their plans being the only record of sites destroyed in later years. But they espoused a foreign origin for the mounds. The moundbuilder controversy was finally resolved in the 1890s, when Cyrus Thomas of the Bureau of American Ethnology carried out large-scale surveys and excavations. He proved beyond all doubt that the mounds and earthworks were the work of ancient Native Americans, not civilizations from other lands.

At the same time, other scholars established that humans had settled in North America much later than they had in Europe. By 1900, there was consensus that the first American remains were only four thousand years old.

Southwestern archaeology had its roots in ethnology, in the researches of Adolph Bandelier and Frank Cushing, who established the notion of working back from the present into the past, a basic principle of later Southwestern archaeology. Collectors and looters followed, notable among them Richard Wetherill, until the Antiquities Act of 1906 protected major sites on public land. Southwestern archaeology was born of the interactions between ethnologists and archaeologists, and professional scholars and wealthy patrons, who supported collecting activities by major museums. This phase ended in the 1920s, with the development of tree-ring chronologies and careful stratigraphic excavations.

Guide to Further Reading

Brunhouse, Robert L. 1973. *In Search of the Maya.* Albuquerque: University of New Mexico Press.

An excellent academic study of early Maya archaeologists.

Fowler, Don D. 2000. *A Laboratory for Archaeology: Science and Romanticism in the American Southwest, 1846–1930.* Albuquerque: University of New Mexico Press.

Fowler has used a career's experience of the Southwest to write a thorough and entertaining portrait of early Southwestern archaeology. An excellent, well-illustrated starting point.

Silverberg, Robert. 1968. *The Mound Builders of Ancient America.* New York: New York Graphic Society.

Published more than 40 years ago, Silverberg's thorough and entertaining book is definitive and full of telling quotes.

Snead, James E. 2001. *The Making of Southwest Archaeology.* Tucson: University of Arizona Press.

Snead's short study is a thorough exploration of the complexity of early Southwestern archaeology. Strongly recommended as a sophisticated introduction to individual ambitions and institutional goals.

Stephens, John Lloyd. 1841. *Incidents of Travel in Central America, Chiapas, and Yucatan.* New York: Harpers.

———. 1843. *Incidents of Travel in Yucatan.* New York: Harpers.

Nothing rivals Stephens's own classic accounts of his discoveries. They are readily available in paperback reprints.

chapter 6

Scriptures and Civilizations

Gold mask of a Mycenaean king, called Agamemnon's mask. National Archaeology Museum, Athens, Greece. Copyright Giraudon/Art Resource, NY.

The value of relics, viewed as evidence, may on this account be said to be in inverse ratio to their intrinsic value. The longer I am engaged in these pursuits, the more I become impressed with this fact, the importance of which, I think, has been too much overlooked by archaeologists.

General Augustus Lane Fox Pitt Rivers,
Excavations in Cranborne Chase, 1898 (p. 211)

chapter outline

While the debates over the antiquity of humankind and human progress continued, much popular interest in the past surrounded an emerging biblical archaeology. At the same time, the classical authors remained a primary source of information for interpreting early civilizations. In this chapter we discuss the origins of biblical archaeology, the sensational discovery of the so-called "Flood Tablets" from Nineveh, the discovery of Homeric Troy, and the beginnings of scientific archaeological excavation.

Underground Jerusalem

The Scriptures still drove much thinking about the past in the mid-nineteenth century. Many people believed in the literal historical truth of the Bible and were fascinated by Jerusalem and the Holy Land. When British army Lieutenant Charles Warren (1840–1927) was posted to Jerusalem in 1864, his assignment was to survey its topography and water supplies. Warren had previously served on the Rock of Gibraltar, where his garrison work had given him extensive firsthand experience of tunneling and accurate surveying. He spent much of his time in Jerusalem underground, in the honeycomb of water channels and reservoirs under the modern city. The young officer had no interest in archaeology until his men made important archaeological finds during their surveys. Along the eastern wall, they uncovered a monumental Roman arch that had once formed the entrance to biblical King Herod's palace. The arch, rebuilt on the ruins of an earlier temple by King Herod in the first century B.C., had been demolished by the Romans in A.D. 70. Part of its wall survived and eventually became the Western, or Wailing Wall, one of Judaism's most sacred sites.

Warren's archaeological discoveries astounded and delighted his country-men. In 1865, a public meeting in London launched the Palestine Exploration Fund, with Queen Victoria as its official patron, its objective to find traces of events and people mentioned in the Scriptures. Two years later, the Fund sent Warren and another detachment of Royal Engineers to Jerusalem with instructions to excavate under the Haram esh Sharif, a walled compound that housed some of Islam's most sacred shrines.

The project was extremely controversial and was vehemently opposed by local religious leaders. Warren placed some judicious bribes, then started to dig shafts downward and then toward the Haram from 46 meters (150 feet) outside the city walls. His men smashed through a blocked passageway alongside the Haram walls and so outraged worshipers in the mosque above that they showered the diggers with stones. Warren now leased private lots well away from the Haram, sunk vertical shafts to bedrock, and tunneled to-ward the shrines. He found that the 24-meter (80-foot) -high walls of the Haram extended more than 30 meters (100 feet) below the surface.

Warren sank 27 shafts and traced the northern and southern limits of the old city, following the walls of Jerusalem far underground. He and his col-leagues crawled through long-buried passages and down murky shafts as they mapped the topography of the biblical city.

Warren returned home in 1870 to write *Underground Jerusalem* and *Tent Work in Palestine*, which described his work for a popular audience and was received with critical acclaim. His academic monograph, *The Survey of Western Palestine*, appeared in eight volumes in 1885, and is still useful today.

Charles Warren never returned to Jerusalem. After a distinguished military career, he became commissioner of police at Scotland Yard in London, during the period of the Jack the Ripper murders. His Jerusalem dis-coveries provided the first framework for biblical archaeology. A century was to pass before anyone reinvestigated the city's ancient walls.

The Jerusalem excavations were followed by large-scale topographic sur-veys of the Holy Land, which yielded a vast body of archaeological informa-tion. These researches set the stage for numerous excavations into biblical, historic, and prehistoric sites from the 1890s onward.

The Flood Tablets

Austen Henry Layard's most important discovery was the tablet library of Assyrian King Assurbanipal, unearthed in the royal palace at Nineveh. Layard packed the thousands of tablets into baskets and crates, then shipped them to the British Museum in London. Cleaning and deciphering the library occupied many years, at the hands of a small number of volunteers, who taught themselves decipherment as they went along. Among them was a bank engraver turned epigrapher, George Smith (1841–1876), who caused a sensation in 1872 when he pieced together some tablet fragments bearing what appeared to be an account of a great flood. He noticed a reference to a ship resting on "the mountains of Nizir," followed by an account of the sending out of a dove, and its finding no resting place and returning. On December 3, 1872, George Smith lectured to an overflow audience of the Biblical Archaeological Society. The crowd included Prime Minister William Gladstone. Smith told the story of a prophet named Hasisadra, who survived a great flood sent by the wrathful gods by loading his family and "the beasts of the field" into a large ship. Six days of torrential rain brought a vast inundation. Hasisadra's ark went aground on a high point of land. He sent out a dove, then a raven, in search of dry land. The raven did not return, so Hasisadra released the animals, became a god, and lived happily ever after.

George Smith was well aware that the texts he had discovered were not the only account of the Babylonian floods. He suspected, rightly, that the tale could be traced back to even earlier myths. We know now that they were part of a masterpiece of Sumerian and Akkadian literature called *The Epic of Gilgamesh.* Years later, a copy of the legend was found in the archives of the ancient Sumerian city at Nippur in southern Mesopotamia, but in 1872 the Sumerians were still unknown except for vague cuneiform references.

The Flood Tablets caused a sensation in ecclesiastical and scientific circles. Public interest in ancient Mesopotamia surged. A display of the tablets at the British Museum drew large crowds. But there were tantalizing gaps, including a passage of 17 lines from the very first column of the first tablet. The *Daily Telegraph* newspaper offered the British Museum the then-enormous sum of one thousand guineas for George Smith to lead an expedition to Nineveh in search of the missing fragments. After some brief work at Nimrud in search of additional inscriptions, Smith started work in the pock-marked Kuyunjik mound at Nineveh on May 7, 1873. Incredible though it may seem, on May 14, after only seven days of digging, he located the missing lines of the flood story in the refuse of Layard's excavations.

Unfortunately, George Smith died of dysentery in the Syrian desert on a later expedition to Mosul, but not before producing several other notable decipherments, among them an account of the building of the seven-stage ziggurat of the god Belus at Babylon.

The Sumerian Civilization

The Flood Tablets had the effect of setting off feverish demand for cuneiform tablets in European capitals. Dealers in Mesopotamia, especially in the south, were only too happy to oblige. Hundreds of tablets from dusty city mounds in the south reached London and Paris before anyone had dug them by even slightly scientific methods. As early as 1872, George Smith had predicted that his flood story would turn out to be a late version of a much earlier folk legend. As cuneiform experts in Europe followed up on his work and deciphered other tablets, they realized that he was on the right track. They discovered that the Assyrians had copied a literary tradition that had come from the Babylonians, who in turn had copied it from yet another people, perhaps an even earlier civilization in the south.

For years, Edward Hincks, Jules Oppert, and Henry Rawlinson had suspected that a more primitive script and civilization had preceded the Babylonian cities. Jules Oppert had gone so far as to argue that the early rulers of the south were often called "king of Sumer and Akkad." Thus, he argued that they should be called "Sumerians," but he was the first to admit that this was just a theory.

In 1877, the French government transferred Ernest de Sarzec, an experienced consular official, to the sleepy port of Basra at the northern end of the Persian Gulf. De Sarzec spent his leisure time exploring ancient city mounds in the south, especially the mound of **Telloh,** where dealers told him that many cuneiform tablets were to be found. Telloh was a huge site, 6.5 kilometers (4 miles) of mounds lying along an ancient canal. De Sarzec set a row of men to work along the edge of a brick platform, once the foundations of a temple mound. The dig soon yielded a rich harvest of tablets, jars, inscriptions, and two large terra-cotta cylinders of a ruler named Gudea (Figure 6.1). After only a few weeks, he realized that he had unearthed the remains of a much earlier civilization than that of Babylon. His finds caused a sensation in scholarly circles. Funds were provided by the French government, and he returned to dig at Telloh almost every year from 1880 to 1900. The excavations revealed a hitherto unknown Mesopotamian civilization, Oppert's Sumerians, arguably the world's first literate civilization. The Telloh tablets documented the history of a Sumerian city-state of the third millennium B.C. named **Lagash,** which was ruled by a series of powerful leaders, among them Gudea.

Ernest de Sarzec was by no stretch of the imagination a scientific excavator, and he kept few records. But he had the sense to realize that systematic, long-term excavations would yield more important finds than would mere hasty scrambles for tablets. His excavations established the Sumerians as a solid historical entity, the ancestral civilization of all ancient Mesopotamia.

Others were soon in the field, among them researchers from the University of Pennsylvania, who began work at the ancient Sumerian city of **Nippur** in 1888. Their excavations, which went through many vicissitudes, traced the city walls, investigated the ziggurat's architecture to water level at nearly 3000 B.C., and uncovered a temple library of more than thirty thousand tablets, including literary works and even lesson tablets used in schools. The University of Pennsylvania has maintained an interest in Nippur to this day and is actively involved in the compilation of a Sumerian dictionary, based in large part on the tablets from this early city.

Figure 6.1   The Sumerian ruler Gudea. A statue from Lagash, Iraq.

Excavations in southern Mesopotamia involved digging structures made of sun-dried brick, which are very difficult to distinguish from the surrounding soil, as they literally melt back into the earth. Austen Henry Layard was defeated by the mounds of the south. So was de Sarzec, whose excavations were too casual, while those at Nippur were at best crude. In the end, it was German archaeologist Robert Koldeway (1855–1925) who mastered the problem during his excavations into King Nebuchadnezzar's Babylon between 1899 and 1912. The city was little more than dusty mounds. Koldeway trained teams of skilled diggers, who used picks to distinguish the subtle differences between mudbrick and the surrounding soil. Thanks to these diggers, he was able to trace Nebuchadnezzar's ways, and to reconstruct the

Figure 6.2   The reconstructed Ishtar Gate from Babylon, Iraq.

magnificent, frieze-covered Ishtar Gate (Figure 6.2). Today's workers use the same method along with compressed air to clear mudbrick structures.

By the time Robert Koldeway started work at Babylon, more scientific excavation methods were spreading slowly through the Mediterranean world, thanks to the work of other German archaeologists and a gradual recognition that the rough methods of earlier generations were no longer adequate. This realization came in large part from Heinrich Schliemann's sensational discoveries at Troy and Mycenae.

Heinrich Schliemann: Troy and Mycenae

The archaeologists of the late nineteenth century still owed much to the classics, which they regarded as a source of great inspiration about the world's earliest civilizations. But the greatest mystery of all was the Greek writer Homer, whose immortal epics, the *Iliad* and the *Odyssey,* were set down in about the tenth century B.C. Nineteenth-century classical scholarship was much concerned with the authorship of these magnificent works. Were they written by one poet? If so, who was he? And, above all, did the two epics describe actual events in Greek history? Like the historical truth of the Scriptures, the question of the true identity of the Homeric city of Troy became a near-obsession for some archaeologists, among them German businessman-turned-archaeologist Heinrich Schliemann (1822–1890), one of the most colorful and controversial of all nineteenth-century excavators.

The son of a Protestant minister in rural north Germany, Schliemann developed an interest in Homer at an early age. His family was so poor that his education ended at age 14, when he was apprenticed to a grocer. After being shipwrecked while emigrating to Venezuela, Schliemann became a clerk in Amsterdam. With the single-minded intensity that marked the rest of his life, Schliemann set out to educate himself. He learned to write properly, then mastered English and French in a year, helped by his exceptional powers of memory. In short order, he then acquired four more European languages, displaying a remarkable aptitude for foreign tongues that gained him a job with the Schroeder brothers, Amsterdam merchants with major interests in the Russian indigo (dye) trade. In 1846, he became the Schroeders' agent in St. Petersburg, Russia, before founding a lucrative indigo business on his own. He then made a fortune during the gold rush by setting up a banking agency in Sacramento, California, in 1850. Two years later, he returned to St. Petersburg, married, and had three children, making another fortune supplying war materials to the Russian army during the Crimean War. In 1863, at age 43, Heinrich Schliemann abruptly retired from business to devote himself to Homer and a search for the archaeological site of Homeric Troy.

Schliemann took his time. He went on an extensive world tour, then studied archaeology in Paris before visiting Greece for the first time in 1868. At the time, most scholars thought that Homer's Troy was a mythical city. Schliemann was convinced that the *Iliad* was the historical truth, so he set out for the plains at the mouth of the Dardanelles in northwestern Turkey, where Troy was said to lie. He came to a hill named **Hissarlik** 4.8 kilometers (3 miles) from the coast, where he met the American vice-consul Frank Calvert, who owned half the large city mound on the hill. Calvert had dug into the mound and declared it was Troy, but it was Schliemann who took the credit for identifying the Homeric metropolis. In fact, Hissarlik had been rumored to be Troy for centuries.

In 1871, Schliemann married his second wife, Sophia Engastromenos, a 17-year-old Greek girl, in what may been a marriage of convenience but evolved into an enduring relationship. In October of that year, the Schliemanns set 80 workers to trenching into the Hissarlik mound. Six weeks later, a 10-meter (33-foot) trench revealed the stone walls of a long-buried city. The following spring, between 100 and 150 men set to work under the supervision of engineers who had worked on the digging of Egypt's Suez Canal. Schliemann reached bedrock at 14 meters (45 feet), digging through layer after layer of human occupation with frenzied haste. He claimed that the third horizon from the bottom was Homer's Troy, largely because the stratum showed signs of burning. Schliemann considered this the conflagration set by the Greeks when they overran the city.

In mid-1873, the Schliemanns made their most controversial discovery: a collection of magnificent gold artifacts and ornaments in the deposits of the third city. Schliemann gave the workers the day off while he and Sophia secretly gathered up the glittering finds of the "Treasure" in Sophia's shawl. Scholars still argue over the Schliemann treasure: Was it a hoard of gold artifacts buried in a time of peril, or did the Schliemanns gather together isolated gold objects from many levels and "package" them to create a truly sensational find (Figure 6.3)? Modern experts are still doubtful about the treasure claim. The finds ended up in the Berlin Museum and vanished during World War II, only to reappear in Russia at the end of the Cold War, years after it was assumed they had been destroyed in an air raid.

Schliemann now turned his restless attention to another Homeric site— King Agamemnon's citadel at **Mycenae** in southern Greece (Figure 6.4). The

Figure 6.3   Heinrich and Sophia Schliemann. She wears the so-called "Treasure of Priam" from Hissarlik. King Priam was the Homeric ruler of Troy.

Figure 6.4   Mycenae from the air. The famous so-called Shaft Graves came from the area inside the main gate to the right.

excavations there began with three teams of 63 men, trenching around the entrance, the Lion Gate, and in an open area just inside the entrance. A circle of tombstones bearing engravings of charioteers came to light, then five graves containing 15 skeletons smothered in gold. Several of the skeletons wore gold-sheet death masks showing clipped beards and mustaches. Fine headdresses, seals, and pottery lay with the burials. Schliemann was in his element, claiming in telegrams to the world's newspapers that he had found the tomb of Agamemnon himself. Two ruling monarchs and the prime minister of Britain were kept informed of the excavations. Today, we know that Schliemann had discovered the glories of the **Mycenaean civilization** of Bronze Age Greece, which flourished in the late second millennium B.C.

In 1878, Schliemann returned to Hissarlik. This time he took well-qualified archaeologists with him. The German Wilhelm Dorpfeld (1853–1940) was trained in scientific excavation methods and worked with Schliemann at Hissarlik from 1888 to 1890. He was a highly trained observer, an expert on stratified city sites and small artifacts. Dorpfeld helped Schliemann identify the sixth, and not the third, city as the Homeric settlement.

Heinrich Schliemann remains something of an enigma—on the one hand a near-megalomaniac and ruthless mythmaker; on the other, by all accounts a kindly and thoughtful man. He brought archaeology to millions of people, but at tragic cost in damage to Hissarlik and Mycenae. At the time of his death, he was negotiating to excavate on a hillside at Knossos, near the coast of northern

Crete, where he believed that another ancient civilization, that of Homer's King Minos, lay. Fortunately for science, his negotiations were unsuccessful.

The Beginnings of Scientific Excavation

Heinrich Schliemann was already an archaeological anachronism when he dug into Hissarlik in 1871. His excavations were crude and destructive, resembling a construction site rather than a scientific dig. Even as he uncovered the Homeric city, a new generation of archaeologists was introducing a new rigor into archaeological excavation. For the first time, a few scholars excavated in search of information rather than spectacular finds, to solve specific archeological problems. Above all, the standards of recording improved considerably.

The Germans were leaders, working in the Aegean Islands and on the Greek mainland under the sponsorship of the King of Prussia. Alexander Conze (1831–1914) excavated the shrine of the Cabiri on the island of **Samothrace** in the northern Aegean with meticulous care in 1871. An architect was on site at all times, a photographer recorded the excavations, and a warship anchored offshore provided logistical support. The Germans under Conze's student Ernst Curtius (1814–1896) now moved to **Olympia,** site of the Olympic Games, where they excavated the stadium, surrounding temples, and other buildings between 1875 and 1880, again with an architect present at all times. The archaeologists renounced all claims to the finds, which were housed in a specially constructed museum on the site. Both the Olympia and Samothrace excavations were published in full in sumptuous detail, complete with architectural drawings and photographs.

Conze and Curtius set new standards for archaeological excavation and recording, which paid careful attention to even small finds—a far cry from the unbridled treasure hunters of yesteryear. Far away, in southern England, General Augustus Lane Fox Pitt Rivers (1827–1900) excavated with equal, if not even greater, rigor than the Germans, but on much smaller, more compact sites, located on his vast country estates on **Cranborne Chase.** Pitt Rivers was of aristocratic birth but modest means. He pursued a successful career as an artillery officer and became an expert on firearms of all kinds. His professional specialty sparked an interest in antique guns and in the evolution of weapons of all kinds. While still in the army, he was strongly influenced by Charles Darwin's *Origin of Species,* which led Pitt Rivers to argue that natural selection also applied to humanly manufactured artifacts. He carried out some minor excavations in which he applied his exact military mind to the observation of stratigraphic trenches cut across Roman and Iron Age earthworks.

In 1880, a series of unexpected family deaths made him the sole heir of his uncle's immense fortune and master of 10,900 hectares (27,000 acres) making up Cranborne Chase in the chalk country of southern England—acreage that was exceptionally rich in archaeological sites of all kinds. Cranborne Chase was a rural landscape, a great tract of medieval hunting country that had never been plowed. Pitt Rivers realized that he had a unique chance to investigate ancient burial mounds, earthworks, and Roman villas on his property. He started with Bronze Age barrows (burial mounds), then moved on to Winklebury Camp, an Iron Age fort. There he cross-sectioned ramparts to date the earthworks.

In 1884, he turned from earthworks to a Roman military camp at Woodcutts Common—several acres of low banks, humps, and hollows. Pitt Rivers had the men clear off the topsoil, then dig out the dark irregularities in the white chalk subsoil and trace the outlines of ditches, hearths, pits, and postholes. This was revolutionary archaeology in the 1880s. In 1893, he turned his attention to Wor Barrow, a Stone Age earthwork used for communal burials (Figure 6.5). His predecessors had simply trenched into burial mounds and removed the human remains and grave furniture (see Chapter 3). Pitt Rivers excavated the entire mound, including 16 skeletons, leaving a row of earthen pillars down the center, which recorded the layering. At one end of the mound he found a rectangular outline of trenches in the chalk, where the uprights of a large building protected six bodies. In a final exercise in archaeological science, he left the ditches that surrounded the mound open for four years, then re-excavated them to see how chalk

Figure 6.5 General Pitt-Rivers and a relative at the Wor Barrow excavations. Courtesy Salisbury & South Wiltshire Museum. © Anthony Pitt-Rivers.

ditches broke down and filled with sediment after abandonment, as a way to better interpret his excavations.

Pitt Rivers was gifted with superb organizational skills. He compiled four privately printed volumes, *Excavations on Cranborne Chase* (1887–1898)—heavily illustrated books describing every detail of his excavations. He ran his excavations along disciplined military lines, working with small teams of trained workers, and also with site supervisors, each of whom had two assistants, one a draftsman, the other a modelmaker. From the very beginning, Pitt Rivers recorded the position of every find, however small, including animal bones and seeds. Throughout his excavations, he thought of his sites in three dimensions—a cornerstone of modern excavation methods. Each site was excavated completely down to bedrock, each layer recorded, human disturbances of the soil noted. Pitt Rivers pioneered the use of photography to record his sites and insisted on prompt publication of the results. Unlike his contemporaries, he was interested in how earthworks were formed and weathered by the elements.

Pitt Rivers had no patience for archaeologists who just searched for objects. He considered science "organized common sense," a principle he followed throughout his excavations. His contemporaries considered him eccentric, but he was unrepentant, providing free Sunday concerts for visitors to the museum housing his collections. There, his collections of firearms, tribal artifacts, and archaeological finds were displayed in evolutionary sequences from the simple to the more complex. Pitt Rivers believed that archaeology should be part of everyone's education, so that the public could learn the links between past and present.

General Augustus Lane Fox Pitt Rivers was years ahead of his time. His methods are among the foundations of modern archaeological excavation. He died in 1900 and was rebellious even in death. He insisted on being cremated, at the time still considered improper. It was not until the 1920s that other European archaeologists took note of his pioneering excavation methods.

Flinders Petrie and the Small Object

Another Englishman, William Matthew Flinders Petrie (1853–1942), first went to Egypt in 1880, just as Pitt Rivers was starting work on Cranborne Chase. A surveyor's son, Petrie had little formal schooling but picked up an excellent knowledge of surveying and geometry from his father. In 1872, the two of them made the first accurate survey of Stonehenge in southern England. Eight years later, Flinders Petrie went to Egypt, where he spent two years making the first scientific survey of the Pyramids of Giza. Petrie lived in an abandoned tomb and kept tourists at arm's length by working in the narrow pyramid passages dressed only in his red underwear. He had plenty of time to collect potsherds and other small objects, which made him realize that many of archaeology's most significant clues came from the small and the seemingly unimportant. At the same time, he was disgusted with what passed for excavation along the Nile. "It is sickening to see the rate at which everything is being destroyed, and the little regard paid to preservation," he wrote in his *Methods and Aims in Archaeology*, published many years later in 1904.

Petrie's monograph on the Giza survey established his reputation. Inevitably, he now turned from survey work to excavation, digging on behalf of the Egypt Exploration Fund from 1883 to 1887. Then he branched out on his own as a freelance excavator, digging in Egypt each winter, then writing up his finds the following summer in England. Petrie's methods were rough by today's standards, but were a vast improvement on those of many of his contemporaries. Living under very primitive conditions and working with minimal funds, Petrie supervised large gangs of laborers, whom he paid for reporting small finds such as beads and papyri. Year after year, he excavated pyramids and tombs, towns and cemeteries, paying careful attention to small objects. Several generations of archaeologists learned excavation under him—a demanding experience. They received little formal instruction, were sent out to work without close supervision for many hours in the hot sun, and spent hours each evening sorting and classifying pot fragments. There were few creature comforts. Petrie was notorious for the austere regime in his camp, where the food was appalling. But those who survived several seasons with him became tough, competent excavators. Among them was the artist Howard Carter, who was to discover the undisturbed tomb of the pharaoh Tutankhamun in 1922 (see Chapter 8).

Flinders Petrie made extraordinary discoveries, among them a cemetery containing mummies of Roman Egyptians of A.D. 100 to 250 at **Hawara** in the Fayyum Depression west of the Nile. Realistic portraits of the dead adorned the mummies. His excavations at the workers' town of **el-Kahun** provided a fascinating portrait of the lives of ordinary folk under the rule of Middle Kingdom pharaoh Senusret II (1897–1878 B.C.). Another community, **Ghurab,** dated to the Eighteenth Dynasty (1570–1293 B.C.) and yielded potsherds of brightly painted Mycenaean pottery from distant Greece, found in a walled enclosure close to the town temple.

Petrie was one of the first to realize that ancient Egyptian civilization did not flourish in isolation, but traded with much of the eastern Mediterranean world. He used the precisely dated and highly distinctive pottery at Ghurab to date Schliemann's Mycenaean civilization to around 1500 to 1000 B.C. This innovative method, known today as cross-dating, used closely dated sites in Egypt to date distant prehistoric sites as far afield as temperate Europe. Obviously, pot fragments at Ghurab when found in the same style in sites on the Greek mainland provided a date for an otherwise undatable occupation level far from the Nile. Petrie's "cross-dating" method is still widely used by archaeologists and was to prove a vital dating tool for establishing the chronology of the Minoan civilization in Crete (see below).

Eccentric he might be, but Flinders Petrie had no doubt about what he was doing. He proclaimed himself a collector of "all the requisite information," as a tester of hypotheses, and as someone who wove "a history out of scattered evidence." A major test of his skills came at **el-Amarna** on the Middle Nile, the capital of the heretic pharaoh Akhenaten, who ruled briefly over Egypt in 1350–1334 B.C. El-Amarna was the only Egyptian capital with no overlying occupation, so Petrie was able to clear large areas of the town, including the pharaoh's palace with its magnificent painted frescoes and pavements. He also discovered a priceless archive of cuneiform tablets that turned out to be the royal archives, chronicling dealings with Hittite and other monarchs at a time of constant political machinations.

In 1892, Flinders Petrie was appointed the first professor of Egyptology at the University of London, a remarkable appointment for a man who never earned a university degree. Two years later, Petrie made one of his most important discoveries with the excavation of a series of enormous desert cemeteries near the town of **Naqada** in Upper Egypt that dated to centuries before the beginning of pharaonic Egypt in about 3100 B.C. He cleared more than two thousand graves in 1894 alone, each containing a skeleton and decorated clay pots. Petrie studied them grave by grave, each as a separate sealed unit, and found that there were gradual changes in the shapes of vessels and their decoration over time. For example, what were once practical handles for lifting pots degenerated over time into mere painted squiggles. So many graves were found that Petrie was able to arrange them in chronological stages of development, working back from a royal grave that linked his stages with older, undated graves. This bold and revolutionary attempt to date cultures much earlier than Egyptian civilization was used for years and became known as "sequence dating."

The same principles of artifact ordering are still used in the elaborate seriations of potsherds and other artifacts commonplace today. Such seriations are based on the principle that artifact fashions are fleeting things, which change through time. By classifying artifacts from successive occupation levels, the archaeologist can plot out the growing popularity, then decline, of different artifact forms, decorative motifs, and so on. The percentages of these artifacts and individual features, or attributes, can be used to compare the artifact contents of different sites.

The historical archaeologist James Deetz demonstrated the validity of the principle of such seriations with a classic study of New England tombstones of known age. His plots of changing percentages of different styles look somewhat like an old-fashioned battleship hull viewed from above, whence the widely used term "battleship curve" to describe such seriation diagrams. Seriation is now much refined with the use of statistical studies of changing features (attributes) of different artifacts and dating methods such as radiocarbon and tree-rings. But the basic principles go back to Petrie's simple analyses of early Egyptian pottery.

By the closing decade of the nineteenth century, the small archaeological world was still largely made up of amateurs, many of them people of independent means. Everyone knew everyone else, which meant that there was a constant interchange of information. Training was at best rudimentary, for one learned excavation on someone else's dig before being sent out on one's own. Many people started major excavations with virtually no experience at all, among them Arthur John Evans, who discovered the Minoan civilization of Crete in the first major excavation of the twentieth century.

The Discovery of Minoan Civilization

Arthur John Evans (1851–1941) was the youngest son of John Evans, papermaker and antiquarian and one of the major protagonists in the controversies over human antiquity in 1859. Of small stature, with keen eyesight and an insatiable curiosity, Evans traveled widely in Greece and southeastern Europe while a young man, serving as a freelance journalist and being arrested as a spy for his pains. In the intervals between covering rebellions in the Balkans, he collected artifacts of all kinds, using his microscopic eyesight to examine even the tiniest objects. His unusual eyesight enabled him to appreciate small finds that his contemporaries ignored.

In 1884, Evans became Keeper of the Ashmolean Museum in Oxford, a post he held for 25 years. He transformed a moribund institution into a dynamic center of archaeological research, traveling constantly and acquiring numerous artifacts for the museum. His travels brought him in touch with many archaeologists of the day, among them Heinrich Schliemann. He visited the excavations at Mycenae and realized that it was a major trading center of a Bronze Age civilization, with important ties to the Aegean Islands and Crete. While in Athens, he bought dozens of tiny seals from antique dealers in the city, bombarding them with questions about his purchases. He soon learned that the minutely engraved seals came from Crete.

Evans first visited Crete in 1894, inspecting the pottery-strewn hillside at **Knossos.** After two years, he managed to purchase the site. Meanwhile, he traveled widely through the island and found traces of at least two undeciphered ancient writing systems, written with tiny symbols on clay tablets. These he named Linear A and B, without any idea which one was the earlier of the two. As the sale of Knossos was being completed, a vicious rebellion broke out on Crete, resulting in the expulsion of the hated Turks, who had ruled the island for centuries. Evans acquired great goodwill by distributing relief supplies as he collected artifacts.

The Knossos excavations finally started in 1900, and they continued intermittently for the next 30 years. Arthur Evans had absolutely no digging experience except for some hasty trenching in prehistoric cemeteries, and certainly he had absolutely no qualifications to excavate a site as complicated as Knossos. No one questioned his abilities in an era when one learned digging by doing. Fortunately, he had the sense to hire an experienced Scottish excavator, Duncan Mackenzie, who shouldered much of the detail.

On the very first day the workers uncovered building foundations; on the second they uncovered a house with faded wall decorations. Evans realized immediately that his new palace was neither Greek nor Roman, but was the home of ancient Cretan kings. He promptly named this hitherto unknown civilization "Minoan," after the legendary King Minos of Crete, who was said to have lived at Knossos thousands of years ago. Within a few months, Evans had uncovered more than two acres of the palace, including a throne room complete with stone throne and wall benches, living quarters, storage chambers, and a magnificent wall painting of a male cupbearer (Figure 6.6).

The Palace of Minos was an extraordinary structure built around a central courtyard, entered from the north through a pillared hall. Rows of storage rooms opened into a narrow passageway to the west of the courtyard, with the capacity to store at least 28,400 liters (75,000 gallons) of olive oil alone. Two staircases of imposing design led to what Evans thought were the royal living quarters below. Unlike some of his faster-working predecessors, Evans filled notebook after notebook with notes about layers and small finds, with architectural details of individual rooms.

In 1908, Evans inherited a large fortune from a relative, much of which he spent on an ambitious architectural reconstruction of portions of the palace. By judicious rebuilding and reconstruction, he tried to give both Cretans and

Figure 6.6   The Palace of Minos at Knossos.

tourists an impression of Minoan civilization. He replaced wooden columns with concrete pillars painted to conform to Minoan decor. Any reconstruction of an archaeological site is controversial, but on the whole Evans succeeded in giving a fair impression of parts of the palace. He hired Swiss artist Emile Guillieron, who helped him reconstruct the palace paintings: young people in formal processions, a young boy gathering saffron, mythical griffins and other beasts, and reliefs of charging bulls. The reconstructions owe a considerable amount to Evans's fertile imagination.

Between 1900 and 1935, Evans commuted between Knossos and Oxford, studying the thousands of potsherds and other small finds from the palace. He did not have the advantage of radiocarbon dating or other modern chronological techniques to date the palace. Fortunately, the Minoans had traded with many other lands, including Egypt, where accurately dated artifacts abounded. By using dated Cretan pottery found in Egypt by Flinders Petrie, Evans produced the first chronological framework for Minoan civilization, beginning with simple village farmers before 3000 B.C. By 3000 B.C., "Early Minoans" were trading with other Aegean islands and with Cyprus. Between 2200 and 1250 B.C., the "Middle" and "Late Minoan" periods saw Cretan civilization at its height. The island was densely settled. Minoan ships traded as far as Egypt and Syria. The palace itself was rebuilt many times over its long life, partly because of earthquake damage, then abandoned before Minoan civilization collapsed in 1200 B.C. Today's chronologies place the end of the Minoans a couple of centuries earlier, but the general outlines of Evans's framework are still in place.

In an interesting footnote to Minoan archaeology, in 1967 the Greek archaeologist Spyridon Marinatos unearthed a Minoan village at Akrotiri in the Aegean island of Santorini (Thera), buried under many meters of volcanic ash deposited by a violent eruption that blew most of the island into space. The date of this cataclysm is controversial, but is probably around 1688 B.C. What effect the resulting ash clouds and tidal waves had on nearby Crete is a matter of debate, but they must have caused significant damage. Some archaeologists believe that the Santorini eruption was remembered in folklore for many centuries, to become the basis of the legend of the lost continent of Atlantis, which sank into the ocean in a sudden catastrophe. This legend, immortalized by the Greek philosopher Plato, has been the subject of much speculation over the centuries. The Santorini catastrophe is but one of many candidates for Atlantis, and an unlikely one. Almost certainly, Atlantis is a fictional continent.

Arthur Evans devoted the rest of his life to Knossos and the Minoans. He published his great four-volume report, *The Palace of Minos at Knossos,* over 14 years between 1921 and 1935—a colossal task by any standards. He painted a picture of a colorful, peaceful civilization with gifted artists, where bulls and a goddess of fertility played a central role in human life. Despite decades of effort, Evans failed to decipher the mysterious Cretan script, which had been one of his original objectives in 1900. Eleven years later, another Englishman, Michael Ventris, unlocked some of the secrets of the script, which is still only partially deciphered to this day.

The Knossos excavations marked the beginning of a new era in archaeology, when a concern with chronology and artifacts—with the development of civilizations—replaced the hasty searches for spectacular finds so characteristic of early excavations. We may deplore the methods of the early excavators, but one must remember that the archaeological science of today developed slowly and steadily during the twentieth century, in the hands of increasingly expert and innovative researchers. Chapter 7 summarizes some of the key developments and archaeological discoveries that laid the foundations for the scientific revolution in archaeology in the past century.

Summary

Chapter 6 describes the beginnings of biblical archaeology with Charles Warren's excavations under Jerusalem in 1864 and the challenges and difficulties of that work. These excavations and regional surveys of the Holy Land were the founding projects of biblical archaeology. Meanwhile, interest in the relationship between archaeology and the Scriptures reached fever pitch in 1872, with the decipherment of the so-called Flood Tablets from Nineveh by George Smith. The flood legend was a late version of a myth told by the Sumerian civilization, identified in ancient mounds in southern Mesopotamia by Ernest de Sarzec at Telloh in 1877. The Sumerian civilization turned out to be as old as the ancient Egyptian state, but excavations were thwarted by a lack of methods for excavating sun-dried brick. Such methods were finally developed by Robert Koldeway at Babylon in the first decade of the twentieth century.

Meanwhile, German businessman-turned-archaeologist Heinrich Schliemann excavated into Hissarlik mound in northwestern Turkey in 1871 and claimed he had found Homeric Troy. He subsequently excavated royal burials at Mycenae, the first archaeological evidence for the Mycenaean civilization of mainland Greece. Schliemann's excavation methods were very rough and were soon outdated by the more refined approaches of German excavators at Samothrace and Olympia. In southern England, General Augustus Lane Fox Pitt Rivers developed scientific excavation methods on prehistoric and Roman sites on his vast estates at Cranborne Chase. His methods were the prototypes for cutting-edge excavation techniques developed in Britain after World War I. In Egypt, another British excavator, Flinders Petrie, excavated both dynastic and predynastic sites. He stressed the importance of potsherds and other small artifacts, developed cross-dating as a means of dating prehistoric sites, and also devised seriation methods for ordering predynastic burials.

Archaeologist Arthur Evans used his microscopic eyesight to study seals from the Minoan civilization of Crete. In 1900, he began excavations at the Palace of Minos at Knossos, and discovered the flamboyant Minoan civilization.

All of these discoveries ended the pioneer era of archaeology. By 1900, there were signs that more responsible excavation methods were finally coming into use.

Guide to Further Reading

Bowden, Mark. 1991. *The Life and Times of Lieutenant-General Augustus Lane Fox Pitt Rivers.* New York: Cambridge University Press.

Bowden's biography is an excellent account of this important figure.

Drower, Margaret S. 1985. *Flinders Petrie: A Life in Archaeology.* London: Victor Gollancz.

Comprehensive and well written. One need not look further for a Petrie biography.

Evans, Joan. 1943. *Time and Chance.* London: Longman.

Evans's book covers three generations of the Evans family. It is arguably the best biography, although there are others.

Silberman, Neil A. 1982. *Digging for God and Country: Exploration, Archaeology, and the Secret Struggle for the Holy Land, 1799–1917.* New York: Alfred Knopf.

The best and most entertaining history of biblical archaeology available.

Traill, David A. 1995. *Schliemann of Troy: Treasure and Deceit.* New York: St. Martin's Press.

A measured assessment of Schliemann, warts and all.

chapter 7

The Birth of Culture History

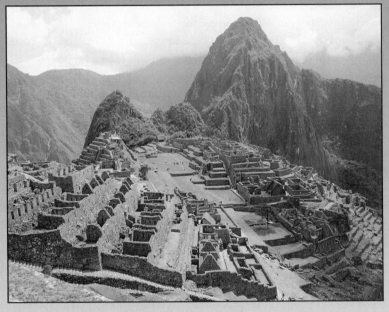

Machu Picchu, Peru

Into this well they have had . . . the custom of throwing men alive as a sacrifice to the gods, in times of drought. . . . They also threw into it . . . precious stones and things, which they prized.

Bishop Diego de Landa on the Sacred Cenote at Chichén Itzá, Mexico, in his *Relacíon de las Cosas de Yucatán*

I felt . . . a strange thrill when I realized that I was the only living being who had ever reached this place alive and expected to leave it again still living.

Edward Thompson, letter on diving in the Sacred Cenote, 1910

chapter outline

In Chapter 4, we saw how the notion of human progress dominated anthropological and archaeological thinking during much of the nineteenth century. Prehistoric archaeologists were frustrated by the incompleteness of the archaeological record, which compelled them to draw on the researches of biological anthropologists, linguists, and ethnologists in their efforts to reconstruct the past. At the same time, they lived in a time when nineteenth-century industrial civilization was considered the pinnacle of human achievement. In this chapter, we describe some of the intellectual developments that moved archaeology away from simplistic ideas of human progress in prehistoric times.

Lubbock's **Prehistoric Times**

We begin with the stereotypical Victorian, John Lubbock—banker, archaeologist, and ardent evolutionist. His *Prehistoric Times, as Illustrated by Ancient Remains, and the Manners and Customs of Modern Savages* appeared in London in 1865. Lubbock was a firm believer in unilinear cultural evolution and was strongly influenced by Darwin's thinking, to the point where he thought of modern Europeans as the product of lengthy biological and cultural evolution. Technologically less advanced people were culturally, intellectually, and emotionally more primitive than civilized societies. Not only that, but the processes of natural selection had operated differentially among Europeans themselves, thereby accounting for the criminal and lower classes. Lubbock used evolution and natural selection not only to account for the superiority of European societies over others, but for the social inequality within European society.

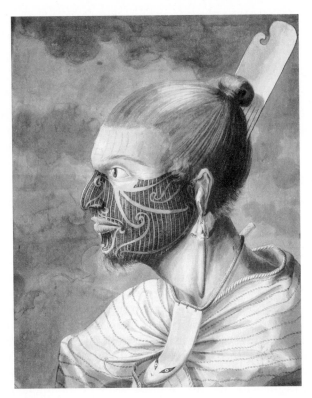

Figure 7.1　A Maori warrior with tattooed features drawn by Sydney Parkinson, who traveled with Captain James Cook, 1769. © Copyright The British Museum.

Prehistoric Times was an immensely popular book on both sides of the Atlantic and went through seven editions between 1865 and 1913. Lubbock's influence on archaeological thinking was enormous, drawing as it did on the Three Ages of prehistory, the latest archaeological discoveries, and a miscellany of information about living non-Western societies, from Native Americans to the Maori of New Zealand (Figure 7.1). His descriptions of non-Western societies were unflattering and stressed that they were morally deficient—which accounted for their exotic customs by Western thinking. Furthermore, according to Lubbock, such societies remained static and never changed, while cultural development and technological innovation led to material progress and spiritual enlightenment. In other words, Victorian industrial civilization with its ardent capitalism and the natural selection resulting from it was nirvana, an earthly paradise. This inevitable progress through innovation had begun deep in prehistoric times, while the most primitive societies were destined to vanish, to become extinct in the face of expanding industrial civilization.

John Lubbock used theories of evolution and natural selection, of human progress, to justify Western colonization of other lands on the grounds that it promoted the general progress of humanity. Whereas scholars of the Enlightenment believed that all humans would participate in progress, Lubbock's vision of the past was linked to doctrines of European superiority, to an expanding empire, and to a future world that would, naturally, be led and dominated by Western civilization. By the end of the book's long life, *Prehistoric Times* had become a relic of a period when much less was known about prehistory. New generations of research showed that the ancient world was much too complex to accommodate simple evolutionary schemes.

Oscar Montelius and the First Culture History

Modern prehistoric archaeology was born in Scandinavia, thanks to the Three Age System and to the researches of Jacob Jens Worsaae, described in Chapter 4. Worsaae's intellectual successor, and the archaeologist who exposed the simplicity of unilinear evolution, was Swedish archaeologist Oscar Montelius (1843–1921), who obtained a doctorate in archaeology at the University of Uppsala in 1867, then went on a series of study tours across Europe, examining stone, bronze, and iron artifacts from dozens of archaeological sites. Like John Lubbock, Montelius was deeply influenced by the evolutionary teachings of Charles Darwin. He soon became an expert on prehistoric artifacts of every kind, especially bronze brooches, bowls, and swords. In 1873, he published a pioneering study of these objects from northern and central Sweden, using evolving series of artifacts to distinguish between an Early and Late Bronze Age in the region.

Montelius published this research as numerous new excavations throughout Europe produced hundreds of new artifacts. Although attached to the Swedish State Historical Museum, he spent much of each year traveling away from Stockholm, visiting museums and newly excavated sites, combing all parts of Europe for new material. He produced a series of brilliant and highly detailed technical reports, culminating in his *Brooches from the Bronze Age* (1881), an artifact study that drew on finds not only from Scandinavia, but also from much richer collections from as far away as Greece and Italy.

Montelius followed this important work with his *On the Dating of the Bronze Age, particularly in relation to Scandinavia* (1885). This closely argued archaeological masterpiece refused to adopt nationalistic perspectives, which were characteristic of European archaeology at the time. Instead, he focused on the artifacts themselves, in an innovative use of typology (artifact classification), which was to dominate European archaeology for more than half a century. "I have given individual consideration to each of the main series of weapons, tools, ornaments, and pottery, together with their ornamentation, so as to determine the course of their evolution, and to find out in what order the types . . . succeed one another," he wrote at the end of his career in 1903 (Montelius 1986:27).

Oscar Montelius was a genius at artifact classification, at tracing minute details of Bronze Age artifacts from one end of Europe to the other. He focused on the shapes of sword blades, the narrow ones being used to stab while the wider ones were slashing weapons. Even the smallest details of brooches used to adorn clothing had significance in Montelius's eyes, for he assumed that changes in fashion and design came slowly and over time. He was careful to base his Bronze Age research on artifacts found with undisturbed burials. His classifications depended on accurate dating, on finds that had never been disturbed by later activity, and on careful observation of stratigraphic layers in archaeological sites. Bronze Age burials were ideal for his purpose, because they were plentiful and contained a wide range of distinctive artifacts. Montelius's artifact classifications traced the development of artifacts from strictly practical prototypes like simple pins, then showed how hitherto strictly functional features like, say, the hasp of a pin became more elaborate and decorative, until, centuries later, a once simple Bronze Age pin had become a highly elaborate ornament worn by important chieftains.

Montelius not only assumed that the simple and functional was the earliest; he set out to document it with reference to other artifacts found in the same graves. For example, Bronze Age axes and adzes first appeared as artifacts with low flanges to set them in their handles. Soon, the makers elaborated them with deeper flanges and set them at an angle in the wooden handle. Montelius traced a spiral design used to hold the two prongs of the shaft set between them to prevent splitting as the wood fused with the ax, then showed how the old haft was modified into a purely ornamental feature as the Bronze Age ax developed a socket to hold the handle. He drew on modern comparisons to make fundamental points. For example, he showed how his system worked by chronicling how railroad passenger cars developed from basically stagecoaches set on flanged wheels into a much more efficient design, which, however, still retained the outside entrance to each compartment.

By 1881, Montelius had subdivided the European Bronze Age into no fewer than six periods, cross-dating the later ones by using artifacts of known historical age in Egypt and southwestern Asia as the basis for a provisional chronology. He showed how bronze first appeared in Egypt by the third millennium B.C., in Greece with the Mycenaeans of the second millennium, with iron appearing there in only about 1000 B.C. Since Bronze Age artifacts found north and south of the Alps resembled each other closely, Montelius was able to show that the Bronze Age began in central Europe in the mid-second millennium B.C. and ended in northern Europe in the fifth century B.C.

Oscar Montelius placed European prehistory on a new, scientific footing, even if his evolutionary conclusions were controversial to some of his colleagues, who did not believe that it was possible to trace minute design changes through time. From the Bronze Age he turned his attention to the

Stone Age (four periods) and the Iron Age (eight periods), using the same approach. His classifications placed European archaeology on a much more scientific footing.

Stratigraphic Archaeology and Culture Change in the Americas

John Lubbock's *Prehistoric Times,* with its evolutionary doctrines, was extremely influential in American scholarly circles, where the idea of progress was much in the air at a time of major economic and territorial expansion. Lewis Henry Morgan's *Ancient Society* was strongly evolutionary in its outlook, tracing human societies from the most primitive to the supreme expression of humanity—industrial civilization. Lubbock's ideas about biological and cultural inferiority reinforced ideas about the inferiority of Native Americans that had been in vogue since the eighteenth century. Darwin's ideas were prestigious, native peoples were declining rapidly in numbers, and their traditional culture was vanishing to the point where it was easy to agree with Lubbock that American Indians were doomed to extinction. Furthermore, it was also easy to argue, as most archaeologists of the day did, that ancient Native American societies had not changed one iota since the earliest times. If one observed changes in the archaeological record, they were certainly not due to human progress.

These viewpoints were widely accepted, but there remained the problem of the spectacular Aztec, Maya, and Inca civilizations that had been overwhelmed by the Spanish conquest. William Prescott and John Lloyd Stephens had portrayed these societies as those of highly civilized people. Had the Americans produced civilizations as sophisticated as those of Egypt and Mesopotamia, as some scholars like Daniel Wilson believed? Wilson's *Prehistoric Man: Researches into the Origin of Civilization in the Old and New World* argued that complex societies had developed in the New World quite independently of the Old. His views were strongly opposed by those who believed that Native Americans were racially inferior. Lewis Henry Morgan went so far as to ignore all archaeological evidence. He accused the Spaniards of exaggerating the sophistication of Aztec and Inca civilization to glorify their own achievement and stated that the traditional way of life of these societies differed little from that of the Iroquois of New York State. No Native American society had progressed beyond a tribal society.

All of this theoretical argument came at a time when stratigraphic excavation was beginning to take hold in American archaeology, notably in the excavation of shell mounds in the eastern United States. Squier and Davis, and also Cyrus Thomas, used stratigraphic methods to examine burial mounds, while the few scholars searching for earlier Stone Age occupation

Figure 7.2   The great Serpent Mound, a Fort Ancient earthwork in Ohio in the form of a snake, with the burial mound in its open jaws. This remarkable monument was saved from destruction by the efforts of Harvard archaeologist Frederick Ward Putnam and a group of Boston ladies in 1886. Hopewell, Adams County, Ohio. Courtesy, National Museum of the American Indian, Smithsonian Institution. (N21598) Photo by Major Dache M. Reeves.

were well aware of stratigraphy from geological researches. But almost invariably, the changes in artifact styles or dwellings observed in these excavations were dismissed as insignificant, even when stratigraphic methods were used (Figure 7.2).

The German archaeologist Max Uhle (1856–1944) was an outstanding exponent of the stratigraphic method. Uhle trained as a philologist in Europe, but switched to archaeology and ethnography. He became a curator in the Dresden Museum, where he met archaeologist and traveler Alphons Stübel. He worked with him during the 1880s at **Tiwanaku,** the great 1,000-year-old ceremonial center close to Lake Titicaca in Bolivia, high in the Andes (Figure 7.3). The young German turned out to be a gifted excavator and carried out some of the first stratigraphic excavations on the Peruvian coast in the 1890s. He also sent large numbers of dessicated mummies from Peruvian cemeteries to various museums. These finds provided vivid portraits of ancient Andeans that were almost unique in archaeology.

Uhle was a careful and perceptive observer, above all a stratigraphy man—an expert at excavating and recording occupation levels in

Figure 7.3 The Sunken Court at Tiwanaku, Bolivia.

archaeological sites. He also knew that the artifacts in each level were valuable markers—evidence of possible cultural change through time. He continued working in Peru for over 30 years.

In 1902, Uhle was retained by the University of California, Berkeley, to excavate a huge shell mound at **Emeryville,** on the east shore of San Francisco Bay. Uhle trenched into the mound stratum by stratum and boldly identified no fewer than ten principal layers. He took his excavation down to the water table and below, until he reached sterile alluvial clay. His carefully drawn cross-section delineated his levels and even counted the number of artifacts found in each one. He pointed out that the artifacts in the upper strata were entirely different from the implements that he found in the lower levels. At the same time, he recognized that there was much cultural continuity from one layer to the next.

In the end, Uhle segregated two major components in the mound, each comprising five of his ten strata. The people of the lowest component had subsisted mainly on oysters rather than bent-nose clams. They buried their dead in a flexed position and made their simple stone tools almost entirely from local chert, a finely crystallized quartz. The later inhabitants cremated their dead, consumed enormous numbers of clams rather than oysters, and used imported obsidian for many of their stone tools.

Uhle had no sophisticated dating equipment to assist him. But he estimated that the Emeryville mound was occupied for more than a thousand years. He used changing styles in projectile points, beads, and other artifacts to identify culture change, just as he had done on the Peruvian coast, using a methodology ahead of its time. The young German's excavation methods were nothing to write home about by modern standards, but they were better than those of most of his contemporaries. He used picks and shovels to uncover stratified layers, but took the trouble to record the occupation levels with drawings and photographs. Unlike most others, he also took the trouble to publish his finds, in a carefully prepared monograph in 1907.

The wrath of the anthropological establishment promptly descended on Uhle's head. His real sin was to identify cultural change at Emeryville instead of a static ancient California society that changed not one iota over many centuries. The all-powerful Berkeley anthropologist Alfred Kroeber, famous for his studies of California Indians and his work with Ishi, the famous Yahi Indian who provided a mine of information on traditional subsistence, condemned Uhle's conclusions out of hand, although he did not mention him by name: "The one published account of a systematic though partial exploration of a shell-heap of San Francisco Bay upholds the view of a distinct progression and development of civilization having taken place during the growth of the deposit. An independent examination of the material on which this opinion is reared, tends to negate rather than to confirm it" (Kroeber 1909:15). In Kroeber's view, there were no major technological advances throughout California prehistory.

With the widespread belief that there had been little cultural change in ancient times, American archaeologists tended to think in terms of different culture areas in space rather than time. In this, they followed many anthropologists, among them the celebrated ethnologist Franz Boas, who rejected evolutionary schemes and argued in 1887 that museums should display their growing collections of Native American artifacts by culture area (see below). Boas's pronouncement led to a proliferation of studies of geographical variations, in which little attention was paid to chronology. In 1914, for example, William Henry Holmes used stylistic and technological features to define an elaborate series of ancient pottery regions for North America, using the same criteria as those used by ethnologists. As the complexity of the past became ever more apparent from new excavations, and as obvious changes were documented in archaeological sites, the changes were attributed to replacements of one people by another, not to cultural change in situ. Ancient times were a palimpsest, a layering, of different cultures, resulting from population movements. Most people had lived where they were for very long periods of time, with little change. As a result, archaeology was seen as enjoying a continuum with anthropology, forming what Bruce Trigger calls a "flat" view of Native American history.

Archaeology was anthropology, and an integral part of it. As Samuel Haven had observed 50 years before: "The flint utensils of the Age of Stone lie upon the surface of the ground. . . . The peoples that made and used them have not yet entirely disappeared" (Haven 1856:37). All of this resulted from popular perceptions that Native Americans were inferior humans.

Franz Boas

Franz Boas was the dominant figure in American anthropology in the early twentieth century. Born in Germany, Boas received a liberal education—a training that brought much idealist, intellectual thought into his anthropological work. His first fieldwork was among Inuit peoples in Baffinland in 1883. From there, he spent a lifetime cataloging and describing Native American societies, trying to establish anthropology as a descriptive science. He had a passion for collecting, classifying, and preserving vast quantities of data. Only the strict methods of science should be used in collecting anthropological data, he believed. Boas had little interest in archaeology, for he wanted to understand the historical development of Indian societies from within, whereas archaeologists worked from the outside. Above all, he was a descriptive scientist, more interested in the distribution of different artifacts than in their subjective significance.

Boas and his many students were preoccupied with publishing a permanent record of the traditional cultures of Native Americans, a follow-up to the early work of the Bureau of American Ethnology. His approach to anthropology rubbed off on archaeology, which went into a period of artifact description and the erection of elaborate typologies, as opposed to interpretation, from the 1920s onward. To some degree, this was a reflection of Montelius's widely read European artifact studies. It was also a consequence of a gradual improvement in the scientific rigor of archaeological excavations. Descriptive typologies came into fashion, comparing artifacts from one site with those from others; it was no longer enough to know, for example, that two sites hundreds of kilometers apart both contained obsidian arrowheads. If the distribution of such artifacts was being discussed, then far more information was required than merely the evidence of presence at two widely separated locations. Modern typological archaeology owes much of its philosophy and importance to Franz Boas.

Diffusionism

Human progress as a popular doctrine lost credibility by the 1880s, when the social problems of the Industrial Revolution became only too apparent—among them urban poverty, slums, and regular economic crises. Industrialism was now thought to bring social disorder at a time when global competition was intensifying and nationalism was enjoying a new popularity. New theories of migration and diffusion entered the archaeological arena. Franz Boas was among those who opposed doctrines of human progress, arguing that every culture was a unique entity, to be understood on its own terms. Boas espoused cultural relativism—the notion that there was no universal standard for comparing the degree of development, or indeed worth, of different cultures. He also believed in historical particularism, seeing each culture as a product of a unique sequence of development, in which the chance operation of diffusion (the spread of culture traits and ideas) played a major part. Boas was no diffusionist, but many of his contemporaries believed that the only way to explain the past was in terms of a succession of diffusions of ideas, which shaped the development of each culture.

Diffusionism (a school of thought that used diffusion to interpret the past) was soon espoused by the Viennese school of anthropology, which envisaged a single series of cultures in Central Asia that had been carried in their various forms to other parts of the world. By far the most extreme exponent of diffusionism was Englishman Grafton Elliot Smith (1871–1937), an anatomist who became interested in ancient Egyptian mummification while teaching anatomy at Cairo University. He is famous for being the first scholar to x-ray a mummy, but he also acquired an obsession with embalming and sun worship. Smith believed that agriculture, architecture, religion, and institutionalized government had all originated in the unique environment of the Nile Valley. Pyramids occurred in many areas of the world; Egyptian pyramids were the oldest, and pharaonic civilization was still considered by many the earliest in the world. Thus, it was logical to argue that civilization, marked by pyramid building, began along the Nile, then spread elsewhere. Smith and others argued that Egyptian merchants then carried these innovations to all parts of the world while seeking raw materials that would help people acquire immortality. These ideas were the stimulus for all manner of civilizations, like that of the Maya, which, however, degenerated once contact with Egypt was lost.

Smith's hyperdiffusionist theories appealed to people with simplistic visions of the past, and they attracted ardent disciples. Cultural anthropologist William J. Perry of the University of London used his ethnographic background to write of "Children of the Sun," ancient Egyptian travelers and sun worshipers who carried civilization as far as the Americas and the Pacific. All these theories assumed that humans were by nature primitive—that civilization was invented by accident, and only once, in a situation where religion, like sun worship, was all-important in spreading civilization in a world where savages never invented anything.

By the 1920s, the sheer complexity of what was known about the past served to discredit Smith's and Perry's hyperdiffusionist ideas, except in the eyes of the most fanatical believers. Clearly, for example, Old and New World civilizations had developed their own civilizations quite independently. For instance, people realized that pyramids are among the easiest forms of monumental architecture to construct, which accounted for their wide distribution. Nevertheless, diffusion continued to be an important means of explaining the past, partly because scholars believed that humans had invented such major innovations as the bow and arrow, agriculture, and metallurgy only once, in one place from whence they spread to all parts of the world. In other words, culture change would occur only when there was a population movement, a biological as well as cultural change. The growing interest in both cultural evolution and diffusion was a reflection of a need for a framework for the past that allowed the archaeologist to account for the well-documented variations in space and time among ancient societies, which was well apparent by the 1920s. In North America, much of the credit for the development of ways of establishing such variations goes to Alfred Kidder.

Alfred Kidder and Pecos

By the dawn of the twentieth century, the notion of working from the present into the past was well understood by many American archaeologists, but was rarely applied on a large scale until the Harvard archaeologist Alfred Kidder excavated the great middens at Pecos, New Mexico, in 1915–1921.

Alfred Kidder (1885–1963) grew up in Cambridge, Massachusetts, in an atmosphere of intellectual curiosity and scholarship, acquiring a lifelong interest in natural history as a result. At age 15, he published an article on birds. During his junior year at Harvard in 1907, he attended a field school in the Southwest run by Edgar Hewitt, a pioneer researcher. As a doctoral student, he received training in field methods from the Egyptologist George Reisner. Art historian George Chase gave him a solid grounding in the analysis of ceramics (clay vessels) of all kinds. It was no coincidence that Kidder's doctoral dissertation was on the style and decorative motifs of Pueblo pottery. He also learned from Franz Boas, who gave Kidder a sense of the importance of detailed analysis of any human society—a point that he took to heart. Kidder also traveled in the Near East, where he had a chance to visit excavations by George Reisner and others on the Nile. There he absorbed excavation methods unknown in the United States, such as systematic burial excavation and careful observation of sequences of human occupation through time. Such techniques were still in their infancy. He also realized just how important the humble pot fragment and other tiny artifacts were for the study of the past.

In 1915, Alfred Kidder embarked on the most important work of his career. He started excavating into the deep, stratified layers of Pecos Pueblo, New Mexico, a pueblo settlement close by a Spanish mission and known to have been occupied far back into ancient times. Up until then, most Southwestern excavation had been less concerned with recording different periods of occupation, and more concerned with clearing ruins and recovering fragile artifacts such as baskets and beautifully decorated Pueblo pots. In 1914, archaeologist Nels C. Nelson had dug into San Cristobal Pueblo, New Mexico, in 0.3-meter (1-foot) levels, from which he had recovered different pottery types. But it was left to Kidder to explain what these differences meant.

Kidder excavated into the deep layers of Pecos on a massive scale. During the early seasons, he refined Nelson's San Cristobal approach by abandoning arbitrary levels and making detailed sketches of the way the refuse discarded by the inhabitants had accumulated. He traced the natural strata of the middens and carefully recorded the pot fragments found in them. Kidder followed Reisner's example in Egypt. He used pegs and strings to record the precise rise and fall of even the smallest ash layers. His potsherd catalogs were also modeled on those used by Reisner, employed along the Nile to develop a meticulous analysis of the profound changes in pottery forms and, above all, surface decoration, over many centuries. For example, Kidder found that the first occupants of the pueblo had made a distinctive black-on-white style of pottery. At the same time, he recovered hundreds of human skeletons.

While waiting for induction into the U.S. Army in 1917, Kidder visited modern-day Hopi and other pueblos in the Southwest and learned much about Southwestern ethnography and about modern Pueblo culture. In all his subsequent researches, he melded anthropology and archaeology, the living culture and the ancient, into definitive summaries of ancient Pueblo society.

Excavations at Pecos resumed in 1920, with the discovery of still more human burials. Kidder called on the expert services of biological anthropologist Ernest Albert Hooton. He insisted that Hooton visit the excavations so he could study the human remains as they emerged in the trenches and witness the actual field conditions of their discovery. This was one of the first cases where a skeletal expert worked in the field alongside a North American archaeologist. Soon Kidder had data on the sex and age of the skeletons, as well as some interesting information on life expectancy and ancient pathology. Hooton showed, for example, that most of the Pecos people died in their twenties.

By 1922, Kidder had turned his attention to the architecture and expansion of the pueblo, and excavated some of the earliest occupation levels. By 1924, when he published *An Introduction to Southwestern Archaeology,* he was confident enough to develop a detailed sequence of ancient Pueblo and pre-Pueblo cultures for the Southwest, using his stratigraphic excavations and pottery studies from Pecos. This was the first culture-historical sequence of any region in North America. Kidder's sequence began with Basketmaker cultures, at least two thousand years old, which eventually evolved into the Pueblo societies of later times. At the same time, he founded an annual Pecos Conference, where he and his colleagues gathered to report on their latest researches and to discuss problems of common concern. The Pecos Conference is still an annual event.

Alfred Kidder established many of the basic principles of North American archaeology. The artifact classification systems he developed at Pecos arranged potsherds by such categories as method of manufacture, decoration, and form, in much the same kind of taxonomy that Carl Linnaeus used for plants. His influence is still felt in Southwest archaeology to this day.

Mesoamerica and the Andes

Archaeological research in **Mesoamerica** and South America proceeded more slowly than that in the north, partly because of the difficulty of access, but also because of unsettled political conditions.

Maya Research, 1880 to 1930

Maya research languished until the 1880s, when a wealthy Bostonian, Charles Bowditch, sponsored a series of expeditions to investigate the spectacular Maya ruins at Copán in Honduras and at nearby **Quirigua** in Guatemala. Other archaeologists soon followed, among them the German scholar Eduard Seler, who was the first to combine archaeology with the study of oral histories, Spanish chronicles, and indigenous documents. He spent much time studying the intricate stelae from Copán and elsewhere and worked out some of the basic details of the Maya calendar.

An independently wealthy Englishman, Alfred Maudslay (1850–1931), visited Quirigua while on a winter vacation. He was so entranced by the ruins that he devoted the rest of his life to recording Maya sites. Maudslay trekked for 17 days through thick rain forest to the city of Tikal, then completely overgrown, with only the tops of the pyramids projecting above the forest canopy. A group of pyramids grouped around a central plaza formed the center of a city laid out on "a rectangular plan." Maudslay was one of the first fieldworkers to use photography to record sites and inscriptions, transporting his bulky equipment along narrow forest tracks on the backs of mules. He visited numerous sites such as Palenque and Chichén Itzá, occasionally making fine papier mâché and plaster casts of Maya carvings (Figure 7.4). Much to the horror of his man-servant, he used his hairbrushes to clean dirt off newly discovered stelae. He accumulated an archive of casts, molds, plans, and photographs that provided the basis for his later studies of Maya script.

Seler and Maudslay were among those who puzzled out the configurations of bars and dots that were the basis of the Maya calendar. They discovered the Maya Long Count, a linear calendar that reckoned time in five cycles ranging from 144,000 years to one day. The research on Maya chronology also owed much to a Catholic priest, Brasseur de Bourbourg (1814–1873),

Figure 7.4   The Castillo at Chichén Itzá, the most prominent structure at this major Maya city.

whose brilliant linguistic abilities enabled him to use a wide variety of Spanish and native sources that had been inaccessible to Prescott and other earlier scholars. His four-volume *Histoire des nations civilisées* appeared in the 1850s and set the study of early Central American civilization on a new footing, even if his conclusions were extremely wild. In 1863, he discovered a copy of Diego de Landa's *Relación de las Cosas de Yucatan,* which had languished in church archives for four centuries, and used it as a potential source for deciphering Maya script. In this endeavor he failed. The glyphs were not deciphered until the 1980s.

Until the twentieth century, only a handful of archaeologists worked on Maya civilization. The self-taught Edward S. Thompson (1856–1935) read Brasseur de Bourbourg's books while studying to become an engineer. In 1885, he arrived in Merida, Mexico, as U.S. consul for Yucatán and Campeche—a self-reliant, hardworking man who had but a smattering of archaeological knowledge. He soon visited nearby Uxmal, so much admired by Catherwood and Stephens, and concluded at once that the lost continent of Atlantis was not the origin of Maya civilization, which was of indigenous origin. Thompson spent much of his time at **Labná,** 117 kilometers (73 miles) from Merida, but his limited archaeological knowledge prevented him from doing serious research. He also made 929 square meters (10,000 square feet) of plaster casts of Maya façades from Labná and Uxmal for the 1893 World's

Fair in Chicago, which caused a considerable stir among the public and wealthy benefactors.

Edward Thompson is remembered as the first archaeologist to explore Chichén Itzá. He began work in 1895 and lived there for more than 30 years, during which time he discovered an important elite burial of five people, cleared many ruins, and devoted much time to probing the depths of the Sacred Cenote, a sacrificial pool described by Bishop de Landa whose algae-covered waters lay 20 meters (65 feet) below ground. Thompson spent many years dredging the muddy depths of the Cenote and experimented with heavy diving apparatus. He ruptured his eardrum for his pains, but he recovered large quantities of ceremonial artifacts and human bones in his scoop. He quietly shipped many of the finds back to the Peabody Museum in Cambridge; others were looted on-site and dispersed. As his Cenote investigations drew to a close, it became clear that there were few artifacts in Mexico to show for the work. In 1923, the Carnegie Institution of Washington began work at the ruins, as a full-fledged scandal erupted over Thompson's activities. Thompson was forced to return to the United States, where he lived out his life in poverty. The Cenote artifacts were published by the Peabody Museum in the 1950s, and the artifacts were discreetly returned to Mexico in 1958.

Thompson was the last of the pioneers. From the early twentieth century onward, major archaeological research was in the hands of large academic institutions. This new generation of expeditions built on the foundations laid by the solitary explorer and scholar of earlier times.

The Andes, 1880–1930

The German naturalist Alexander von Humboldt (1769–1859) traveled through the Andes in 1800–1802. He observed the ceaseless war waged by **Andean** farmers in mountain valleys against cold and frost, as they planted crops ever higher on precipitous slopes. He also observed some fine examples of Inca masonry. In 1865, Ephraim Squier of moundbuilder fame visited Peru on a diplomatic mission. He observed Inca ruins and traditional rope bridges in the Andean highlands and described imposing adobe pyramids on the arid coast.

Serious research began with the excavations of the German Max Uhle, a pioneer of stratigraphic excavation, whose California exploits were described earlier. He learned his craft through working on the finds from Tiwanaku made by the traveler Alphons Stubel, then spent 20 years working on coastal sites, notably at the great shrine at **Pachacamac** near Lima, celebrated as the home of a powerful oracle. Uhle dug through Inca layers at the surface, then probed the earlier levels beneath. He developed the first culture-historical sequence for the southern coast, then moved to the North Coast, where he investigated Moche and **Chimu** sites. All subsequent Andean archaeology is based on Uhle's remarkable excavations.

Uhle preferred to work out of the limelight. His researches remained little known, even as another traveler, Hiram Bingham (1878–1956), rediscovered the Inca city of **Machu Picchu** high in the Andes in 1911. Bingham was a Yale historian with a taste for adventurous travel. He traveled from Cuzco up the Urubamba River, paying money to local Indians if they showed him unknown ruins. Climbing up a precipitous slope high above the Urubamba River, Bingham scrambled through abandoned terrace fields and emerged among magnificent Inca buildings and a shrine surrounding a white stone. He was entranced by the deserted city and its spectacular surroundings. He returned the following year to clear the buildings and proclaimed it the lost city of Vilcabamba, the last capital of the Inca empire during its final resistance against the Spaniards in 1572.

Bingham's discovery caused great popular interest, largely because it was well publicized with photographs in the pages of *National Geographic* magazine, which had supported his fieldwork. As it happens, Bingham was wrong. Years later, in the 1950s, explorer Gene Savoy located the last Inca capital at Espiritu Pampa deep in the forest. As for Machu Picchu, it is now thought to have been a country estate of the great Inca emperor Pachacuti. But the spectacular ruins remain a symbol of the remarkable achievements of Inca, and Andean, civilization. Hiram Bingham went on to serve as a pilot in World War I. He subsequently became governor of Connecticut and a United States senator.

By the 1930s, archaeology was becoming an increasingly professional discipline. The days of epic excavation and small armies of laborers were over, as new scientific methods and stricter antiquities laws regulated archaeological research as never before. At the same time, a few archaeologists were beginning to move beyond artifacts into wider issues such as environmental change and ancient lifeways.

Summary

Chapter 7 begins with Sir John Lubbock's *Prehistoric Times,* which epitomizes late-nineteenth-century notions of human progress and racial superiority. Major advances in scientific knowledge about prehistory showed that unilinear evolution theories were too simplistic to reflect reality. Modern prehistoric archaeology was born in Scandinavia, with the work of Oscar Montelius, who developed the first culture-historical framework for prehistoric Europe in the 1880s and 1890s. He was the founder of modern artifact typology, using both artifact forms and stratigraphic observations to place ancient cultures in chronological order.

Lubbock's book was very influential in the Americas, where doctrines of human progress were fashionable and Darwin's work was prestigious. Many scholars denied that there was any evidence of cultural change in ancient American societies, though stratigraphic excavations in Peru and California in the hands of Max Uhle and others showed that they were wrong. Archaeology was considered part of anthropology, and ancient times in the Americas were considered to be of short duration.

The researches of anthropologist Franz Boas, with his passion for describing living societies, rubbed off onto archaeologists, who became increasingly preoccupied with artifact descriptions and typology. As human progress lost favor as a theory, so diffusionist theories came into fashion during the early twentieth century, triggered in part by the Viennese school of anthropology. Hyperdiffusionism enjoyed a brief popularity in the hands of Grafton Eliot Smith and William Perry, but was soon discredited because of its simplistic vision of the past. Meanwhile, archaeologist Alfred Kidder embarked on large-scale excavations at Pecos Pueblo, New Mexico, where he developed a long sequence of Southwestern cultures using potsherds and working back from the present into the past.

Mesoamerican and Andean archaeology developed in the hands of a few archaeologists, among them Alfred Maudslay and Edward Thompson, who worked on Maya ceremonial centers. Hiram Bingham's expedition to Machu Picchu high in the Andes in 1911 marked the end of the pioneer period of archaeology in the Americas, as Max Uhle conducted stratigraphic excavations on the coast.

Guide to Further Reading

Elliot, M. 1995. *Great Excavations: Tales of Early Southwestern Archaeology, 1888–1939*. Santa Fe: School of American Research.

This book gives a good description of Kidder at Pecos.

Klindt-Jenson, O. 1975. *A History of Scandinavian Archaeology*. London: Thames and Hudson.

The definitive account of early archaeology in northern Europe.

Lyman, R. L., M. O'Brien, and R. Dunnell. 1996. *The Rise and Fall of Culture History*. New York: Plenum Press.

A definitive account of culture history in archaeology. For advanced students.

Willey, Gordon R., and Jeremy A. Sabloff. 1993. *A History of American Archaeology*. 3rd ed. New York: W. H. Freeman.

An excellent basic description of early American archaeology.

Woodbury, Richard B. 1973. *Alfred V. Kidder*. New York: Columbia University Press.

Woodbury's biography is an excellent starting point.

chapter 8

Egypt, Iraq, and Beyond

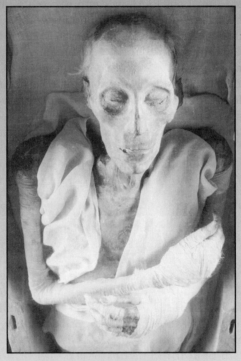

Restored mummy of Rameses II.

The whole thing may seem childish, but in fact it is such things that make the work go well, and when digging at Jerablus ceases to be a great game and becomes, as in Egypt, a mere business, it will be a bad thing.

Leonard Woolley on greeting important finds at Carchemish with a ceremonial revolver volley, Diary, 1912

In 1904, an Englishman named Leonard Woolley, then an undergraduate at New College, Oxford, was summoned to the warden's office to discuss his career plans. Woolley murmured something about becoming a schoolmaster or taking holy orders. The warden leaned back in his chair. "I have decided that you shall become an archaeologist," he announced. And Woolley did—in fact, he became one of the most successful fieldworkers of the twentieth century. In this chapter, we summarize the development of archaeology between about 1900 and 1930, when the foundations of the modern science were laid and archaeology "came of age," as the archaeological historian Glyn Daniel once put it.

Tutankhamun: The Golden Pharaoh

The early decades of the twentieth century were still the domain of the wealthy private individual, who supported excavations in distant lands, although major institutions like the British Museum and the University of Pennsylvania Museum played an increasingly important role in major discoveries.

The world of archaeology was still a very small one, with only a handful of full-time professionals. Many fieldworkers were still people of private means, and almost all were men. Women were not generally welcome, to the point that the young archaeologist Harriet Hawes (1871–1945) was forbidden to excavate in mainland Greece, as her American colleagues thought it inappropriate. None other than Arthur Evans and Sophia Schliemann, widow of Heinrich, encouraged her to work in Crete instead, where she excavated the small Minoan town of **Gournia** in 1899. She excavated the site almost single-handed, with the aid of over a hundred local workers.

For most scholars, archaeology was strictly men's work. The classical archaeologist J. P. Droop wrote a manual of archaeology in 1915 and left his readers in no doubt as to the role of women in the field. He felt that it was better if they dug on their own, away from the male sex. He remarked that he found women charming before a dig and after it, but during the excavation, "however, because they, or we, were in the wrong place, their charm was not seen." He also complained that a mixed dig meant problems at those moments "when you want to say just what you think without translation, which before ladies, whatever their feelings about it, cannot be done" (1915:111). Archaeology remained a largely male preserve until after World War I. Even then, only a handful of female archaeologists were in the field until the 1950s. The numbers are closer to 50 percent today.

Along the Nile, professional Egyptologists worked in increasing numbers, many of them trained by Flinders Petrie. A large number of them worked to copy tomb paintings and inscriptions before they vanished in the face of a tidal wave of destruction. Among the workers was a young English artist named Howard Carter.

Howard Carter (1874–1939) was of humble birth but showed talent as an artist from an early age. In 1891, at age 17, he obtained employment as a cat-aloger and illustrator with William Tyssem Amherst, a local landowner and noted collector of Egyptian antiquities. Carter's work was of such high quality that he came to the notice of the British Museum. Soon, he was sent to Egypt to copy tomb paintings of royal governors at Beni Hassan in Middle Egypt. His work set new standards, so much so that he was sent for field training under Flinders Petrie at the pharaoh Akhenaten's capital at el-Amarna in 1892. Within a few weeks, Carter was left to fend for himself. He worked on his own in the ruins of Akhenaten's great temple. The young artist was much in demand for his copying skills, acquiring a detailed knowledge of the royal tombs in the Valley of the Kings and elsewhere on the west bank of the Nile at Luxor in Upper Egypt. Between 1899 and 1905, he served as inspector of monuments for Upper Egypt, a post that gave him an unrivaled knowledge of the terrain.

Returning to work as a freelance artist, Carter obtained employment with Edward Stanhope, the Earl of Carnarvon (1866–1923), a wealthy English aristocrat and sportsman with a faultless taste in fine antiquities, who spent the winters in Egypt for his health. Carnarvon soon acquired a passion for excavation, despite making few important discoveries. Like many other rich patrons, he had his eye on the Valley of the Kings, the most desirable excavation concession of all. The ten-year permit came in 1914. The objective was to find the rock-cut tomb of an obscure New Kingdom pharaoh named Tutankhamun who had died in 1325 B.C. while still a teenager. Tutankhamun's sepulcher was the only one whose location was still unknown.

Work began in 1917. For six years, Carter cleared rubble from the floor of the Valley of the Kings in a systematic survey and found absolutely nothing.

By 1922 Carnarvon had spent the equivalent of several million dollars without any major results. Reluctantly, he agreed to a final season, focused on a small area near the tomb of Pharaoh Rameses VI, where Carter had started work in 1917. Just three days after starting work, on November 1, the workers uncovered a flight of rock-cut stairs leading to a sealed doorway. For the next three weeks, Carter waited for Carnarvon to arrive from England. Then, on November 26, 1922, the two men stood in front of the sealed doorway, which bore the seal of the pharaoh Tutankhamun. Carter made a small hole in the plaster and shone a flickering candle into the opening. Impatiently, Carnarvon asked him what lay within. "Yes, it is wonderful," Carter replied, as gold glinted in the faint light. Howard Carter had discovered the undisturbed tomb of Tutankhamun, the only unlooted king's sepulcher ever found in Egypt and one of the greatest archaeological discoveries of all time.

The find caused a worldwide sensation. The press and hundreds of curious visitors descended on the Valley of the Kings, threatening to overwhelm the delicate work of recording the tomb. Both Carter and Carnarvon were under severe stress, from the experience of finding the tomb and from the unprecedented media attention, which overwhelmed them. They had a series of blazing arguments that ended up with the two barely on speaking terms. Shortly afterwards, Carnarvon was bitten by a mosquito, then nicked open the bite with his razor while shaving. The bite turned septic. He was only reconciled with his partner a few days before his death on April 5, 1923, his already delicate health undermined by blood poisoning. Inevitably, the press wrote of a deadly "curse of the pharaohs," which had struck Carnarvon down. Many of Tutankhamun's excavators lived into their eighties!

Carter worked on alone. He spent ten arduous years clearing Tutankhamun's tomb, usually with grossly inadequate funding; but he did not live to publish his extraordinary findings. The American Egyptologist Henry Breasted (1865–1935) described in a letter one of the many dramatic moments, when he and Carter opened the innermost shrine and observed the pharaoh's stone sarcophagus within. He described how he experienced a sense of being in the presence of the pharaoh. Nearby, the ostrich feather plumes carried by the king's servants lay on the floor, reduced to brown dust (Figure 8.1).

The clearance of Tutankhamun's tomb was a spectacular achievement and placed Egyptology on a new footing. The magnificent finds from the tomb brought archaeology to public attention as never before and unleashed a fashion for things Egyptian that influenced architecture, fashion, even furniture. It also brought home the incredible wealth of ancient Egypt, and the magnitude of the loss from looting and uncontrolled excavation. As a result of the discovery, antiquities regulations were tightened and the export of artifacts made harder. More and more foreign expeditions became concerned with copying and recording finds—not only new discoveries, but also tombs and monuments that had been ravaged during the nineteenth century. The

Figure 8.1   Howard Carter opens one of Tutankhamun's golden shrines.
Photography by Egyptian Expedition, The Metropolitan Museum of Art.

Oriental Institute of the University of Chicago under James Breasted assumed
a leading role in recording projects, in research that continues to this day.

Howard Carter was a difficult and often moody man who was well aware
that he lacked the social position of most of his archaeological contemporaries. He was always an outsider, even at the height of his fame. His only
official honor was an honorary degree from Yale University. Carter died
in London in 1939 with no formal recognition of his work from the British
government.

Leonard Woolley and Gertrude Bell:
Carchemish and Ur

Leonard Woolley (1880–1960) learned his excavation techniques on a brief
dig on a Roman fort at Hadrian's Wall in northern England. He was
appointed assistant director of the Ashmolean Museum under Arthur Evans

in 1905, and then spent five seasons from 1907 through 1911 working in the Sudan on large cemeteries. This gave him hard experience with handling local people, at which Woolley became exceptionally skilled. At the time, hands-on experience in the Nile Valley was the best archaeological training in the world.

In 1912, Woolley became field director of the British Museum excavations into the **Hittite** city at **Carchemish** near a strategic crossing on the Euphrates River in Syria. His assistant was T. E. Lawrence, later to achieve immortality as Lawrence of Arabia. The Carchemish excavation was a classic example of large-scale excavation at the height of the imperial era. From the beginning, Woolley took a firm hand with local officials and with his workers, who adored him. When a local official refused to issue an excavation permit, Woolley drew a revolver and held it against his head until he signed. He could get away with it, for British power and prestige in the area was then at its height.

The Carchemish excavations began with the removal of much of the Roman city. Woolley was able to dispose of the stone to the German engineers who were building a railroad line to Baghdad nearby. At the same time, he and Lawrence quietly spied on German activities for the Foreign Office. Once the lower, Hittite levels were exposed, Woolley divided his workers into teams of pickmen, supported by shovelers and basketmen—a method he used for a half century at all his excavations. There was nothing new in this approach, which had been established practice since Austen Henry Layard's excavations at Nineveh three-quarters of a century earlier. Woolley introduced one new wrinkle. Important finds were rewarded with a cash payment and a volley of rifle fire. A silly practice to the outside observer, perhaps, but Woolley knew that his men prized this noisy symbol of success. He worked closely with his assistant Sheikh Hamoudi, a man who admitted to two passions in his life: archaeology and violence.

Carchemish was the final stage in Woolley's apprenticeship, but he could never relax because of the volatile political situation. The archaeologists carried firearms for protection. Woolley found that the best strategy was to behave like the surrounding desert chieftains, so that he was treated as one of their equals. As a result, he was trusted on all sides and uncovered a magnificent Hittite city at the same time.

Woolley and Lawrence entertained a steady stream of visitors, among them a young desert traveler, Gertrude Bell (1868–1926). Bell, the daughter of a wealthy iron foundry owner, had a passion for travel. After graduating from Oxford University, she became interested in mountain climbing and soon became one of the leading female climbers of her day. She discovered archaeology during a long stay in Jerusalem in 1893–1894, learned Arabic, and visited Petra. At the same time, she studied the now-largely-destroyed Byzantine churches at Birbinkilise in Turkey. In 1909, she made a memorable journey to the eighth-century Abbassid palace at **Ukhaidir** in the Syrian desert, where

Figure 8.2   Gertrude Bell surveying at Ukhaidir, Iraq.

she not only surveyed the palace, but also had her first introduction to the ever-shifting cross-currents of desert political life. Her account of Ukhaidir, *From Amurath to Amurath,* appeared in 1911 to wide acclaim (Figure 8.2). By the time Bell visited Carchemish in 1911, she had an international reputation as a traveler and an expert on desert politics. She annoyed Lawrence by remarking (correctly) that the Carchemish excavations were unscientific compared with the refined work of the German archaeologist Walter Andraae, who was working at the Assyrian capital, **Assur,** in northern Iraq.

During World War I, Woolley served as an intelligence officer in the Mesopotamian theater and became a prisoner-of-war of the Turks for two years. Bell was appointed to the Arab Intelligence Bureau in Cairo, Egypt, the only woman among dozens of military officers. The army regarded her with suspicion, both on account of her sex and because of her fluent Arabic. But she soon became indispensable, flattering desert chiefs, interviewing them, making use of her unrivaled knowledge of desert lands to keep a finger on the political pulse. The authorities transferred her to Basra on the Persian Gulf in 1916, where she served as a political officer during the critical years when Iraq became a monarchy under King Feisal. Bell worked with British High Commissioner Sir Percy Cox, serving as his Oriental secretary. She was in her element, working with powerful desert sheikhs, defusing quarrels before they boiled over, and paving the way for the creation of a unified state in

Mesopotamia. But as the structure of government became more formalized, the outspoken Gertrude Bell was tactfully shunted aside. Eventually, her only administrative responsibility was archaeology. From this responsibility came the Iraq Museum.

When World War I ended in 1918, scholars from America and Europe were anxious to resume excavations in Mesopotamia. German archaeologists had been reconstructing ancient Babylon for more than a decade before the war. French archaeologists were anxious to excavate at least one ancient city in the heart of Mesopotamia. The British Museum and the University of Pennsylvania sought an excavation permit to conduct a major excavation at the biblical site of **Ur**, celebrated in the Old Testament as Abraham's city. They planned a dig to be headed by Leonard Woolley. By this time, Woolley was a formidable figure. "He was a man of slight stature and no commanding appearance," a contemporary wrote many years later. "But presence, yes—even a blind man would have known what manner of man he was" (Mallowan 1977:26). For 12 seasons, from 1922 to 1934, Leonard Woolley uncovered the Sumerian city of Ur with a ferocious energy that exhausted those around him. His work was complicated by constant negotiations with Gertrude Bell, who supervised the division of finds with the Iraq Museum. Two strong personalities met over the finds, and while Woolley complained of the hard bargains she drove, both sides were satisfied—although the Iraqis have long lamented her generosity to outsiders.

Woolley was an exacting taskmaster, who ran the excavations with the smallest of European staffs, relying heavily on his foreman Hamoudi and his three sons to handle the laborers. The excavations began every day at dawn, and, for the European staff, rarely ended before midnight. Among those who worked at Ur was a young archaeologist named Max Mallowan, who married the detective novelist Agatha Christie after she visited the dig. Christie wrote her mystery *Murder in Mesopotamia* as a result of her Ur experiences, basing the characters on those at the excavation. Woolley himself would work until two or three in the morning, then be at the excavation at dawn. But he was the ideal archaeologist for the job, capable of unraveling layers of long-abandoned buildings from jumbles of mudbrick with uncanny insight. He could dissect a temple or recover the remains of a fragile wooden lyre from the ground with equal skill. He also had a genius for knowing when to wait. One of his 1922 trial trenches uncovered gold objects, perhaps from a royal cemetery. Woolley waited four years to gain the experience to excavate it fully. He wrote: "Our object was to get history, not to fill museum cases with miscellaneous curiosities" (1929:4).

To Woolley, Ur was not a dead city, but a crowded settlement with busy streets. His huge excavations uncovered entire urban precincts. He would rejoice in taking visitors from mudbrick house to mudbrick house, identifying their owners from cuneiform tablets found inside. The excavations studied the architecture of the great *ziggurat* (pyramid) temple at Ur and probed to the depths of the city mound, to the earliest settlement of all—a tiny hamlet of reed huts, now known to date to before 5500 B.C. He even claimed to have found the biblical flood—a thick layer of sterile clay covering a tiny farming village at the base of the ancient city. The claim in fact originated with Woolley's wife Kathleen, a somewhat eccentric artist whom he married in 1927. The find caused a great sensation at the time, but is, in fact, evidence for a much later inundation.

The climax of the Ur excavations came in the late 1920s, when Woolley finally exposed the Royal Cemetery, with its spectacular burial pits. The scale of the excavation beggars the imagination. Woolley cleared more than two thousand commoners' burials and 16 royal graves, using teams of specially trained workers. A series of "death pits" chronicled elaborate funeral ceremonies where dozens of courtiers dressed in their finest regalia took poison, then lay down in the great pit to die with their master or mistress. Unfortunately, Woolley's notes are too inadequate for modern archaeologists to establish whether his vivid reconstructions were, in fact, accurate ones.

Woolley's lucid and dramatic accounts of the royal burials and the "flood" made him one of the most widely read archaeologists of the day. "At one end, on the remains of a wooden bier, lay the body of the queen, a gold cup near her hand; the upper part of the body was entirely hidden by a mass of beads of gold, silver, and lapis lazuli . . . long strings of which, hanging from a collar, had formed a cloak reaching to the waist," he wrote in a popular book, *Ur of the Chaldees,* published in 1929 (167). The spectacular finds rivaled those of Tutankhamun's tomb but were overshadowed by the golden pharaoh (Figure 8.3).

Woolley closed the Ur excavations in 1934, in the belief that a period of study and analysis was needed before more digging took place. He himself wrote most of the massive ten-volume report on the excavation, which took a half century to complete. After World War II, he conducted excavations in Syria and elsewhere, but nothing on the scale of his Ur campaigns, which rank as one of the classic excavations of history.

Leonard Woolley was one of the last independent archaeologists. He never held an academic or museum post, but relied on modest private funds and earnings from his writings for a salary.

Meanwhile, Gertrude Bell sat down to organize an Iraqi Department of Antiquities, with responsibility for granting excavation permits, and a new Iraq Museum to house artifacts found in foreign digs. She was in a difficult position. Expeditions mounted from abroad wanted as many finds as possible. Iraqis felt strongly that at least half the artifacts from any excavation should stay in the country. She drafted a new antiquities law that steered a careful course between foreign and local viewpoints. The first test of the new regulations came at Ur, where Bell and Woolley battled over the finds. Both were strong personalities, the arguments were ferocious, but in the end both were satisfied—which is why many of the finest Ur artifacts are now in the

Figure 8.3 Artist's reconstruction of the royal burial at Ur, Iraq. © Copyright The British Museum.

British Museum and the University of Pennsylvania Museum in Philadelphia and not in Baghdad.

Aurel Stein: Archaeology in Central Asia

The late nineteenth and early twentieth centuries were the apogee of British imperial power, so much so that archaeologists and solitary explorers could wander freely in the remotest of places. For generations, bold young Indian army officers and political officers climbed in the Himalayas and trekked far into Central Asia in search of adventure, or, in some cases, geographical and historical knowledge.

A Swedish traveler, Sven Hedin, was the first archaeologist to explore the ancient Silk Road region of Central Asia in 1895. He and other visitors were ruthless in their explorations, removing manuscripts from Han Chinese garrisons and hacking frescoes from Buddhist temples. The best known of these early archaeologists—one uses the word in a loose sense—was Aurel Stein.

Sir Aurel Stein (1862–1943) studied Asian languages and archaeology at Oxford University, then joined the Indian Archaeological Survey in 1910. By that time, he already had a reputation as a traveler to remote places, having explored the Chinese–Indian frontier. He had studied the territory of the little-known **Khotan Empire,** an early center for the spread of Buddhism from India to China. Khotan fell to the Arabs in the eighth century A.D. and grew rich on the **Silk Road** caravan trade between China and the West. Stein's primary objective was to examine the trade in artifacts and sacred books that were being sold to European collectors at the time. Stein was among the first Europeans to venture into Khotan country, so his collections and his first two books, *Chronicle of Kings of Kashmir* (1900) and *Ancient Khotan* (1907), aroused considerable interest.

In 1906–1913, Stein explored the least accessible parts of China. It was on this expedition that he visited the Caves of a Thousand Buddhas, carved into sandstone at **Dunhuang,** in extreme western China (Figure 8.4). "I noticed at once that fresco paintings covered the walls of all the grottoes. . . . The 'Caves of the Thousand Buddhas' were indeed tenanted not by Buddhist recluses, however holy, but by images of the Enlightened One himself," he wrote in *The Ruins of Desert Cathay* (1912:123). Almost all the shrines contained a huge seated Buddha, with divine attendants. Chinese monks had founded the earliest cave in A.D. 366, forming important communities in the region, which was an important crossroads for the Silk Road. There are 492 caves containing elaborate Buddhist artworks of every kind.

Stein had heard rumors of a cache of ancient manuscripts. He made discreet inquiries and admired a scroll, "a beautifully preserved roll of paper, about a foot high and perhaps fifteen yards long" covered with undecipherable characters. Stein bought this priceless manuscript for a small piece of

Figure 8.4   The Caves of a Thousand Buddhas, Dunhuang, China.

silver. Some weeks later, he witnessed a great festival at the shrine, attended by thousands of pilgrims. He learned of a hidden deposit of ancient manuscripts and bribed his way in. A walled-off chamber contained "a solid mass of manuscript bundles rising to a high of nearly ten feet," undisturbed for almost a thousand years. In a neighboring room, Stein unrolled manuscript and paintings on silk and linen, many of them designed to be hung in shrines. The manuscripts—Chinese versions of Buddhist texts—had been compiled in the third and fourth centuries A.D. With infinite care, Stein examined the entire collection and bought seven cases of priceless manuscripts and more than three hundred paintings for four horseshoes of silver. He discreetly packed them and carried them away on his camels and ponies. Today, they reside in the British Museum. His methods are condemned as unethical robbery nowadays, but it is an open question whether the manuscripts would have survived for posterity had Stein not passed them into expert hands.

During his later career, Stein undertook many difficult journeys into Central Asia, many of them along the ancient Silk Road, which had once linked China and the West. Almost singlehandedly, and in the face of intense rivalries from archaeologists of other nations, Stein amassed huge collections and priceless information about an archaeological wilderness where East had met West. By today's standards, Stein's looting activities and associations with treasure hunters and tomb robbers are ethically indefensible, and his reputation is discredited, especially in China. His great contribution was to link the ancient East and West. His contemporary Sir Leonard Woolley once remarked that Stein performed "the most daring and adventurous raid on the ancient world that any archaeologist has attempted" (Mirsky 1977:421). There is much truth in this remark. Stein's methods were questionable, but he opened up the eyes of the scholarly world to a huge cultural and archaeological blank on the world map. By the time he died, Aurel Stein was an anachronism—a throwback to the early days of archaeological adventure.

As Stein and others explored Central Asia, the first archaeological investigations began in eastern and southeastern Asia. The Royal Asiatic Society, based in London, played a leading role in exchanging knowledge about the little-known world of the Far East and Southeast Asia. Branches of the society flourished in Hong Kong, Shanghai, Singapore, and Korea, founded by missionaries and government officers, as well as by local businesspeople with an interest in antiquities, languages, and other aspects of Asian culture. Japan promulgated a cultural properties protection law along Western lines in 1876. A year later, the American Edward Morse, an instructor at the Imperial University in Tokyo, conducted excavations on the Omori shell mound near Tokyo. He identified distinctive, cord-decorated pottery made by the now well-known Jomon people, who flourished from about 10,000 to 300 B.C. Morse followed local scholars in attributing his shell midden and its pottery to the remote ancestors of the living Ainu people of Hokkaido Island. His work aroused wide interest. None other than Charles Darwin remarked that "several Japanese gentlemen" were accumulating large collections from Tokyo Bay's shell mounds. It was not until 1936 that the Jomon culture was shown to be of considerable antiquity. Today, more than ten thousand Jomon sites are known.

The formal teaching of archaeology began at Kyoto University in 1907, with a department being founded in 1913 under the direction of Hamada Kosaku, who had learned archaeology under Flinders Petrie in London. Archaeologists from this department worked in Korea and Taiwan. Kosaku himself carried out the first stratigraphic excavations on Jomon and later Yayoi sites in 1917 and wrote the first archaeology textbook in Japanese. The legacy of Kosaku and others continues today; Japanese archaeology thrives on a large scale.

In 1432, the great Khmer palace at **Angkor Wat** in what is now Cambodia was abandoned to the forest (see Figure 13.4). Some European visitors stumbled on the overgrown ruins in the sixteenth and seventeenth centuries, but Angkor Wat was largely forgotten until the French colonized what was then called Indo-China two centuries later. From the 1850s on, there was a steady flow of visitors to the site. The French School of the Far East was founded in 1889, modeled on equivalent institutions in Cairo and elsewhere. Many temples were cleared, and some statuary was removed to France. In 1900, the first major archaeological survey of South Vietnamese and Khmer monuments was undertaken by Henri Parmentier.

Many archaeologists followed in Aurel Stein's footsteps, among them Harvard geologist Raphael Pumpelly (1873–1959), who made the first extensive survey of the Gobi Desert and in 1903 excavated **Anau,** an ancient city in southern Turkmen, where he found occupations dating back to 3000 B.C. Pumpelly and the geologist Ellsworth Huntington developed the first "oasis" theory for the origins of agriculture, arguing that farming and civilization in Central Asia resulted from increasing aridity. This was the first ecological explanation of these major developments in human history. During the 1920s, University of Chicago Egyptologist Henry Breasted coined the term *Fertile Crescent* to describe a broad arc of land from the Nile up the Jordan Valley and across the Iranian highlands into Mesopotamia where both agriculture and civilization began. The term is still occasionally used today. A decade later, Australian-born prehistorian Vere Gordon Childe developed the first widely accepted theories of agriculture and civilization, which built on Pumpelly's early research (see Chapter 9).

Early Archaeology in Africa

Early explorers of southern Africa found traces of ancient life in the form of rock paintings in caves and rock shelters. In 1776, the Swedish naturalist Andrew Sparrman dug into a number of stone mounds near the Great Fish

River in what is now South Africa. He found nothing, but concluded that the sites were proof that a more powerful and numerous people had lived in the region before the present "degraded" inhabitants.

The same explorers found themselves among a great diversity of peoples—hunter-gatherers like the Khoisan-speaking San of the desert regions to the north and west of the Cape of Good Hope; Khoe Khoe cattle herders, who moved constantly from one grazing ground to another; and Bantu-speaking farming groups, who were settled north of the Great Fish River and were pressing on the lands of other groups to the south when they first came into contact with European settlers. It was not until the nineteenth century that the remarkable range of black African societies were revealed to the outside world, and when they were, explorer and anthropologist alike assumed that they had acquired agriculture, metallurgy, their art traditions, and other more complex features of their societies from either the ancient Egyptians or other Mediterranean civilizations.

In 1880, the great German Egyptologist Karl Lepsius argued that two major groups made up the population of tropical Africa—lighter-skinned Hamites in the north and black "Negro" populations to the south. Lepsius's Hamites became fashionable as conquerors and colonizers of Africa— creative herders who overran the more primitive black peoples south of the Sahara and imposed on them a rudimentary form of more advanced technology and culture from southwestern Asia.

In 1871, a German geologist, Carl Mauch, investigated rumors of spectacular stone ruins north of the Limpopo River in southern Africa. To his astonishment, he stumbled across an overgrown freestanding enclosure with walls more than 6 meters (20 feet) high. Despite the presence of Africans living near the site, he proclaimed the **Great Zimbabwe** ruins the long-lost palace of the Phoenician Queen of Sheba (Figure 8.5).

Mauch's discovery came as European settlers were pressing northward to colonize the gold-rich lands north of the Limpopo. Cecil John Rhodes's British South Africa Company sent a column northward in 1890. Rhodes himself, a brash imperialist, adopted the Zimbabwe ruins as his own, as proof that Phoenicians had lived in southern Africa long before the modern black inhabitants. His company commissioned antiquarian Theodore Bent, an investigator with experience in the eastern Mediterranean, to dig and report on Zimbabwe in 1891. Bent believed that the ruins were built by outsiders, but professed complete ignorance as to their constructors. He also proclaimed that he was tired of hearing of the Queen of Sheba.

In 1902–1904, a local journalist named Richard Hall was retained to clear the site for tourists, which he did zealously, clearing the gold-rich deposits inside the main enclosure of all archaeological deposits. Hall was convinced that Phoenicians had built Great Zimbabwe, but his depredations were so extensive that the British Association for the Advancement of Science commissioned the Egyptologist and Flinders Petrie protégé Randall MacIver to

Figure 8.5   The Great Enclosure with its freestanding walls, at Great Zimbabwe,
Zimbabwe.

dig at Zimbabwe in 1906. MacIver was an expert in small finds and roundly
stated that the site was of African and medieval origin. His findings
prompted such an outcry among local settlers that no further excavations
took place until 1929, when the British Association again stepped in with
new excavations headed by Gertude Caton-Thompson. Like MacIver, Caton-
Thompson had worked in Egypt, where she had experience with exotic
imports and cross-dating, and she had also studied Stone Age encampments.
Her meticulous excavations focused on the hill, known as the Acropolis, that
overlooks the Great Enclosure. She recovered imported glass beads and
Chinese porcelain of known date, which enabled her to date what she called
"a mature civilization" of wholly African origin and inspiration dating to
immediately before Portuguese explorers arrived on the East African coast
in A.D. 1597.

Caton-Thompson's findings were well received in archaeological circles,
but were attacked savagely by settler interests (and a few scholars) threatened by the very idea that Africans were capable of constructing such
sophisticated buildings. Such doubts were popular in the 1930s. According
to an ethnologist of the day, Charles Seligman, the black Africans were
culturally static and backward. His ideas were widely accepted by his colleagues. The notion that sub-Saharan Africa was a stagnant bystander
through most of human history remained a popular assumption until the
1960s. Meanwhile, the clash between racist colonial ideologues and archaeologists at Great Zimbabwe continued to simmer for half a century, becoming a hot political issue when Rhodesia declared independence in 1965.

The controversies surrounding Great Zimbabwe were akin to the mound-builder debates in North America during the nineteenth century, with the difference that the international archaeological community accepted the African origin of the site after MacIver's 1906 excavations. Thereafter, the controversy was purely a local issue. Today, Zimbabwe is under the control of black Zimbabweans, some of whom, for their part, declare that no white person can interpret the ruins. It is a classic example of political ownership of archaeological sites.

The early study of Stone Age prehistory was confined, in the main, to Europe and Mediterranean lands. But Charles Darwin had pointed to Africa as the most likely cradle of humanity in his *Descent of Man* in 1871. Finely made Stone Age artifacts were found in South Africa in the 1850s. By the 1880s, geologist J. P. Johnson was studying the geological context of Stone Age artifacts in the Orange Free State and Transvaal provinces of South Africa. In 1911, another scholar, Louis Péringuey, divided the prehistory of the country into a Paleolithic phase and a later Bushman phase, based on rich finds in caves and rock shelters.

Stone Age artifacts came to light in the East African Rift Valley as early as 1893, but the first systematic work began with Louis Leakey's East African Archaeological Expedition in 1926, described in Chapter 9.

At first, Stone Age cultures in sub-Saharan Africa received European names like **Acheulian,** Mousterian, and Aurignacian, because early researchers assumed that the same cultures had flourished everywhere during early prehistory. Leakey and others soon realized that there were major differences between African and European cultures reflected in stone tools and other artifacts. Leakey himself proposed an entirely different culture-historical sequence for East Africa, which he correlated with "pluvials" and "interpluvials"—periods of wetter and drier climate that he linked to European glacials and interglacials. At about the same time, two South African prehistorians, John Goodwin and C. van Riet Lowe, wrote a classic work, *The Stone Age Cultures of South Africa,* in which they developed specifically African cultural labels that remain in use, albeit much modified, to this day.

One major turning point in African archaeology came with the discovery of *Australopithecus africanus* at **Taung** in South Africa by anatomist Raymond Dart in 1924 (see Chapter 9), even if his find was not accepted as relevant to human prehistory until the 1950s. Until then physical anthropologists had been mesmerized by the forged Piltdown skull from southern England (see Chapter 9). Another new chapter began in the 1960s, when radiocarbon dates showed that farmers had settled on the banks of the Zambezi River in what is now southern Zambia as early as the first century A.D. At the time, most experts believed that the ancestors of modern African societies had lived in their homelands for little more than a few centuries. The new radiocarbon dates were a major factor in the development of a multidisciplinary African archaeology and history during the 1960s, which coincided with the granting of independence to many black African nations.

Archaeology in sub-Saharan Africa was a product of colonialism, and of colonial administration, as part of an effort to better understand indigenous societies. But very often the finds that came from such archaeology differed from the racist interpretations of Africa's past that remained prevalent until the 1960s.

Australia and New Zealand

Australia

In A.D. 1772, a small band of seamen led by French explorer Marion du Fresne landed on a sandy beach in southern Tasmania, south of Australia. As du Fresne's boat landed, a band of about 30 naked, black-skinned Aborigines carrying sharp sticks and stones emerged from the trees to greet the strangers. Perhaps it is surprising that the hunters recognized their visitors as fellow humans. Marion du Fresne was the first outsider the Tasmanians had seen in at least eight thousand years, since rising sea levels flooded the Bass Strait and isolated Tasmania from mainland Australia.

The Tasmanians and the Australian Aborigines aroused intense curiosity in an outside world that was becoming increasingly familiar with non-Western societies of all kinds. Both Australians and Tasmanians were constantly on the move, with only minimal, and very simple, tool kits. By the 1850s, thousands of Aborigines had perished at European hands or had been driven from their lands by convicts and colonists. At the same time, racist thinking dominated anthropological discussion about the Aborigines. John Lubbock was among those who considered the Australians and Tasmanians obvious examples of societies that were still in the Stone Age. Their artifacts served as models for archaeologists studying early prehistoric societies in Europe. Given the intellectual climate of the day, it was hardly surprising that the Tasmanians were soon referred to as "the connecting link between men and the monkey tribes." Even as late as 1899, Baldwin Spencer and F. J. Gillen wrote *Native Tribes of Central Australia,* which placed the study of Aboriginal societies on a modern basis. But Spencer later wrote that the Aborigines were "a relic of the early childhood of mankind left stranded . . . in a low condition of savagery."

When no traces of humanly manufactured artifacts appeared in the same levels as the bones of extinct animals, the experts assumed that the Aborigines had arrived recently, and that their cultures had not changed since their arrival—an assumption eerily similar to that made about many Native American societies. From 1910 to the 1950s, this view was unchallenged, the main archaeological activity being in the hands of collectors. Any differences in artifacts were attributed to the qualities of diverse raw materials used to make them.

Archaeology did not become the subject of study at an Australian university until 1948, when a department of archaeology was founded at the University of Sydney—to study Europe and the Near East. This lack of interest in indigenous archaeology was almost entirely due to racist attitudes toward Aboriginal culture. Only a few scholars, among them the archaeologist Norman Tindale, carried out stratigraphic excavations. Tindale observed artifact changes that he attributed to environmental change. The modern era in Australian archaeology came with the appointment of John Mulvaney at the University of Melbourne in 1953. He was trained in ecological archaeology by Grahame Clark at Cambridge University. A steady stream of young archaeologists from England followed Mulvaney. They soon established that humans had lived in Australia for at least forty thousand years.

New Zealand

New Zealand's first archaeologist was not appointed until 1954, although archaeological discoveries had been made for over a century, especially of stone tools associated with the bones of an extinct, flightless bird called the giant moa. By the 1870s, the moa hunters were being described as a vanished Stone Age people who had lived on fish and shellfish and were distinct from the much later if somewhat similar sweet-potato-farming Maori, the inhabitants of New Zealand when Europeans arrived in the 1770s. Serious archaeology began in the 1920s, when Henry Skinner, a Cambridge University–trained anthropologist, studied moa hunter sites on South Island. He carried out his research at a time when both settlers and Maori historians were much preoccupied with vanishing Maori traditional culture, and with Maori origins in Polynesia. The Maori were thought of as recent colonists who had seized their new homeland from much more primitive peoples. Skinner combined archaeology with oral traditions and other sources to show convincingly that the moa hunters were Maori, and also of Polynesian origin. They were New Zealand's first people. The serious archaeological study of Maori culture did not begin until the 1950s, with most research being focused on the moa hunters. Since then, the chronology of Maori settlement has been extended, and a great elaboration of ancient Maori culture has been documented. Once again, as Bruce Trigger has pointed out, research was held back by the assumption that indigenous culture changed little over many centuries, when quite the contrary was the case.

Summary

Chapter 8 describes some of the greatest archaeological discoveries of the early twentieth century and the first archaeology in Central Asia, Australia, and New Zealand. Howard Carter and Lord Carnarvon discovered the undisturbed tomb of the Egyptian pharaoh Tutankhamun in 1922. The find caused a worldwide sensation, since it was the first discovery of an undisturbed pharaoh's sepulcher. As a result, antiquities regulations were tightened in Egypt and other countries. Sir Leonard Woolley, one of the greatest archaeologists of the twentieth century, excavated a Hittite city at Carchemish in Syria before spending 12 years digging the Sumerian city of Ur in southern Iraq. There he discovered spectacular royal burials and evidence of early village settlement, as well as excavating entire urban precincts. Gertrude Bell was a contemporary of Woolley's, a remarkable desert archaeologist, and founder of the Iraq Museum.

While these spectacular archaeological discoveries were being made, Sir Aurel Stein was making a series of expeditions to remote parts of Central Asia, where he searched for archaeological sites and manuscripts. He was responsible for collecting hundreds of Buddhist manuscripts from the Caves of a Thousand Buddhas at Dunhuang, in western China. Many archaeologists followed in his footsteps, among them Raphael Pumpelly of Harvard University, who was the first scholar to propose an oasis theory for the origins of farming and cities.

African archaeology began with the discovery of stone tools in the nineteenth century, and with the controversies over Great Zimbabwe ruins north of the Limpopo River. Zimbabwe was alleged to be a Phoenician city—a theory that appealed to white settler interests. Excavations by Randall MacIver and Gertrude Caton-Thompson, the latter in 1929, showed that the stone buildings were built by Africans in medieval times. The controversy smoldered on until the 1960s. The discovery of *Australopithecus* by Raymond Dart in 1924, and young Louis Leakey's early researches in Kenya, showed that African prehistory had a very long time scale and that the continent was the cradle of humankind. Chapter 8 ends with a brief survey of early archaeology in Australia and New Zealand, where scientific archaeology began considerably later than in Europe and north America.

Guide to Further Reading

Allsebrook, Mary. 1992. *Born to Rebel: The Life of Harriet Boyd Hawes.* Oxford: Oxbow Books.

   A lovely biography of Harriet Hawes by her daughter, which gives a wonderful flavor of a long-vanished archaeological era.

Mirsky, Jeannette. 1977. *Sir Aurel Stein: Archaeological Explorer.* Chicago: University of Chicago Press.

   Mirsky's biography summarizes Stein's remarkable and varied career.

Wallach, Janet. 1996. *Desert Queen.* New York: Nan A. Talese and Doubleday.

   A definitive biography of Gertrude Bell, which is especially good on her character.

Winstone, H. V. F. 1990. *Woolley of Ur.* London: Secker and Warburg.

   A thorough biography of one of the greatest archaeologists of the twentieth century.

chapter 9

Archaeology Coming of Age, 1920 to 1940

The Sutton Hoo ship under excavation in 1939, showing the ghosts of the planks and frames, and the nails, still in position. © Copyright The British Museum.

On Monday, May 8, I arrived at Sutton Hoo and had an interview with Mrs. E. M. Pretty, during which arrangements were made regarding personnel and equipment for the excavation. We then went to the barrows and upon my asking Mrs. Pretty which mound she would like opened, she pointed to the largest of the group . . . and said 'What about this?' and I replied that it would be quite alright for me." . . . So simply and almost casually was the decision made which led to the dramatic finding of the unique treasure ship.

James Brown on the Sutton Hoo excavation, 1939, in Charles Green,
Sutton Hoo: The Excavations of a Royal Ship Burial, 1963 (p. 14)

chapter outline

The years 1920 to 1950 were the decades when archaeology changed from a largely amateur pursuit into a professional discipline. These 30 years were marked by remarkable archaeological discoveries and by a growing professionalism. Archaeology came of age with a new sophistication and a greater concern for knowledge rather than spectacular discoveries. In this chapter, we describe some of the most important developments of these highly productive years.

Field Archaeology and Aerial Photography

Archaeology was a gentleman's pursuit, and often a country gentleman's calling, in the first half of the twentieth century. There was a long and vibrant tradition of European archaeology—walking the countryside in search of earthworks, burial mounds, artifacts, and less conspicuous archaeological sites. The tradition went back to medieval times in Britain and Scandinavia and involved a wide spectrum of amateur and professional archaeologists. They came to what they called "field archaeology" with a keen eye for country and landscape and with strong instincts for archaeological discovery. The sophisticated settlement archaeology of today was born in such researches, in the hands of countrymen like O. G. S. Crawford (1886–1957), a trained geographer who spent the early years of his career surveying earthworks and ancient landscapes. Crawford became the first archaeology officer of Britain's Ordnance Survey and was responsible for the first archaeology maps produced by the British government.

Crawford served as an observer in Britain's Royal Flying Corps in World War I. He flew over the western front, spotted ancient earthworks from the air, and realized at once the potential of aerial photography for studying archaeological sites in the context of a wider landscape. Both French and German aviators working in military intelligence also studied archaeological sites from the air, especially in Mesopotamia. Crawford and Alexander Keiller, a gifted, independently wealthy archaeologist, hired an aircraft in 1927 and photographed more than two hundred archaeological sites in southern Britain over two months. Their joint volume, *Wessex from the Air,* was the first archaeological monograph devoted entirely to aerial photography of the past.

Meanwhile, landscape geographers exercised a strong influence on British archaeology. Cambridge-trained archaeologist Cyril Fox came under the influence of geographers studying humanly modified landscapes and applied his geographical interpretations of the past to a region within a 40-kilometer (25-mile) radius of the city of Cambridge. Fox studied the distributions of archaeological sites against a background of the natural environment and ancient vegetational cover. He then applied his approach to all of England, Scotland, and Wales, where he distinguished between the highland and lowland areas of Britain, describing his research in a landmark book, *The Personality of Britain,* which appeared in 1932 and caused a major stir.

Both Crawford and Fox's work, like that of human geographers, was based on simple notions of environmental change and ecology, combined with aerial photography and long hours of surveying archaeological sites on the ground. They were not alone in this approach, which was also on the minds of some French human geographers and a few German scholars.

At the time, most British and European archaeologists were enmeshed in artifacts and artifact classification, just as their nineteenth-century predecessors had been. They were preoccupied with artifact classification, chronology, and cultural groups—work stemming directly from the researches of Worsaae, Montelius, and other Danish scholars. In a sense, archeology of this genre was a little like stamp collecting, an activity more concerned with artifacts than with the people who made them. There were a few voices raised to the contrary, many of them pointing to the remarkable organic finds that came from the Swiss lake dwellings and from Mesolithic sites in Denmark. The Cambridge University archaeologist Miles Burkitt, a Stone Age specialist, argued that the prime objective of prehistoric archaeology was not to classify and date artifacts so much as to reconstruct the lifeways of the people who made them. A few years later, his student Grahame Clark, later to become a world-famous prehistorian, rebelled even more strongly. "I was concerned to attack . . . the kind of archaeology promoted by museum curators" (Clark 1989:35). And attack it he did, influenced by the researches of the Australian-born archaeologist Vere Gordon Childe, whose work is described below.

Mortimer Wheeler and Scientific Excavation

Before World War I, and in many places even into the 1930s, archaeological excavation was a crude, fast-moving operation that paid little attention to fine detail or the need to record sites for posterity. Most excavators were self-taught and had only a rudimentary understanding of the complexities of stratigraphic layers or using artifacts to establish chronologies.

The development of scientific excavation in Britain before World War II was, to a considerable extent, in the hands of one man—the British archaeologist Mortimer Wheeler (1890–1976). Wheeler's colorful life spanned the decades when archaeology was transformed into a scientific discipline. After studying classics at London University, Wheeler researched Roman pottery in Germany's Rhineland. He then became an investigator for the Royal Commission on Historical Monuments for England, but joined the army at the outbreak of World War I. He served with distinction in the Royal Artillery, ending the war with the rank of major.

By the end of World War I, Wheeler had acquired the background and experience that were to guide his career. He had a fluent writing style inherited from his journalist father, a background in classics and archaeology from university, and a gift for logistics and organization, acquired in the army. For a short while, he returned to the Royal Commission, but he was appointed keeper of archaeology at the newly founded National Museum of Wales and lecturer in archaeology at University College, Cardiff, in 1920. Four years later, he became director and set the museum on a sound financial basis.

Between 1920 and 1926, Wheeler and his wife Tessa revolutionized Welsh archaeology with a series of major excavations on Roman frontier forts. At the time, most archaeological excavation was little more than an uncontrolled search for spectacular artifacts. The Wheelers adopted and refined the almost forgotten excavation methods of the Victorian archaeologist General Augustus Lane Fox Pitt Rivers (see Chapter 6). They paid careful attention to observing even minute layers in the soil, recovered even the smallest of potsherds and other artifacts, and published technical reports promptly, illustrated with Wheeler's own fine drawings.

Wheeler's time in Wales established his credentials as a serious archaeologist. He was offered the first professorship of prehistoric archaeology at Edinburgh University, but turned it down in favor of a nonacademic career. In 1926, he became keeper of the much neglected London Museum, which he promptly resuscitated. Each summer, he continued excavations, each one designed to clarify the relationships between indigenous British and Roman society and to train a new generation of young archaeologists. In 1928–1929, he worked at a Roman sanctuary at Lydney in Gloucestershire. Then he turned his attention to the late-Iron-Age and Roman city of **Verulamium** (modern-day St. Albans) just north of London, where he spent four years from 1930 to 1933. Verulamium lay in open country, unlike many Roman towns that are buried under modern cities. He and his wife Tessa exposed 4.45 hectares (11 acres) of the city, as well as tracing the complicated history of its outlying earthworks and the smaller forts and settlements that had preceded it. By the time the report on Verulamium was published in 1936, Wheeler was tired of the Romans and looking for new topics to research.

The culmination of Wheeler's British excavations came when he turned his attention to the enormous Iron Age hill fort at **Maiden Castle** in southern England. During the summers of 1934 to 1937, he and Tessa developed the art of archaeological excavation to heights never achieved before. They excavated deep trenches through Maiden Castle's serried earthen ramparts (see Figure 9.1). They investigated broad areas of the interior with area trenches. Hundreds of visitors toured the excavations each summer, for the Wheelers believed in keeping the public informed about their work. An entire generation of young archaeologists worked at Maiden Castle, many of whom made major contributions to the field after World War II. Despite the tragic early death of Tessa and the coming of World War II, Wheeler published the final report on Maiden Castle in 1943.

With his bristling mustache and flowing hair, Wheeler was a formidable personality who tolerated little criticism and did not suffer fools. No one denied his talents as an organizer and leader, as the archaeologist who brought British and much European excavation and fieldwork into the modern world. Wheeler returned to the Royal Artillery with the outbreak of World War II in 1939. His coolness and decisive leadership under fire led to rapid

Figure 9.1   Mortimer Wheeler's excavations at Maiden Castle, 1938.

promotion. He was soon promoted to brigadier and would have risen higher, had he not been invited by the viceroy of India to become director general of the Archaeological Survey of India in 1943.

The Harappan Civilization

The ancient cities of **Harappa** and **Mohenjodaro** in the Indus Valley of what is now Pakistan had been identified as archaeological sites in the nineteenth century. Harappa's bricks provided much of the ballast for the Karachi-Lahore railroad line. Indian archaeologists Daya Ram Sahni and R. D. Banerji's excavations during the 1920s revealed unknown pottery styles and an urban society that was clearly much older than historic times—a hitherto unknown indigenous state (today known as the **Harappan civilization**). Two British archaeologists, Sir John Marshall and Ernest MacKay, carried out large-scale excavations before World War II, but their work had none of the rigor that Mortimer Wheeler was to bring to the ancient cities.

The Archaeological Survey of India confronted Wheeler with an extraordinary challenge. The Survey was moribund, with an untrained and demoralized staff and an entire subcontinent to cover. Wheeler arrived with a mandate to train an Indian staff in high standards of excavation and publication and to provide a sound chronological framework for India's past. Fresh from military command, he strode into the Survey offices to find people dozing at their desks. A loud shout woke them up. Within ten days, the office was functioning efficiently.

Wheeler then set off on a whirlwind tour of India, met outlying staff, and, like a general on a military campaign, devised a strategy for major changes. He started a rigorous six-month training program at **Taxila,** a city in northern India once visited by Alexander the Great. Sixty-one students worked long hours and learned a standard of excavation unheard of in India. His methods are still faithfully used in India and Pakistan to this day. Wheeler also founded an academic journal, *Ancient India;* then he excavated Arikamedu, a trading station on the southeast coast. Arikamedu yielded Roman pottery, allowing him to establish chronological connections with the Roman world of the day.

Harappa and Mohenjodaro, two great prehistoric cities in the Indus Valley of what is now Pakistan, provided Wheeler's greatest challenge. He deployed his now skilled fieldworkers at both cities and uncovered great citadels and massive defense works, along with standardized grids of streets and brick houses. The excavations applied all his excavation experience on Roman sites in Britain to huge cities, whose size did not intimidate him in the least. His work culminated in a classic account of the Harappan Civilization, which appeared as part of the *Cambridge History of India* in 1950.

Wheeler served in India for five years, leaving a year after independence in 1948. He was to return to the subcontinent on several occasions as an adviser to the government of Pakistan. A generation of local archaeologists perpetuated his research methods in both India and Pakistan.

To Mortimer Wheeler, archaeology was an international endeavor, something much broader than merely Iron-Age or Roman Britain. His influence on the development of excavation methods and on the proper reporting of archaeological research was enormous.

Vere Gordon Childe: Prehistoric Revolutions

While Mortimer Wheeler and his contemporaries revolutionized excavation, another scholar, Vere Gordon Childe (1892–1957), brought the study of Old World culture history into the modern era.

Gordon Childe was the son of a conservative Church of England minister in Sydney, Australia. He soon rebelled against his staid upbringing. While an undergraduate at Sydney University, he became a militant liberal, with strong views on workers' rights. He espoused Marxist beliefs for the rest of his life. Childe graduated with degrees in Greek, Latin, and philosophy in 1913. After two years studying classical archaeology at Oxford University, Childe returned to Australia and became actively involved in Labor Party politics—an experience that alienated him permanently from political life. He returned to England and resumed his studies of European archaeology, supporting himself by translating foreign archaeological books into English.

Throughout the 1920s, Childe traveled widely throughout Europe, visiting archaeological sites and studying museum collections, especially in eastern and southeast Europe, where few British scholars ventured. Unlike most of his archaeological contemporaries, Childe was a brilliant linguist, so he was able to converse with ease with archaeologists all over Europe, even in obscure museums in the Balkans. He was also blessed with a powerful visual memory, which enabled him to note and remember similarities among artifacts from widely separated locations. For example, he traced the distinctive round-based clay vessels made by the earliest farmers in the Danube River Valley in southeastern Europe right across Germany, through the Rhine Valley to the Netherlands, far to the northwest. Years of arduous traveling and library research trained Gordon Childe to become a master of the broad sweep of European history, one of the few scholars with an ability to summarize obscure archaeological data from widely separated lands into a coherent story.

Three books established Gordon Childe as one of the leading archaeologists of his day. The first was *The Dawn of European Civilization,* published in 1925. He wrote the book as a form of narrative history, using artifacts and ancient societies instead of kings, statesmen, and people. *The Dawn* uses what Childe called "archaeological cultures," similar assemblages of artifacts and other culture traits, to trace the movements of ancient peoples across Europe. He believed that the great changes in the European past resulted from the movements of people and the spread of new ideas such as farming and metalworking, many of them originating in southwest Asia, then spreading into temperate Europe.

The Danube in Prehistory (1929), one of Childe's major writings, was a detailed study of a vital region from which many pivotal ideas for ancient Europe developed, among them metallurgy and agriculture. Childe was an advocate of culture history—the use of artifacts and chronologies to define long series of changing prehistoric cultures through time, which could be compared with others from neighboring areas. He turned European prehistory into an intricate jigsaw puzzle of artifacts, human cultures, and archaeological sites, building on the earlier work of Oscar Montelius and others. His work still forms the basis of much of what we know about ancient Europe today.

In 1927, Gordon Childe was appointed the first professor of prehistoric archaeology at Edinburgh University. He was not a good teacher and had few students, so he spent most of his time traveling and writing articles and books. Between 1928 and 1955, he also carried out excavations at more than 15 sites in Scotland and northern Ireland. His most important excavation was that of **Skara Brae,** a Stone Age village in the Orkney Islands north of the mainland, where he found internal furnishings still intact (Figure 9.2). He interpreted the furnishings by the simple expedient of comparing them to nineteenth-century rural dwellings in the Scottish highlands. As a result, he was able to show which parts of the dwellings were used to house humans, and which housed cattle, and to distinguish the hearth areas where women prepared food. This was one of the first attempts ever made to distinguish between mens' and womens' activities in ancient houses.

Meanwhile, Childe continued to write about wider issues of archaeology. His interests shifted from artifacts to broad economic developments in the past, especially agriculture and the origins of urban civilization. For these developments, he looked to southwestern Asia. In a third influential book entitled *The Most Ancient East* (1928), he argued, like Raphael Pumpelly, that extensive droughts at the end of the Ice Age had caused human societies in the region to settle in oases, where they came in close contact with wild goats and sheep and with wild grasses. Within a short period of time, they began farming and herding animals, innovations that had a profound effect on human history—what he called the Agricultural Revolution. (He used the term "revolution" deliberately, a reflection of his Marxist perspective.)

A later book, *New Light on the Most Ancient East* (1934), developed his revolution hypothesis even further. Childe argued that the Agricultural Revolution soon led to an Urban Revolution—to the emergence of state-organized

Figure 9.2
The interior of a house at Skara
Brae, Scotland, excavated by
Gordon Childe.

societies. Each revolution produced more productive technologies, greater
food surpluses, and greater population increases. He believed these two cat-
alytic events had as much impact on human history as the Industrial Revolution of the eighteenth century A.D. From southwestern Asia, the innovations
and technologies from the two revolutions had spread far and wide—to
Europe, Africa, and eastern Asia. "From the east came light," he proclaimed—
and generations of archaeologists and historians believed him.

In 1935, Childe visited the Soviet Union, where he toured museums and
was exposed to communist doctrines. He began writing about human cultural evolution—about the ways in which increasing scientific knowledge
gave humans greater control over the natural environment. Later, he argued
that social, political, and economic institutions played important roles in
such changes, and flirted with notions of class struggle and other features of
Marxist dogma, but without much success.

In 1946, Childe left Edinburgh to become professor of European archaeology at the Institute of Archaeology, London University. He remained there
until he retired in 1956. Giving up excavation, he threw himself into writing
more theoretical works, among them *Piecing Together the Past* (1956), a model

of clear explanation of the basic principles of archaeological method that is still of use today. He began to write about the ways in which environmental differences produced different Stone Age farming cultures in Europe and southwestern Asia, but he concentrated mostly on his unrivaled knowledge of artifacts. These were the meat and drink of his great syntheses of ancient Europe. The last of these was *The Prehistory of European Society* (1956), where he stated that the nature of society was a powerful factor in determining ancient kinship patterns, political systems, and other forms of social relations.

By this time, Childe was thoroughly depressed about the limitations of archaeology, a discipline based on artifacts and material remains of the past. He felt there was no chance of studying religious beliefs or other intangibles of the past from such finds. His depression became more intense after his retirement. Childe was very much a loner who never married, and he became increasingly lonely in later life. Three months after his retirement, he returned to Australia and committed suicide by jumping off a cliff in the Blue Mountains.

The Search for Human Origins

We must now turn the clock back to the late nineteenth century, to a time when scientists were much preoccupied with the notion of a "missing link" between apes and humans. More Neanderthal skeletons came to light in the caves and rock shelters of the Dordogne during the 1860s and 1870s. By this time the explanatory power of evolution was becoming increasingly apparent. Charles Darwin himself had written *The Descent of Man* in 1871, in which he drew attention to Africa with its many ape forms as the most likely cradle of early humanity. Nevertheless, the first important fossil discoveries after the Neanderthals came from southeast Asia.

Homo erectus and Piltdown

A young Dutch physician, Eugene Dubois (1858–1941), became convinced that the origins of humans lay in Asia, as apes were denizens of the tropics. He wangled a posting as a government medical officer in Java in 1890 and spent his spare time over the next two years exploring the gravels of the Solo River near **Trinil**. Dubois promptly discovered the skull cap, upper leg bone, and two molar teeth of an apelike human. This he named *Pithecanthropus erectus* ("ape-human who stands upright"), and proclaimed that it was the "missing link" between apes and humans. European scientists were thoroughly skeptical, so much so that the obsessive Dubois withdrew from the fray in frustration. He is said to have hidden *Pithecanthropus* in a box under his bed.

Few anthropologists took Dubois seriously, largely because most human fossils of the day came from Europe. To many people, the Neanderthals were *the* prehistoric humans, largely because an influential study proclaimed them so. A Neanderthal skeleton unearthed in the **La Chapelle-aux-Saints** cave near Les Eyzies in 1908 came under the scrutiny of the eminent human pale-ontologist Marcellin Boule (1861–1942). Boule did not believe that the Neanderthals were the ancestors of modern humans and painted a portrait of the Neanderthal as a shambling, bow-legged primitive. Unbeknownst to him, the Chapelle-aux-Saints man had chronic osteoarthritis. Generations were to pass before later experts corrected this misconception.

The European scientific establishment was also mesmerized by Piltdown Man. In 1908, a lawyer and amateur archaeologist named Charles Dawson announced the discovery of a series of primitive-looking skull and jaw frag-ments from a gravel quarry at Piltdown in southern England. He claimed that he had found the "missing link"—a claim that remained virtually un-challenged until 1953, when Piltdown was exposed as a clever forgery. No one knows who perpetuated the fake, but it was probably Dawson, who spent many years seeking a spectacular find to put him in the limelight. With Piltdown, he succeeded beyond his wildest dreams, for his combination of a six-hundred-year-old human skull and an orangutan jaw hoodwinked a gen-eration of anthropologists who were anxious to believe that Britain had made a contribution to human evolution.

Dubois's *Pithecanthropus* fossils remained in limbo until the 1920s, when Swedish geologist Johan Andersson, working for the Chinese geological sur-vey, excavated a deep cavern at **Zhoukoudian** 100 kilometers (46 miles) southwest of Beijing. Chinese scholar Pei Wenzhong was the first to unearth the bones of a primitive-looking human at Zhoukoudian, which was named *Pithecanthropus pekinensis*. The new fossils proved to be virtually identical to Eugene Dubois's *Pithecanthropus erectus*. Soon, the two forms of *Pithecan-thropus* were united under a single taxonomic label, *Homo erectus*. Eugene Dubois was vindicated, but he took no further part in the search for human ancestors. In a tragic footnote to the Zhoukoudian finds, the precious fossils were lost during the chaos resulting from the outbreak of World War II and have never been found.

Australopithecus: **The "Southern Ape-Human"**

"It is . . . probable that Africa was formerly inhabited by extinct apes closely allied to the gorilla and chimpanzee," wrote Charles Darwin in his book *The Descent of Man,* published in 1871. "It is probable that our early progenitors lived on the African continent" (Darwin 1871:233). But his prophecy was not widely accepted until the 1950s, for the first discoveries of fossil ape-humans in Africa during the 1920s and 1930s fell on deaf scientific ears in a Europe mesmerized by Piltdown.

In 1923, a young Australian anatomist with an interest in human fossils, Raymond Dart (1893–1988), took a post as an anatomy lecturer in the medical school at the University of Witwatersrand in Johannesburg, South Africa. In 1924, Dart received delivery of two wooden boxes of rock-encrusted fossils from a limeworks mine at **Taung** near Kimberley, in Cape Province. He was dressing for a wedding at the time. Oblivious of the dust and impending nuptials, he broke open the crates and promptly found limestone blocks containing the skull and jaw of what appeared to be a fossilized ape. Dart chiseled away at the cemented rock for months. In December 1924, he extracted the face of an infant primate from the hardened matrix and gazed on the skull of a unique creature, with anatomical features that were both apelike and human. He published the Taung fossil in the prestigious journal *Nature* in 1925, naming it *Australopithecus africanus* ("southern ape of Africa") and boldly proclaimed it a representative of "an extinct race of apes intermediate between living anthropoids and man" (Figure 9.3) (Dart 1925:195).

The Taung fossil seemed an anomaly. Its brain was small compared with the large brain of the Piltdown skull, which dominated contemporary thinking about "missing links." Taung did have a humanlike jaw and teeth, but Dart was savagely criticized for his claims of human ancestry. Sir Arthur Keith, at the time the leading authority on human evolution, dismissed Dart's claim as "preposterous." He called Taung a young anthropoid ape.

Dart was a volatile yet visionary scholar, as well as a brilliant anatomist. He was so embittered by the reception of his paper that he withdrew from

Figure 9.3
Raymond Dart with
Australopithecus africanus from
Taung, South Africa.

any further study of *Australopithecus* for more than 20 years. But another anatomist, Robert Broom (1866–1951), was firmly convinced that Dart was correct. A probably apocryphal story had him entering Dart's office in the medical school and falling on his knees before the Taung baby. The indefatigable and crusty Broom fanned out over the limestone country of the Transvaal around Johannesburg. Soon Broom found other *Australopithecus africanus* fossils in the cemented fillings of what had once been limestone caves—at Sterkfontein, Swartkrans, and Kromdraai. He also identified a more heavily built Australopithecine, which he named *Australopithecus robustus*, on account of its massive skull with a sagittal crest (see Figure 11.3b).

Broom's discoveries received international attention after World War II, when the sheer number of fossil discoveries finally convinced European scientists that *Australopithecus* was indeed an early hominid form, and close to the ancestry of humankind.

Louis and Mary Leakey

As Dart suffered the fury of the scientific establishment, another archaeologist was establishing his reputation as an expert on early prehistory. Louis Seymour Basset Leakey (1903–1972) was the son of a Protestant missionary. He spent his childhood among the Kikuyu people of central Kenya and became interested in archaeology as a teenager. In 1922, he entered St. John's College, Cambridge, where he was banished from a University tennis court for wearing shorts—a scandalous deed at the time. He graduated with a first-class anthropology degree in 1926 and immediately mounted a shoestring archaeological expedition to Kenya. Leakey excavated a series of sites, including **Gamble's Cave,** where he found human occupation going back an estimated twenty thousand years. His first book, *The Stone Age Cultures of Kenya Colony,* was published to much acclaim in 1930. In this now-classic volume, Leakey outlined a long sequence of Stone Age cultures in East Africa totally unlike those found in Europe—a major scientific advance for the time.

During the 1930s, Leakey found some controversial fossil specimens, but ran into trouble when he was unable to establish their exact stratigraphic position and original find spots. He was careless in his excavation, and was given to extravagant claims. But a major site reestablished his reputation. In 1931, Leakey visited **Olduvai Gorge,** a 40-kilometer (25-mile) -long slash through the Serengeti Plains of what is now northern Tanzania. He traveled with the German paleontologist Hans Reck, who had previously visited the gorge and found fossil elephant remains there. Reck had bet Leakey the then-huge sum of 10 English pounds (about $40) that he would not find any human artifacts in the gorge. Leakey collected the wager with a fine Stone Age hand ax on the very first day and soon realized that Olduvai offered a unique chance to study the very earliest humans of all.

In 1936, Leakey married his second wife, Mary (1913–1996), a gifted artist with an interest in archaeology. Mary was a quiet, determined person who was the exact opposite of the flamboyant Leakey. They shared a passion for archaeology and were to work together for three decades. They made many visits to Olduvai Gorge, where they developed a new method of studying early human settlements, clearing scatters of artifacts and broken animal bones, recording even the smallest finds in place, then lifting them, as a way of studying ancient lifeways. Using this approach, they excavated magnificent 300,000-year-old Acheulian kill sites at **Olorgesaillie** in the Kenya Rift Valley during World War II, turning the site into a small museum—a unique approach at the time.

By the 1950s, and after the exposure of the Piltdown forgery, it was clear that the earliest chapter of human evolution had unfolded in sub-Saharan Africa. The earliest known hominids were the Australopithecines, known from the South African caves. After them came *Homo erectus,* at the time discovered only in East Asia and Europe; then the familiar Neanderthals; and then the modern Cro-Magnons of the late Ice Age. It was a simple, linear family tree, which reflected just how few human fossils were known, and the very limited scope of excavations on the earliest archaeological sites at the time. All this was to change in the 1950s, when a new chapter in paleoanthropology dawned and the study of human origins became an international science.

Excavating a Ghost Ship: Sutton Hoo

The 1920s and 1930s were remarkable for many important discoveries, among them that of a Late Bronze Age and Early Iron Age fortified town of the eighth to seventh centuries B.C. at **Biskupin** in northwestern Poland, excavated from 1933 to 1939 by Jósef Kostrzeweski (1885–1969), an influential figure in Polish archaeology. Biskupin lay on a peninsula that extended into a lake, surrounded by a wooden rampart filled with earth and sand that enclosed 2 hectares (5 acres). A single entrance with a watch tower and double gates lay on the southwestern side. A road ran around the inside of the rampart, enclosing a system of 11 streets made of logs laid side by side. More than a hundred houses made of horizontal logs reinforced with pegs lay along the streets, each house large enough to accommodate humans and beasts. Preservation conditions were so good that many wooden and bone artifacts, as well as textile fragments, survived. The earliest Biskupin settlement was built almost entirely of oak, while later buildings were constructed of pine, reflecting a shortage of timber caused by the use of over 8,000 cubic meters (10,500 cubic yards) of timber in each building phase.

On the eve of World War II in 1939, a landowner in eastern England, Elizabeth Pretty, asked local archaeologist James Brown to investigate the largest of 14 mounds on her property at **Sutton Hoo** in Suffolk. Brown soon found iron ship nails and suspected at once that he had found a funerary boat. Using trowels and brushes, he uncovered 11 frames and the bow of what he realized was an Anglo-Saxon ship. A sealed bulkhead now appeared. At this point, Brown wisely called in Charles Phillips of Cambridge University, an expert on Anglo-Saxon sites and on ancient timber structures.

With great skill, Phillips followed gray discolorations in the sandy soil, tracing the lines of the boat and the burial chamber amidships, while leaving the hull nails in position. His workers used long-handled coal shovels that shaved back the sand in thin slices, allowing the digger to follow even minute gray discolorations in the soil. In this way, the excavation revealed the outline of the ship preserved in sand with impressions of the long-rotted wood. He established that the 27-meter (89-foot) ship had been towed nearly a kilometer (0.6 mile) from the nearest river to its final resting place. The diggers even found traces of repairs to what had still been a seaworthy vessel. The boat had no mast and was propelled by 38 oars. The burial chamber contained a variety of metalwork, including cauldrons, bowls, spears, a sword, axes, bottles, and a purse. Phillips and British Museum experts were able to date the burial to within 25 years of A.D. 625 by examining the coins found with the dead man in the chamber. His identity is still uncertain, but he was probably a member of the historically known Wuffing family—perhaps Raedwald, a documented king of the East Angles.

In recent years, archaeologists have returned to Sutton Hoo with metal detectors, ground-penetrating radar, and ultraviolet lights, among other technologies that have enabled them to detect the ghostly outlines of other bodies in the sand, perhaps sacrificial victims, which could be consolidated with chemicals. They hope one day to be able to establish the sex and age of the victims.

Biskupin and Sutton Hoo involved much more sophisticated excavation methods than those of earlier decades. One can safely say that only a fraction of the information obtained from both sites could have been recovered with the rough methods of previous generations of excavators. Both sites represent an important coming of age of archaeology, which came to full fruition after World War II.

Summary

The 1920s and 1930s saw archaeology come of age, in a transition from the largely amateur traditions of earlier times to a more scientific, professional discipline. There were major advances in field survey methods, especially when used with aerial photography, whose potential was first realized during World War I. Scientific excavation methods were introduced in England by Mortimer Wheeler and others, following the blueprint of General Pitt Rivers in the 1880s. Wheeler excavated important Iron Age and Roman sites, including Verulamium and Maiden Castle. In 1944, he went to India as director of the Archaeological Survey, where he carried out major excavations at many sites, including Harappa, Mohenjodaro, and Taxila. These excavations put the Harappan (or Indus) civilization into much sharper focus.

Australian-born Vere Gordon Childe had a major influence on prehistoric archaeology with his typological studies of European cultures. From these he wrote a series of important syntheses of later prehistory, based on the notion that major agricultural and urban revolutions transformed human existence, and spread from the Near East into Europe. His work was influential into the 1960s and beyond. Meanwhile, Eugene Dubois's discovery of *Pithecanthropus erectus* in Java, and the finding of *Pithecanthropus pekinensis* in the 1920s, added new complexity to early human evolution, which was muddied by the Piltdown forgery, only exposed in 1953. *Australopithecus africanus* came to light at Taung, South Africa, in 1924, ushering in a new chapter in palaeoanthropology. But *Australopithecus* was not fully accepted by the scientific establishment until after World War II, by which time Louis and Mary Leakey had found evidence for very early human settlement at Olduvai Gorge and Olorgesaillie in East Africa. The 1920s and 1930s were also remarkable for many other important discoveries, including the Iron Age town of Biskupin in Poland and the Anglo-Saxon ship burial at Sutton Hoo, England.

Guide to Further Reading

Carver, Martin. 1998. *Sutton Hoo: Burial Place of Kings?* Philadelphia: University of Pennsylvania Press.

An authoritative account of this most remarkable site.

Childe, Vere Gordon. 1956. *The Prehistory of European Society.* Baltimore: Pelican.

The last of Childe's great syntheses in posthumous edition. This gives an excellent flavor of his work.

Crawford, O. G. S., and Alexander Keiller. 1928. *Wessex from the Air.* Oxford: Oxford University Press.

A classic, and worth browsing for the photographs.

Hawkes, Jacquetta. 1982. *Adventure in Archaeology: The Biography of Sir Mortimer Wheeler.* New York: St. Martin's Press.

The only biography of Mortimer Wheeler.

Lewin, Roger. 1987. *Bones of Contention.* New York: Simon and Schuster.

A popular account of early paleoanthropology that navigates through the personalities and controversies.

Morrell, Virginia. 1995. *Ancestral Passions.* New York: Simon and Schuster.

This comprehensive biography of the Leakey family pulls no punches and is based on many sources.

Trigger, Bruce G. 1980. *Gordon Childe: Revolutions in Archaeology.* London: Thames and Hudson.

Trigger gives us a sophisticated assessment of Childe's work.

Wheeler, Mortimer. 1958. *Still Digging.* London: Pan Books.

Wheeler's autobiography is a forthright account of pioneering days of scientific excavation in Britain and India. Worth reading for a sample of Wheeler's panache.

chapter 10

Culture History and Beyond

Alexander Keiller's Avebury excavations of the 1930s included re-erecting many of the stone uprights.

Let us hold fast to the idea that in essence culture symbolizes a relationship, or rather an intricate web of interrelations, between society and environment, and that culture change involves a more or less complete series of adjustments between them.

Grahame Clark, *The Study of Prehistory: Inaugural Lecture*, 1953 (p. 23)

This chapter returns to North America, to discuss the increasing preoccupation with chronology, culture history, and artifact ordering that developed during the 1930s. We also discuss some of the major changes in archaeology that emerged during the 1930s and 1940s: a new concern with ecology and economic archaeology, with cultural ecology, and with settlement patterns.

North American Archaeology: Tree-Rings and Taxonomy

The pace of archaeological research in North America accelerated in the early twentieth century, at a time when there was an increasing realization that ancient Native American cultures had changed quite profoundly through time and space. Cultural distributions, in particular, drew early attention, notably in the definition of several moundbuilder societies, among them the **Fort Ancient** and **Hopewell** cultures, by William C. Mills in Ohio as early as 1902—the first use of the word "culture" in an archaeological context in North America. These and other cultures were predominantly geographical entities, defined by site distributions rather than chronologies—an approach that stemmed in part from Franz Boas's use of the ethnographic culture as a basic unit of study. Boas favored diffusionism and cultural relativism. He was himself little interested in North American archaeology, but his approaches strongly encouraged the assumption that Indian cultures had changed in the past.

Dendrochronology

One of the greatest problems facing American archaeology was that of dating. Stratigraphic excavations had taken place since the 1860s, and were used successfully by Nels C. Nelson in the Southwest in 1916. In the same year anthropologist Alfred Kroeber made surface collections of painted potsherds in the Zuñi region, then used simple ordering methods, working back from the present, to place them in rough chronological order. Alfred Kidder excavated the Pecos middens in New Mexico after 1914. He applied Kroeber's ordering approach, also stratigraphic observations, and pottery from sealed graves, to work back from the present into the past (see Chapter 7). He produced the first culture-historical sequence for the Southwest, published in his *Introduction to the Study of Southwestern Archaeology* in 1924. Kidder's synthesis appeared a year before Gordon Childe's *Dawn of European Civilization*, the other classic work of culture history from the between-the-wars years (see Chapter 9). Kidder used archaeological finds from nine river drainages to define four stages of cultural development in the Southwest: Basket Maker, Post-Basket Maker, Pre-Pueblo, and Pueblo. Within these stages were various regional cultures.

Kidder's scheme offered a long chronological sequence and raised considerable interest, but it lacked an accurate time scale. A University of Arizona astronomer, A. E. Douglass, produced the solution. Since 1901, he had been working on climatic changes and their relationships to sunspots. He had concentrated on the annual growth rings in trees, using much more accurate observations than those of the Reverend Manasseh Cutler on trees growing on earthworks at Marietta, Ohio, in 1788. Douglass started with firs and pines, taking a tree-ring chronology back two centuries. Next, he extended his time scale with beams from colonial Spanish churches, then Ancestral Pueblo buildings. Douglass almost gave up his work, but continued it at the urging of local archaeologists. He developed a borer for sampling ancient beams without removing them, then used tree-ring sequences from them to work out a relative chronology for pueblos. For years, he looked for a beam to link his master curve that was anchored to historical trees to an earlier "floating" chronology for ancient pueblos. In 1929, Douglass finally recovered a beam from a ruin at Show Low, Arizona, which linked the ancient and historic tree-ring sequences. Within a few weeks, he produced an accurate chronological framework for Southwestern archaeology and the major pueblos. This, in turn, enabled him to date Pecos and its sequence of changing pottery styles (Figure 10.1).

Dendrochronology (tree-ring dating) placed Southwestern archaeology on a new footing, but it was confined to a single region. The chronology of the rest of North American archaeology was a matter of informed (and usually inaccurate) guesswork until the 1960s. Not that many archaeologists of the time were that concerned, for they believed that North American prehistory had a relatively short time scale—no more than a few thousand years.

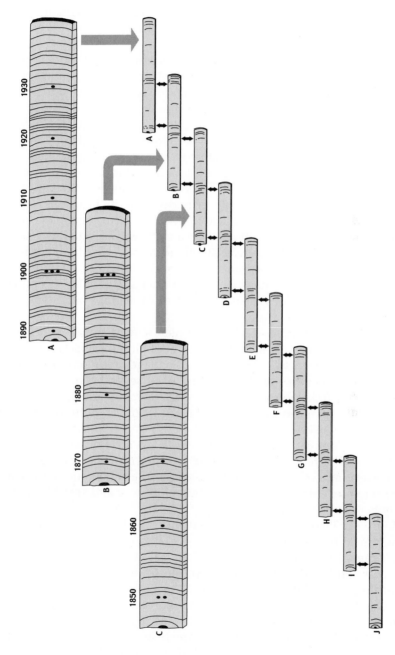

Figure 10.1   Dendrochronology matches ancient timbers with a master sequence of tree rings, as shown here.

The Midwest Taxonomic System

While dendrochronology became the established chronological method for the Southwest, others devoted themselves to developing new taxonomies for North American archaeology.

The Pecos sequence soon came under close scrutiny. A husband-and-wife team, Harold and Winifred Gladwin, pointed out that Kidder's scheme referred more to the northern Southwest than to the south. They proposed a hierarchical classification of cultural units for the entire Southwest, with three general "roots"—Basketmaker (later called Anasazi [now Ancestral Pueblo]), Hohokam, and Caddoan (later to become Mogollon). The Gladwins proposed a treelike classification stemming from these roots, with different regional branches and twigs, based on an implicitly chronological assumption—that Southwestern cultures diversified through time.

In 1932, W. C. McKern and a group of midwestern archaeologists developed what they called the Midwest Taxonomic System to classify enormous amounts of data collected by both amateur and professional fieldworkers in a region where stratified sites were relatively uncommon. Although this was a purely taxonomic system based on artifact forms, there was, once again, an implicit assumption that cultural differences at a single location occurred over time, and that the widespread distribution of cultures over wide areas was a sign of contemporaneity.

McKern and his colleagues developed a hierarchy of archaeological entities, starting with artifact *assemblages*, the sum of all the artifacts found in a site. Then he moved on to *components*, assemblages representing a single period of occupation at a site. A *focus* comprised several components with almost identical artifact types. Then there were *aspects*, made up of foci with "a preponderating majority of traits," and finally *patterns*, cultural reflections of the "primary adjustments of peoples to environment, as defined by tradition." McKern identified three patterns: *Archaic*, which lacked pottery but included ground slate artifacts; *Woodland*, with semi-sedentary sites, cord-marked pottery, and stemmed or side-notched projectile points; and finally *Mississippian*, a sedentary pattern with incised pottery and small triangular stone points.

The Midwest Taxonomic System owed much to Franz Boas's historical particularism, to his assumption that cultures were collections of individual traits that came together as a result of historical accidents (see Chapter 7). Whereas Gordon Childe paid much attention to human behavior and the uses of artifacts, the Midwest Taxonomic System made no inferences about human behavior, just recorded the presence or absence of artifacts. Any form of quantification, such as percentages of artifacts, was considered suspect, since the archaeological record was incomplete and such counts were inaccurate. But it was conceded that "quantitative similarity" in percentages of shared artifact types had significance as a way of fitting individual occupation levels and sites into a broader framework.

Stratigraphy, Seriation, and Culture History

Both the Gladwin system and the Midwest Taxonomic System, with their treelike organizations, came into widespread use between the 1930s and the 1950s. They stimulated a great deal of local research, where stratigraphic observation and careful artifact ordering (seriation) produced convincing local chronologies. Much of this work came from extensive Army Corps of Engineer canal and dam-building projects in the South and Southeast during the 1930s—the famous River Basin Surveys, when many young archaeologists, among them James A. Ford and Gordon R. Willey, developed culture histories of entire river drainages from extensive field surveys and selective excavations. They and others moved away from the treelike assumptions of a few years earlier, to a view that cultures formed elaborate mosaics of different units, each with its own chronology and local distribution. Some of these cultures and artifact types diffused over larger areas to form cultural traditions, very much along the lines proposed by Gordon Childe in Europe, who derived much European prehistoric culture from southwestern Asia (see Chapter 9).

The River Basin work culminated in a major article by James Ford and Gordon Willey in the *American Anthropologist* for 1941. "An Interpretation of the Prehistory of the Eastern United States" used the River Basin Survey data and a mass of other publications to group eastern cultures into five stages of development ranging from Archaic through two stages of "Burial Mound" (Woodland) and two of "Temple Mound" (Mississippian). Each stage was thought to have come from the south, from Mesoamerica, before spreading north through the Mississippi Valley.

The Ford and Willey synthesis made very cautious use of both diffusion and migration, as if native North Americans were conservative imitators rather than innovators. For instance, the changes from Archaic to Woodland and from Woodland to Mississippian were thought to be the consequence of population movements into the region from outside, a perspective that lingered right into the 1950s.

With the notable exception of Ford and Willey's work, almost all interpretations in American archaeology were largely descriptive, with little effort made to explain the meaning of the archaeological record. Cultural change and development had indeed taken place, but only in limited ways—"a continuous process of adaptation to local environments, of specialization, and of independent invention" that led to a series of regional cultures, as three authors of a major synthesis of North American archaeology put it in 1947 (Martin, Quimby, and Collier 1947:520).

As the preoccupation with artifact typologies and jigsaw puzzles of cultures intensified, North American archaeology rapidly became decoupled from ethnology, and from any concern with living Native Americans. Acceptance of change in ancient times was minimal; methodologies of culture history dominated all archaeological thinking; there was still a patronizing, even "colonial" attitude to native people that permeated archaeology. It was as if Indians were museum specimens. American archaeology became intensely conservative, often a mindless collecting and ordering of artifacts without any theoretical or even historical context. Inevitably, many younger scholars became disillusioned. Gordon Willey and Philip Phillips developed the concepts of North American culture history to their most refined in *Method and Theory in American Archaeology,* a short book published in 1958 that remains on the reading list of any prospective professional archaeologist. Among other things, the authors penned the now-famous statement "Archaeology is anthropology or it is nothing else."

The culture-historical approach encouraged American archaeologists to excavate and define ancient cultures. Excavation of this mind-set focused on middens, where artifacts tended to be most abundant—an approach that was to persist in many parts of North America into the 1960s and even later. This was cheap, easy excavation, focused on artifacts and their classification, a basis for increasingly elaborate artifact seriations to create sequences of sites based on artifact percentages—what Alfred Kroeber had once called "frequency seriation." In Europe, artifact classification made use of much earlier evolutionary typologies developed by nineteenth-century archaeologists, much of the work being devoted to splitting or refining existing types established by Oscar Montelius and other luminaries. American archaeologists did not have this evolutionary perspective or background, so they spent enormous amounts of time debating the theoretical significance of artifact classification—a debate that began in the 1920s and continues to this day.

Initially the debates surrounded the issues of objectivity. Then James Ford and others argued that types should be recognized only if they were useful chronological or spatial markers. Types were tools for historical analysis. The debate then shifted: Did archaeological types coincide with those created by their original makers? What were the relationships between the type and the various attributes (or features) used to define them? By the 1950s, archeologists like Albert Spaulding, a pioneer of statistical methods, proposed "natural types," defined by statistically grouped clusters of attributes that would reveal more about human behavior. Spaulding's approach is still commonplace today. These prolonged, and often dreary, debates about types represented the first attempts to make the analytical basis of American archaeology more explicit.

Grahame Clark and the Birth of Ecological Archaeology

Even as excavation focused on artifacts and single sites, a new precision in archaeological methods was developing, notably in Europe, where there was a new concern with wider questions than merely tool classification. How had people lived in the past? What had they worn? What were their domestic arrangements? Answering such questions required much better standards of excavation, and also the recovery of far more comprehensive data.

Between the 1920s and the 1940s, a series of exceptional excavations, usually building on the methods espoused by Pitt Rivers and now Mortimer Wheeler, raised fieldwork standards to new heights and produced much more complete information about ancient lifeways. Much of this work was in Britain, where Alexander Keiller carried out years of exploratory excavations on sites around the Avebury stone circles. This research was highly selective, much of it devoted to restoration, including the erection of stones felled by quarrymen. Keiller marked the sites of monoliths identified by marks in the chalk subsoil with cement markers and carried out meticulous stratigraphic excavations. The Avebury research was remarkable for its concern not just with the stone circles and with artifacts, but for the Avebury landscape as a whole—a kaleidoscope of stone circles, burial mounds, and avenues that formed an intricate jigsaw puzzle of Stone Age ceremonial. In this, Keiller followed in the tradition of the eighteenth-century antiquarian William Stukeley, who had made perceptive observations of Avebury two centuries earlier (see Chapter 1).

Other archaeologists, among them Dutch, German, and Scandinavian fieldworkers, paid careful attention to waterlogged sites and locations where structures like Neolithic longhouses were preserved by posthole discolorations in glacial soils or sand. Careful plotting of artifact distributions produced exciting information about daily life and domestic activities. The German-trained archaeologist Gerhard Bersu was a pioneer in the excavation of long-vanished wooden structures, using meticulous digging and three-dimensional plans to reconstruct the dwellings of an Iron Age village at **Little Woodbury** in southern England. But the greatest advances were in ecological archaeology, much of it in the hands of the Cambridge archaeologist Grahame Clark (1907–1995).

In 1931, the trawler *Colinda,* working in the southern North Sea, dredged up a lump of peat from the shallow seabed that had once been moorland and was later covered by rising post–Ice Age sea levels. As the lump split open on the deck, a bone spearhead fell out. Fortunately for science, the trawlermen kept their find, which was soon identified as a classic example of a **Mesolithic** bone point.

One of those who examined this chance discovery was a young Cambridge archaeologist, Grahame Clark, who was just completing a study of Mesolithic cultures in England for his doctoral dissertation. The discovery was a turning point in Clark's career. He was friends with a pioneer of pollen analysis in Britain, Harry Godwin, and realized the great potential that such finds offered for studying major environmental change and the ways in which prehistoric people adapted to changing climatic conditions. For the rest of his long life, Clark argued for the importance of wet sites, where organic and environmental data might be found in close association. He was strongly influenced by research on waterlogged sites in Denmark and Sweden, and by continuing research on Swiss lake dwellings. Like the Scandinavians, Clark also advocated multidisciplinary archaeological research, a novel idea at the time.

In 1932, Clark was one of a small group of scientists who founded the Fenland Research Committee, a loose association of scientists who worked on the Fens—the wetlands and lowlands close to Cambridge. In the years that followed, Clark carried out small-scale excavations at a series of locations, including a site at **Peacock's Farm,** where he found stratified peat deposits, clays, and sands associated with a scatter of Mesolithic stone tools, and, in a higher level, some Neolithic pottery. Peacock's Farm, despite its few archaeological finds, was very important at the time, for it placed the Mesolithic and Neolithic within an environmental context of changing vegetation, and it provided an entirely new direction for research that was radically different from merely studying stone tools.

Grahame Clark now widened his intellectual horizons. He wrote a memorable book, *The Mesolithic Settlement of Northern Europe,* published in 1938, in which he placed changing human societies after the Ice Age in their environmental context, an important innovation at the time. During World War II, during breaks in military service, he wrote a series of important essays on economic archaeology, which looked at major topics like beekeeping and honey, seals, sheep farming, and whaling—to mention only a few topics. He had set out his views on archaeology in *Archaeology and Society,* a textbook published in 1939 in which he stated that archaeology's primary concern was to find out how people lived. He published a famous diagram showing the relationships between habitat, economy, and biome (habitat in which animals and plants live together). This drawing, albeit much elaborated, was the foundation of much of Clark's archaeological thinking.

Clark's interest in simple forms of ecological systems and ancient economic life culminated in his classic series of essays, *Prehistoric Europe: The Economic Basis,* published in 1952. Based on archaeology, ethnographic analogy, and folk culture from European peasant societies, this important book broke firmly away from culture history and looked at general economic practices. The book was based on the assumption that all human societies operated in a state of equilibrium within ecological systems, and changed constantly, often in response to climatic change. *Prehistoric Europe* was, as Clark wrote, "essentially an act of propaganda." The more conservative of his colleagues criticized him for eschewing culture history, but many welcomed its sophisticated insights into a realm of archaeology that had been little explored. In many respects, this book, arguably the most influential of all Clark's works, foreshadowed much of 1960s archaeology's concern with ecological systems and ancient subsistence; but few of the proponents of the "new archaeology" of that era read it.

In 1948 Clark got wind of a Mesolithic site in peat at **Star Carr** in north-eastern England. Between 1949 and 1951, he excavated this most famous of Stone Age sites on a shoestring, publishing the results in *Excavations at Star Carr* in 1954, one of the classic monographs of twentieth-century archaeology. Star Carr was a tiny hunting stand set on a birch platform in the reeds at the edge of a long-dried-up glacial lake surrounded by birch forest (Figure 10.2). The excavations involved pollen expert Harry Godwin, animal bone specialists from the British Museum, geologists, and others, who collaborated to produce a portrait of a tiny Mesolithic site dating to the Pre-Boreal period, when birch forests spread across northern Europe. One of the first radiocarbon dates ever obtained on a Stone Age site dated Star Carr to about 7530 B.C. The overall portrait of the site was remarkably complete, including evidence for canoes, seasonal occupation, and bone technology, dissected with a thoroughness unheard of in Britain. A generation of British students, and many overseas, were brought up on the Star Carr report, which was a blueprint for a new form of archaeology concerned as much with environment and subsistence as with technology.

The Star Carr site has been reinvestigated in recent years and Clark's somewhat simplistic vision of the site much modified. AMS radiocarbon dates (explained in Chapter 11) now place the occupation a millennium

Figure 10.2
Excavations at Star Carr: the birch bark platform.

earlier, to between 8700 and 8400 B.C. But this does not detract from what was, at the time, a remarkable piece of field research, conducted with minimal funds and only volunteer labor.

Clark's research went in parallel with a new concern with Julian Steward's pioneering research on cultural ecology on the other side of the Atlantic.

Julian Steward and Cultural Ecology

Julian Steward (1902–1972), an approximate contemporary of Grahame Clark's, was one of the first American anthropologists to stress the importance of ecological factors in shaping ancient societies. His research focused mainly on the Great Basin, where he investigated caves near the Great Salt Lake and spent much time studying small bands of Shoshonean hunter-gatherers. Steward urged the use of both archaeology and anthropology to study culture change and to examine not just the details of artifacts, but ancient subsistence, settlement patterns, and population changes. He asked the question: "Are there ways of identifying common cultural features in dozens of societies distributed over many cultural areas?"

Disagreeing with the ardent evolutionists, who argued that all societies had passed through similar stages of cultural development, Steward assumed that certain basic culture types would develop in similar ways under similar conditions. For generations, many archaeologists had thought of culture as analogous to a layered cake, with technology as the bottom layer, social organization the middle, and ideology the top. Steward added another layer to the cake—that of environment—and looked to it as the cause of cultural change. To do so, he developed a method for recognizing the ways in which such change is caused by adaptation to the environment.

Calling his study of environment and culture change "cultural ecology," Steward laid down three principles:

- Similar adaptations may be found in different cultures in similar environments
- No culture has ever achieved an adaptation to its environment that has remained unchanged for any length of time
- Differences and changes during periods of cultural development in any area can either add to social complexity or result in completely new cultural patterns

Steward used these principles as a basis for studying cultures and culture change in widely separated areas. To study different cultures, he would isolate and define distinguishing characteristics in each culture, a nucleus of traits he called the "cultural core." For example, he observed that African San, Australian Aborigines, and Fuegian Indians of South America were all organized in patrilineal bands, in which descent came through the father, forming a cultural type. Why? Because their ecological adaptation and social organization were similar. Despite major environmental differences, the practical requirements of the hunter-gatherer lifeway grouped all these peo-ple in small bands, each with its own territory. In all the areas, the social structure and general organization of the bands were very similar, and their adaptation to their environment was fundamentally the same, despite many differences in detail.

Steward also spent much time studying the relationships between envi-ronment and culture that form the context and reasons for critical features of culture. He applied cultural ecology to such problems as the spread of dwelling types, attempting not to identify diffusion or other forms of culture change, but to *explain* them. Cultural ecology, he believed, could answer questions about why human societies adjust to different environments using certain general types of behavior. Steward added changing adaptations to the natural environment to the study of diffusion, evolution, and migration. In other words, the study of culture change involved analyzing human cultures and their changing environmental conditions as well.

Julian Steward's thinking about cultural ecology and settlement patterns had a great impact on young researchers like Gordon Willey, and, later, Great Basin scholars like David Hurst Thomas. He was one of those who brought twentieth-century archaeology to the threshold of great theoretical change. Steward established, once and for all, the close relationships between ar-chaeology and anthropology and the need for multidisciplinary research. He also stressed that one of archaeology's primary goals must be to develop ad-equate explanations for human prehistory—an aim far more sophisticated than those of survey, excavation, and description. Most theoretical debates in archaeology since 1960 have focused on the need to explain the past.

Settlement Archaeology in the Americas

In the United States, federal government relief agencies funded large-scale excavations through park services, museums, and universities during the depression years of the 1930s. Much of this funding went into the River Basin Surveys, in which entire sites were excavated before they were flooded by dam construction. This was a very different form of excavation from that designed to produce artifact samples, for not only was everything exposed, but the accompanying survey work placed the excavated site in a much wider geographical and landscape context. This research had a pow-erful effect on the young Gordon Willey, a major participant in the River Basin Surveys. He realized the potential of studying changes in settlement patterns through time and across changing ancient landscapes, often called settlement archaeology.

In 1943, Willey was appointed to the Smithsonian Institution in Washington, D.C., to help Julian Steward edit the monumental *Handbook of South American Indians*. He came under the pervasive intellectual influence of Steward and his thinking about cultural ecology. He listened as Steward proclaimed that archaeologists should spend less time looking at single sites and should look at them set in their landscapes as these changed over time.

After World War II, Willey applied Steward's settlement and landscape approach to the **Virú Valley** on Peru's North Coast. Here he studied an entire river valley's changing settlements through more than 1,500 years of prehistoric time, using aerial photography, foot surveys, and limited excavations. Willey believed you could not study ancient societies without looking at them as part of complex economic, political, and social landscapes. The Virú research, published in 1953, helped found a new field of settlement archaeology in the 1950s and 1960s, which fostered large-scale archaeological surveys of such areas as the Valley of Mexico before Aztec civilization, ancient Nubia (Sudan), and Mesopotamia.

Willey's Virú Valley research had an enormous influence on the future direction of archaeology. He himself shifted his interests to Mesoamerica, on being appointed Bowditch Professor of Central American Archaeology and Ethnology at Harvard University. He now applied his settlement experience at the Maya center of **Barton Ramie** in Belize. Here, farmers had cleared the forest for their fields, so Willey and his students were able to walk freely across the landscape. Willey spotted some promising house mounds in 1953 and returned a year later for a larger-scale survey. The result was one of the first Maya settlement patterns ever to be mapped.

Willey expanded his settlement researches to other sites, first at **Altar de Sacrificios** in Guatemala's Petén in 1959, where a Maya ceremonial center lay on an island in a swamp. The forest cover here was thick, and the survey yielded few house mounds. So the team moved to **Seibal** further upstream on the Pasion River, where the center lay on higher, better drained ground. Willey laid out a 3-mile-by-3-mile (5-km-by-5-km) square, which he surveyed intensively, while training a generation of now-distinguished Maya archaeologists, among them William Rathje and Jeremy Sabloff. By the time the fieldwork at Altar de Sacrificios and Seibal ended in 1968, Willey had founded a new tradition in Maya archaeology.

In all his researches, the focus of Willey's surveys and excavations was not only on the city itself, but on the hinterland—the hierarchy of lesser settlements that flourished in the shadow of the larger centers. His successors carry on the tradition. Such settlement research continues to be a major part of Maya archaeology. The result: a much better understanding of the changing fortunes of individual Maya centers.

The Dead Sea Scrolls

While Willey began his settlement research, new discoveries were causing headlines around the world. In 1947, a Bedouin shepherd looking for some lost goats near Qumran, Jordan, close to the Dead Sea, came across a cave full of jars containing scrolls wrapped in linen cloth. A few of the scrolls ended up in a Jerusalem dealer's hands, and it became apparent that one included a copy of most of the Book of Isaiah. Fortunately for science, most of the scrolls were recovered before being sold or destroyed.

The 40 or 50 scroll-filled jars in the cave were once the treasured possession of a Jewish community at nearby Khirbat Qumran. The Qumran community was an austere one, charged to live righteously and to seek God. Excavations at the community showed how Qumran had flourished twice, the first time before an earthquake drove everyone away in A.D. 31, and again until A.D. 68, when Roman persecution made life unbearable. It was then that the community buried its precious scrolls in a nearby cave.

The scrolls themselves are important religious texts, which bear witness to the historical milieu in which Christianity was emerging. Inevitably, they became revered relics—sacred texts reclaimed and proudly exhibited by the new state of Israel (Figure 10.3). To many people, they became tangible tokens, icons of sanctity to be venerated, not necessarily to be studied. They became political symbols of immense value—religious tourist attractions

Figure 10.3 A Dead Sea Scroll fragment—a portion of the Book of Isaiah.

commemorated in the Shrine of the Book. At the same time, the ebb and flow of politics placed Qumran in Jordan, not Israel. On both sides of the border and overseas, insiders, establishment figures, and government officials controlled access to, and study of, the scrolls for many years. Archaeology became a weapon in a generations-long political battle.

The scrolls themselves came under the intellectual control of scholars more interested in narrow pastimes like the study of ancient scripts, analyzing texts, and protecting their intellectual preserves. It is only in recent years that their control has been challenged and the texts made available to scholars and interested people everywhere.

The Sepulcher of the Maya Lord Pacal

The Dead Sea Scrolls attracted international headlines, but the discovery of the spectacular burial of a Maya lord in the steaming Mesoamerican rain forest in 1952 went almost unnoticed outside archaeological circles.

In 1949, Mexican archaeologist Alberto Ruz was appointed director of research at the Maya city of Palenque, visited by John Lloyd Stephens during the first of his two Central American journeys in the 1840s (see Chapter 5). He decided to investigate the Temple of the Inscriptions, the architectural centerpiece of the ceremonial precincts (see Figure 5.2). Finding a flagstone with plugged holes in the floor of the temple, Ruz levered it up and unearthed a stairway sealed with tightly packed boulders. It took five months to clear the stairway of 66 steps with a sharp U-turn in the middle. In July 1952, Ruz's workers unblocked the entrance to a burial chamber at original ground level, guarded by the remains of six young sacrificial victims. Ruz found himself in a rock-cut chamber decorated with great stucco figures of priests marching around the walls. A huge stone slab adorned with intricate hieroglyphs adorned the floor. He drilled carefully through two corners and found a hollow space. Using automobile jacks and timber beams, Ruz and his workers raised the five-ton slab, revealing a cavity sealed with a highly polished stone plug. Inside lay the skeleton of a Maya lord wearing a jade diadem, his hair divided into strands with small jade cylinders. The body was literally smothered in jade ornaments. The lord wore a magnificent mask made of jade mosaic, with eyes of shell, each iris of shiny obsidian.

At the time when Ruz made his discovery, no one could decipher the glyphs on the sarcophagus lid. Ruz himself noted that the lid depicted a man falling in death into the Otherworld. It was not until Maya glyphs were deciphered in the 1980s that epigraphers were able to identify the magnificent personage in the tomb. He was Lord Pacal the Great (known as "Shield"), a member of the ruling dynasty of Palenque, who reigned for 67 years in the seventh century A.D. The glyphs on his sarcophagus lid recounted his genealogy and divine ancestry, an abiding preoccupation of Maya lords.

Functional Archaeology

While the resumption of excavation after World War II led to exciting discoveries in many parts of the world, archaeological analysis and interpretation were changing only slowly. The first cracks in the comfortable world of culture history had appeared with the researches of Grahame Clark, Gordon Willey, and others, who proclaimed the virtues of a multidisciplinary approach to archaeology. They were aware of environmental changes, of changing settlement patterns, and of the intricacies of ecological approaches. But, for the most part, their work fell on deaf ears. Clark's researches at Star Carr and elsewhere in Europe were virtually unknown in North America until the 1960s except to a handful of scholars who followed European archaeology.

Under the complacent surface, however, lay widespread frustration about the sterility and limitations of doctrinaire culture history, especially among the younger generation of fieldworkers. (For W. W. Taylor's work, see Chapter 11.) Many of them became interested in the ways tools were made and used—what was sometimes called *functional archaeology.*

They were not the first to have such interests. The North American archaeologist Harlan Smith (1872–1940) attempted to reconstruct how the inhabitants of the Fox Farm site, a Fort Ancient settlement, had once lived. His *Prehistoric Ethnology of a Kentucky Site,* published in 1910, analyzed the artifacts from the site by their functional categories, including "securing food," "tools used by man," "tools used by women," and "processes of manufacture." Smith made considerable use of ethnographic analogy, but also used inspired guesswork. His fieldworkers consulted local Indians, drew heavily on ethnography, and experimented with making modern-day replicas of ancient artifacts.

William S. Webb (1882–1964) was the best known of Smith's coworkers. He worked extensively on Kentucky mounds and shell middens. Webb was also well known for studying how ancient peoples made and used artifacts—and how these artifacts reflected nonmaterial aspects of human existence. Webb was trained as a physicist, was strongly influenced by Harlan Smith's work, and was largely self-taught. After initial efforts to study ancient human behavior, epitomized by his *Ancient Life in Kentucky* (1928), Webb turned to culture history and minutiae of artifacts in his later career.

This preoccupation with artifacts and minor attributes of projectile points and clay vessels came at a time of very large-scale excavations in some parts of North America, notably as part of the River Basin Surveys in the eastern and southeastern United States during the 1930s. Here, horizontal excavation revealed house floor plans, other features often only identified by their postholes, and even the layouts of entire settlements. Most of this research was carried out to expand knowledge of artifact traits, with only a few archaeologists being interested in how people had lived in the past. Even when the authors of books or papers turned their attention to human behavior, it was almost always in the context of lists of artifact traits in a form of pseudo-ethnography modified to accommodate archaeological evidence. The advent of the Midwest Taxonomic System and a major emphasis on chronological studies largely suppressed all other kinds of archaeological research for a generation.

Nevertheless, a growing number of younger archaeologists were beginning to look at the past in more functionalist terms, in part because of the widely read field researches of British anthropologist E. E. Evans-Pritchard among the Nuer pastoralists of the Sudan, and those of the Polish-born scholar Bronislaw Malinowski, whose functionalist studies of the Trobriand Islanders of the southwestern Pacific were already classics of their kind. A wider academic audience was now aware of the researches of Gordon Childe and Grahame Clark with their strong emphases on ancient human behavior.

A number of important researches renewed archaeological ties with ethnology, at a time when many well-known anthropologists were proclaiming that archaeologists, with their material finds, could say nothing about the intangibles of human behavior. William D. Strong (1899–1962) worked on the Nebraskan Plains, which many people believed to have been sparsely populated before Europeans introduced horses. He excavated at **Signal Butte,** Nebraska, and revealed a Great Plains inhabited by hunter-gatherers and horticulturalists for thousands of years before Europeans and horses turned the Plains into a carnival of nomads. Strong's work showed how archaeology could be used to check ethnological information. He used the direct historical method employed by Kidder at Pecos, while another Plains archaeologist, Waldo Wedel, examined the relationships between ancient cultures and environments on the Plains, and showed how archaeological cultures were shaped by other factors than mere accident.

By the late 1940s, functionalist approaches were a significant trend in American archaeology, not only in the north, but also in Mesoamerica and the Andes, where studies of the well-known **Chavín** art style of the first millennium B.C. moved beyond mere diffusion to a consideration of the social and religious characteristics of the artifacts.

In 1940, the Harvard anthropologist Clyde Kluckhohn wrote of Mesoamerican archaeology that its practitioners had two choices—either continue historical studies that sought to re-create unique events in pitiless detail, or adopt a more scientific approach that examined significant trends and uniformities in cultural change through time. His remarks reflected an emerging concern about the future of archaeology that surfaced in the 1950s and 1960s—developments described in Chapters 11 and 12.

Summary

Chapter 10 describes the development of North American culture history and its preoccupations with artifact classification and chronology, which resulted in the development of dendrochronology (tree-ring dating). The result was an increasing focus on the minutiae of culture history and artifact typologies at the expense of other aspects of the past. Meanwhile, in Europe, Cambridge archaeologist Grahame Clark became involved in ecological and economic archaeology, a specialty that stemmed from a realization that wet sites offered excellent opportunities for studying climate change and human adaptations to ancient environments. His work culminated in the publication of *Prehistoric Europe: the Economic Basis* in 1952. Clark also excavated the Mesolithic site at Star Carr, England, one of the first comprehensive portraits of a prehistoric site in its environmental setting.

Anthropologist Julian Steward, who worked among the Shoshone people of the Great Basin, developed new theories of culture change and cultural ecology during the 1930s and 1940s, which resulted in a new approach to prehistory—cultural ecology, the relationship between people and their changing environments. Steward also stressed the importance of studying not individual sites but changing distributions of sites across a changing landscape—settlement archaeology. His approach was espoused by Gordon Willey, first with his settlement survey of Peru's Virú Valley, and later in the Maya lowlands. The same period witnessed important discoveries such as the Dead Sea Scrolls in Jordan and the spectacular burial of the Maya lord Pacal at Palenque, Mexico. However, the full significance of this find was not appreciated until the decipherment of Maya glyphs in the 1980s.

The late 1940s and 1950s saw a rising concern over the sterile approaches of hard-core culture history, which manifested itself in an increasing interest in functional archaeology—the uses of artifacts in the past. All of these developments culminated in a theoretical furor in archaeology, which emerged during the 1950s and exploded during the 1960s.

Guide to Further Reading

Clark, J. G. D. 1952. *Prehistoric Europe: The Economic Basis.* Cambridge: Cambridge University Press.

Classic essays on European economic prehistory crammed with useful analogies and examples.

Davies, Philip R., and others. 2002. *The Complete World of the Dead Sea Scrolls.* London and New York: Thames and Hudson.

This lavishly illustrated survey of the scrolls and their historical context is an ideal starting point.

Fagan, Brian. 2002. *Grahame Clark: An Intellectual Biography of an Archaeologist.* Boulder, CO: Westview Press.

This biography describes Grahame Clark's engagement with ecological archaeology, and also with many of the developments in Chapter 11.

Steward, Julian H. 1955. *A Theory of Culture Change.* Urbana: University of Illinois Press.

An essential book for any student of cultural ecology.

Willey, Gordon R., and Philip Phillips. 1958. *Method and Theory in American Archaeology.* Chicago: University of Chicago Press.

The classic primer on culture history and terminology in the Americas. Every serious archaeology student reads this book.

chapter 11

Radiocarbon Dating and World Prehistory

A plastered ancestral skull from Jericho, Jordan.

We almost cried with sheer joy, each seized by that terrific emotion that comes rarely in life. After all our hoping and hardship and sacrifice, at last we had reached our goal—we had found the world's earliest human.

Louis Leakey on the discovery of *Zinjanthropus boisei* at Olduvai Gorge, Tanzania, 1959

By the 1950s, increasing numbers of archaeologists were uncomfortable with the narrow culture-historical perspective that dominated most archaeological thinking. This discomfort was reflected in the new interest in ecological archaeology and cultural ecology, the emergence of the functionalist perspective, and Gordon Willey's pioneering settlement research. This chapter continues the story of a changing archaeology in the 1950s, of changes triggered both by dissatisfaction among a younger generation of archaeologists and by the development of radiocarbon dating. This new chronological method made it possible to think of a truly global archaeology—a world prehistory.

Taylor's A Study of Archaeology

Inevitably, the widespread concern over the narrow perspectives prevalent in archaeology produced a defining study. In 1948, a young scholar, Walter W. Taylor, published a scathing review of American archaeology. *A Study of Archaeology* was an extended polemic. It was written to provoke discussion, and it did. Taylor pointed out that most American archaeologists were culture historians, who said that they sought to reconstruct the past. Instead, they preoccupied themselves with what he called "mere chronicle"—culture history in space and time. As for culture change, that was attributed to diffusion and migration.

Taylor wrote a critique of an archaeology with limited goals, in which fieldwork methods were careless, analysis incomplete. Stone tools and potsherds received meticulous attention; other categories of evidence such as animal bones, plant remains, and even basketry, were virtually ignored, and sometimes not even collected. The excavators compiled long lists of culture traits, quantified them, and then compared them, mainly on the basis of the absence or presence of different artifact types. An obsession with chronology had put blinkers on many archaeologists' perspectives. They ignored the exact positions of artifacts and data on relationships between houses and hearths—much valuable data that would tell one a great deal about the way people behaved, lived, and interacted with one another, to say nothing of what they ate.

Walter Taylor balanced his criticisms with a proposal for what he called a "conjunctive approach," which added studies of the interrelationships between artifacts and features to the traditional culture history. Taylor urged careful consideration of quantitative aspects of artifacts, of the spatial distribution of all finds, as well as evidence as to how they were used and made. Like Grahame Clark's thinking, Taylor's conjunctive approach defined cultures as mental constructs, their material remains as products of culture rather than culture itself. Many aspects of culture, which was, in the final analysis, intangible, survived in the archaeological record, not just material objects.

Above all, the archaeologist should strive to recover just as much information from a site as possible. Taylor stressed the importance of environmental reconstruction, of ethnographic analogy. His conjunctive approach aimed to understand how people lived at a site as a "functionally integrated pattern." Ultimately, the archaeologist should aim at a functional understanding that was the equivalent of the ethnologist's insight into living cultures. Under this rubric, archaeologists should work alongside anthropologists in the study of culture.

A Study of Archaeology caused a considerable stir. Predictably, ardent culture historians and many in the archaeological establishment of the day savaged the book. It is said to have wrought permanent damage to Taylor's career. But a decade later many people hailed the volume as a major break with the past—as a precursor of the major theoretical advances of the 1960s (see Chapter 12). In fact, *A Study* resembles in many respects the by-then-familiar approach of Grahame Clark, who also advocated the study of how people lived in the past, as well as close use of ethnographic sources and the need to pay attention to social, political, and other institutions of the past. But Taylor was no ecologist and had no interest in human cultures as adaptive systems, as Clark did—a perspective that was to become one of the foundations of archaeological theory in the 1960s. Taylor was basically a functionalist, whose ideas coincided more closely with the Boasian notion that cultures were made up of shared concepts and traits. During his career, he carried out important fieldwork in northern Mexico.

A Study of Archaeology was, however, a powerful call for improved standards of archaeological research and more detailed analysis of artifacts. Taylor reinforced the functionalist approach and, with his polemic, foreshadowed the theoretical furors of the 1960s. But he did not initiate the major revolution in archaeological thinking that came a decade later.

Multidisciplinary Research

Both Taylor, and more explicitly, Julian Steward, advocated multidisciplinary research in the field, an approach to the past strongly backed by Grahame Clark in his widely read papers on general aspects of economic archaeology in Europe published during, and immediately after, World War II. Clark himself put his fieldwork where his mouth was with his multidisciplinary Star Carr excavations in 1949 (see Chapter 10), but American scholars were also active in influential multidisciplinary projects.

During the 1950s, Robert Braidwood (1907–2003) of the University of Chicago's Oriental Institute recruited an interdisciplinary research team to investigate both hunter-gatherer and early farming sites in the Kirkuk region in the Zagros foothills of northern Iraq as part of a study of the origins of agriculture and animal domestication. Braidwood brought together geologists and zoologists, botanists and other specialists, to examine a small farming village named **Jarmo,** which was soon radiocarbon-dated to about 6000 B.C., at the time a very early date indeed for agriculture. Braidwood used this research to draw attention to experiments with plants and wild animals on what he called "the hilly flanks" of southwestern Asia. He also rejected Gordon Childe's theory that desiccation and oases played a major role in the changeover to agriculture.

Braidwood's team approach to early agriculture was extremely influential in fostering a new generation of research into such major questions as the origins of farming and animal domestication.

While Braidwood worked at Jarmo, British excavator Kathleen Kenyon probed the depths of the ancient city mound at **Jericho** in Jordan. Kenyon had learned her excavation techniques at Great Zimbabwe under Gertrude Caton Thompson, and on several of Mortimer Wheeler's large excavations. She was, above all, an expert on pottery and stratification, but like Braidwood, she made sure that she had access to experts in such specialties as animal bones and plant remains. The Jericho excavations caused considerable excitement, not only for their important Iron Age and Bronze Age levels, but also because of the long sequence of Stone Age farming villages that began with a humble camp near the spring that was the focus of all settlement at Jericho. Radiocarbon dates traced the beginnings of Jericho to as early as 7800 B.C., in the days before tree-ring calibration made the chronology even earlier. The later communities were much larger than the original settlement, with the earliest one nestling behind a massive stone wall and ditch, complete with watchtower (Figure 11.1). Kenyon also unearthed a cache of ancestral skulls in one of the houses, with the features of their owners plastered on them (see chapter opener).

Figure 11.1   Stone watchtower at Jericho, Jordan.

At about the same time, the American archaeologist Richard MacNeish studied dry caves and open sites in the **Tehuacán Valley** in highland Mexico in a search for the origins of maize agriculture. Combining survey with excavation, MacNeish identified a sample of 456 sites spanning a period of ten thousand years. Using radiocarbon dates and the well-preserved botanical and faunal remains in the Tehuacán caves, MacNeish was able to chronicle major shifts in subsistence practices, and, by an estimated 5000 B.C., the cultivation of maize. The small maize cobs from MacNeish's caves are still among the earliest corn specimens in the world.

Richard "Scotty" MacNeish was one of the great characters of late-twentieth-century archaeology. He spent more than half a century excavating sites in the Americas, and, in his last years, in China. His finest work was at Tehuacán in the late 1950s and early 1960s. In his later years, he became increasingly preoccupied with research into the first Americans, which led to controversial excavations at a cave in New Mexico. He also dug in southern China in a search for the earliest rice.

The Braidwood and MacNeish projects were among the first major archaeological endeavors financed with federal dollars through the National Science Foundation. They were also among the first field projects to collect radiocarbon samples. In both cases, the resulting dates, together with those obtained by Kathleen Kenyon at Jericho, pushed back the origins of agriculture several thousand years from the traditional date of 4000 B.C., a thousand years before the appearance of civilization in Mesopotamia and along the Nile. Thus, agriculture had taken hold far more slowly than once believed.

Radiocarbon Dating

Jarmo, Jericho, and Tehuacán were among the first archaeological sites to be dated by a dramatic scientific discovery that was about to revolutionize the dating of the past.

In 1949, Willard Libby and J. R. Arnold of the University of Chicago announced a new way of dating organic materials from archaeological sites. Radiocarbon dating was a direct offshoot of Libby's work on the atomic bomb during World War II. He based the new chronological method on the fact that cosmic radiation produces neutrons that enter the earth's atmosphere and react with nitrogen. The neutrons produce carbon-14, a carbon isotope with eight rather than the usual six neutrons in the nucleus. With these additional neutrons, the nucleus is unstable and is subject to gradual radioactive decay. Libby calculated that it took 5,568 years (now recalculated to 5,730 years) for half the carbon-14 in any sample to decay, and he devised a method for counting the number of emissions in a gram of carbon. He knew that carbon-14 entered the carbon dioxide in the atmosphere, together with ordinary carbon. Because living vegetation builds up its own organic matter through photosynthesis and by using atmospheric carbon dioxide, the proportion of radiocarbon in it is equal to that in the atmosphere. As soon as an organism dies, no further radiocarbon is incorporated into it, but the amount present will continue to disintegrate slowly, so that after 5,730 years only half the original amount will be left, and less proportions as time passes.

Libby and Arnold tested their new dating method on objects of known historical age, such as wooden Egyptian mummy cases. When these dates agreed well with known chronologies from written sources, they extended the method to prehistoric sites. Soon, charcoal samples were pouring into the University of Chicago laboratory by the dozen, sent in by archaeologists from all over the world. Everyone realized that this was the first dating method that promised accurate dates for sites dating back as far as forty thousand years.

Radiocarbon dating revolutionized many well-established chronologies for such events as the origins of agriculture in southwestern Asia, which was thought to date to somewhat before 4000 B.C. At one swoop, the chronology of early food production from Jarmo and Jericho jumped back in time more than three thousand years. (Current estimates are in the 11,500 B.P. range, obtained from highly refined radiocarbon chronologies based on many samples and on tree-ring calibrations.)

The surprises were not confined to the origins of agriculture. The chronology of the European Neolithic and Bronze Age was pushed back at least a thousand years, overthrowing years of carefully reasoned guesswork based on artifact typologies by Oscar Montelius, Gordon Childe, and others.

Within a few years, it became apparent that radiocarbon dates offered the first opportunity to reconstruct a truly global chronology for the last forty thousand years of human prehistory, from the late Ice Age to as recently as A.D. 1500. It also allowed the comparison of cultural sequences in widely separated parts of the world and the first measurements of the *rates* of cultural change, a critically important consideration.

Radiocarbon dating has been much refined since Libby's day, especially with the use of growth rings from tropical coral and tree-rings, which convert radiocarbon dates into calendar dates—a necessary procedure because of changes in the amount of C14 in the atmosphere. Since the 1980s, accelerator mass spectrometry (AMS) has been used to process samples—a method that uses ionized carbon atoms from the sample to count the number of remaining ions, thereby dating the sample. AMS is not only more accurate, but it can be used on the tiniest of samples, even individual seeds.

New Chapters in Human Evolution

As radiocarbon dating began to transform the chronology of later prehistory, startling new hominid discoveries transformed knowledge of human origins.

It was a blazing hot day at Olduvai Gorge, East Africa, in 1959. Back in camp, Louis Leakey lay in his tent, suffering from a bout of influenza. Meanwhile, Mary Leakey, sheltered by a beach umbrella, was excavating the small scatter of broken bones and crude artifacts deep in the gorge. For hours she brushed and pried away dry soil. Suddenly, she unearthed part of an upper jaw with teeth so humanlike that she took a closer look. Moments later, she jumped into her Land Rover and sped up the track to camp. "Louis, Louis!" she cried, as she burst into their tent. "I've found Dear Boy at last." Louis leapt out of bed, his flu forgotten. Together, they excavated the fragmentary remains of a magnificent robust hominid skull. The Leakeys named it *Zinjanthropus boisei* ("African human of Boise" [now known as *Australopithecus boisei*]), a Mr. Boise being one of their benefactors. With this dramatic discovery, they changed the study of human evolution from a part-time science into an international detective story (Figure 11.2).

Part-time science it had very much been, for the Piltdown discovery had continued to dominate much thinking about human evolution until the 1950s. By then, it was clear that Piltdown was an anomaly. In 1953, British Museum experts finally exposed it as a clever forgery, probably at the hands of its discoverer. By that time, the anatomist Robert Broom had discovered

Figure 11.2   Paleoanthropologist John Robinson,
himself a discoverer of australopithecines in South
Africa, examines the *Zinjanthropus* skull with Louis
Leakey (right).

many more specimens of *Australopithecus,* in both lightly built and robust
forms, known respectively as *Australopithecus africanus* and *Australopithecus
robustus* (Figure 11.3a, b). The eminent biological anthropologist Wilfred Le
Gros Clark traveled to South Africa, examined the Australopithecine fossils,
and proclaimed them to be potential human ancestors. A vindicated
Raymond Dart now resumed work on *Australopithecus,* digging into a fossil-
rich cavern at **Makapansgat** in northern South Africa, where he recovered
large numbers of well-preserved Australopithecine fossils embedded in a
hard, concretelike breccia. He also recovered thousands of what appeared to
be systematically fractured antelope bones. Dart, who was a scholar of
violent passions, soon attributed the fractures to the Australopithecines.
They had used bones as tools and weapons, he proclaimed, as a unique
"osteodontokeratic culture," a culture of bone, teeth, and horn. He implied

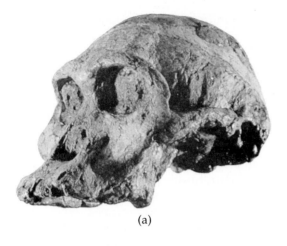

(a)

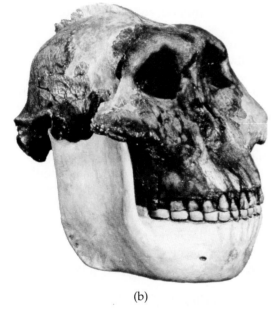

(b)

Figure 11.3
Australopithecines.
(a) *Australopithecus africanus,*
the more gracile form;
(b) *Australopithecus robustus,*
a much heavier form.

that the earliest humans were aggressive and violent. The "osteodontoker-atic culture" did not survive the close scrutiny of zoologist C. K. Brain, who compared the bones to those from carnivore dens. The fractures were identical, and the "osteodontokeratic culture" passed into intellectual oblivion.

Meanwhile, Louis and Mary Leakey had resumed excavations at Olduvai Gorge, on Tanzania's Serengeti Plains, in 1951, after finding a 20-million-year-old primate fossil, *Proconsul africanus,* on **Rusinga Island** in northwestern Lake Victoria, Kenya, in 1948. Between 1951 and 1958, they worked on the five geological beds of the gorge—fine clays and sands laid down by a shallow lake at a time when the surrounding landscape teemed with ani-mals. Instead of systematic collecting, they concentrated on locating ancient "living floors," places where early humans had camped or butchered ani-mals. By 1958, they had recovered large numbers of stone tools and the remains of dozens of extinct animal species, some of them from the locations where the animals were butchered with crude stone choppers and flakes. Except for a few fragmentary hominid teeth, there were no traces of human fossils. Then they unearthed *Zinjanthropus* in 1959. Almost overnight, the Leakeys became international celebrities. They were lauded by the National Geographic Society, which published articles on Olduvai and *Zinjanthropus* while giving them a large research grant for further work.

Louis Leakey estimated that *Zinjanthropus* was about 600,000 years old. He, and the rest of the scientific community, were stunned when two geophysicists from the University of California, Berkeley, used the new potassium-argon dating method for measuring radioactive decay in volcanic rocks to date the *Zinjanthropus* site to 1.75 million years. (Potassium-argon dating can date volcanic rocks millions of years old, whereas radiocarbon dating is limited to the past 40,000 years.) At one stroke, human origins had become twice as old—a far cry from the 4004 B.C. of pre-1859 days!

Mary Leakey now undertook a major excavation of the *Zinjanthropus* site, which she excavated grid square by grid square with meticulous care. All the soil from the site was passed through fine-meshed screens to recover even the smallest rodent bones. From this remarkable excavation, Mary not only recovered thousands of bone fragments and stone tools, but also developed methods for excavating early human sites that are still in use today.

Larger-scale excavations at nearby locations yielded yet more hominid fossils, this time from a slender, more gracile creature, quite different from *Zinjanthropus.* The finds included an almost-complete foot. The South African biological anthropologist Philip Tobias named the new hominid *Homo habilis,* "handy person," the first toolmaking human. In 1960, Louis found a massive skull of an anatomically more advanced human, *Homo erec-tus* (sometimes called *Homo ergaster* in modern classificatory parlance), at a high level in the gorge.

By the 1960s, Mary was bearing the brunt of the field research, living almost full-time at Olduvai Gorge. She wrote the definitive study of the ear-liest human culture in the world, a simple technology of stone choppers and flakes, named the Oldowan, after Olduvai Gorge. Now she was internation-ally recognized as a scientist in her own right, and as a more patient and thor-ough excavator than Louis would ever be. Meanwhile, Louis was always proposing new theories of human origins and becoming interested in research into living primates as a way of better understanding very early human behavior. He sponsored a number of soon-to-be-well-known researchers, among them Jane Goodall, who worked among chimpanzees in Tanzania, and Dian Fossey, who became world famous for her research on mountain gorillas.

Louis Leakey died in London in 1972, just as his son Richard was achieving international fame with new hominid discoveries in the East Turkana area of northern Kenya (see Chapter 12). Meanwhile, Mary worked quietly on the Olduvai artifacts and opened excavations at **Laetoli** in Tanzania in 1978. Here she amazed the world with the discovery of a trail of footprints left by two hominids preserved in hardened volcanic ash dating to 3.6 million years ago (Figure 11.4). "Now this is really something to put on the mantlepiece," she remarked of one particularly nice footprint. This remarkable discovery was the capstone of an archaeological career as illustrious as that of her husband. "The tracks," she wrote, "indicate a rolling and probably slow-moving gait, with the hips swiveling at each step, as opposed to the free-striding gait of modern man" (Leakey and Harris 1990:74).

The Leakeys' spectacular finds revolutionized the study of human origins, coming as they did at a time of growing international involvement in what was now called *paleoanthropology,* the study of early human behavior. With the new potassium-argon dating method, it was possible for the first time to gain a sense of the length and speed of human evolution. The chronology for

Figure 11.4   3.6-million-year-old hominid footprints at Laetoli, Tanzania.

the appearance of the first toolmaking humans had expanded dramatically, from 600,000 years in 1959, to just under 2 million years in 1960, and then out to 2.5 million during the 1970s, when an explosion of research into human origins brought new discoveries and fresh perspectives on very early human ancestry.

Discoveries: Pazyryk, Tollund, and Olsen-Chubbock

The pace of archaeological discovery accelerated during the 1940s and 1950s, a reflection of more funding, expanded graduate training, and an increase in development, road construction, and general industrial activity that exposed many new sites. Much of this research was basic culture history. We can describe only a few of the more exceptional, spectacular finds here.

The Pazyryk Horsemen

The horsemen of **Pazyryk** in Siberia's Altai Mountains provided dramatic confirmation of the preservative properties of deep-frozen soils.

The Russian archaeologist Sergei Rudenko discovered a group of five large and nine small burial mounds at Pazyryk in 1924. After a preliminary dig in 1929, he returned for large-scale research in 1948–1949. The mounds, erected in about 400 B.C., were covered with stones, with the largest mound measuring between 36 and 46 meters (119 and 152 feet) in diameter. Each covered a central tomb shaft between 4 and 5 meters (13 and 16 feet 5 inches) deep. The shafts were dug during the summer, deep into partially thawed ground. The mourners built long boxlike timber chambers inside them for the burials and grave furniture. Once the mounds were completed, moisture and condensation permeated the corpses and grave goods, which froze solid during the subsequent winter. The mounds insulated the sepulchers and kept them from thawing, preserving them in ice for more than two thousand years. Only the depredations of grave robbers disturbed the tombs, but spectacular finds remained.

The Mound 2 burial was the best preserved, its wooden chamber lined with felt wall hangings. The embalmed bodies of a man and a woman lay in a hollowed-out wooden coffin adorned with cut-out leather silhouettes of deer. The man's body bore intricate tattoos of imaginary and real animals. Clothing and textiles, leather items, and wooden furniture accompanied the dead. Between 7 and 14 horses complete with their elaborate harnesses lay in the tombs, set aside from the main burial chamber. One horse burial included a four-wheeled cart with a felt canopy.

The Pazyryk people were consummate horse riders, who wandered over vast tracts of Central Asia. The styles of their textiles and silks show that they had contact with China and Persia.

Tollund and the Bog People

Scandinavian archaeologists had always been interested in wet sites, in locations where organic remains were well preserved. Peat was a staple for winter fuel, so peat-cutting operations probed many wet areas that had lain undisturbed since prehistoric times. For centuries, peat diggers had unearthed wooden artifacts, the remains of fishing nets, and other organic finds, including even dugout canoes. In 1950, two men digging peat for winter fuel at **Tollund** in the Jutland area of Denmark stumbled across a corpse. Thinking that they had discovered a murder victim, they reported their find to the police. Fortunately, the authorities were aware of other bog bodies and called in local archaeologists. They in turn alerted Peter Glob, archaeologist at the University of Aarhus, who was an authority on such discoveries. He found himself looking at a man's body lying on its side, the face bearing a peaceful expression, the eyes lightly closed (Figure 11.5). On his head the dead man wore a pointed skin cap fastened securely under the chin by a hide

Figure 11.5
Tollund Man.

thong. The man was otherwise naked except for a smooth hide belt, his hair cropped short, a short stubble on chin and upper lips.

When Glob removed a small lump of peat from beside the man's head, a rope made of two twisted leather thongs came to light, encircling the victim's throat in a tight noose, the end lying behind the back. Glob lifted the entire body in its original peat matrix, a laborious task that had to be completed by hand, as the ground was too soft for a crane. One of the helpers collapsed of a heart attack and died. Back in the laboratory, the long task of reconstructing the victim's medical history began. Thanks to the acidic soil, the body was exceptionally well preserved, especially the head. An autopsy showed that Tollund Man had been hanged. His intestines contained the remains of his last meal, probably a thin gruel made from barley, linseed, and other seeds and cultivation weeds, consumed between 12 and 24 hours before his death.

Archaeological and medical science have advanced a long way since Tollund Man was discovered, but his head remains one of the best preserved and most haunting images of the past. This important discovery emphasized the potential for detailed study of ancient human remains, which has come full circle with the discovery of frozen people in the North American Arctic and with the sensational finding of the Ice Man in the Italian Alps in 1991 (see Chapter 13).

Olsen-Chubbock: A Paleo-Indian Bison Kill

When Joe Ben Wheat of the University of Colorado investigated bison bones eroding from a filled gully at **Olsen-Chubbock,** 26 kilometers (16 miles) southeast of Kit Carson, Colorado, he discovered the remains of a long-forgotten bison kill from about 6500 B.C. The subsequent excavations ushered in the modern era of investigating such hunting sites and set new standards for the study of the animals killed in the hunt.

With meticulous care, he uncovered the jumble of closely packed bison bones from the ancient arroyo (dry gully). He discovered that the Paleo-Indians had located a large bison herd and had stampeded the beasts into a dry gully. The leading animals had teetered at the edge, but were driven into the narrow defile by the sheer weight of the panicked animals behind them. About 157 beasts were immobilized and trampled to death; the rest were speared as they flailed around helplessly. Given Joe Ben Wheat's reasonable assumption that hunters had approached the herd from downwind, the direction of the skeletons suggested that the wind had been blowing from the south on the day of the hunt (Figure 11.6).

Months of analysis reconstructed the butchery that had followed. First the hunters maneuvered the carcasses into a position on their bellies where they could be cut up at the edge of the arroyo. The bison wedged in the gully were cut up where they lay. The butchers worked in teams, systematically, first removing the hide and stripping it down the animal's sides, so that the flesh

Figure 11.6
The excavated bison bed at
Olsen-Chubbock, Colorado.

could be piled on it. In the course of several days, the Olsen-Chubbock hunters butchered 75 percent of the animals they killed. Wheat estimated that they acquired about 24,752 kilograms (54,560 pounds) of meat in the process. They also obtained 2,449 kilograms (5,400 pounds) of fat and 1,812 kilograms (4,000 pounds) of edible internal organs. Much of the flesh and fat must have been pounded into pemmican, the food that the people consumed on the march.

Large kill sites like Olsen-Chubbock are a rarity, perhaps events that unfolded once a generation or so. Wheat's careful and imaginative excavation set new standards and showed the great potential of animal bones for studying ancient subsistence, a major preoccupation of the 1960s.

The 1950s saw much remarkable fieldwork in western North America. Among the excavations were a series of large-scale cave and rock-shelter excavations in the Great Basin, including the Hogup and Lovelock caves with their remarkable organic finds that showed how the inhabitants exploited local lakes and wetlands.

A Global Prehistory

Until well into the 1930s, most archaeology focused on the eastern Mediterranean and Europe, North America, and Mesoamerica. With only a handful of university archaeology departments, this was hardly surprising.

The Department of Archaeology at Cambridge University was almost unique in having a long tradition of teaching prehistory on a somewhat broader canvas, partly in response to a steady stream of students destined for the Colonial Service who passed through its courses. The perspective of international archaeology dated back to the 1920s, with a visit by the Stone Age archaeologist Miles Burkitt to South Africa, and to Louis Leakey's researches in Kenya (see Chapter 9). The eclectic interests of Ellis Minns, a Russian specialist, also came into play. The greatest agent of internationalism was Dorothy Garrod, who was elected to the Disney Professorship of Archaeology in 1939.

Dorothy Garrod, Mount Carmel, and World Prehistory

Dorothy Garrod (1892–1968) was a quiet, self-effacing person, but an extremely competent Stone Age archaeologist. She was elected to the Disney Professorship at a time when it was almost unheard-of for women to hold chairs in British universities. After digging a Neanderthal cave in Gibraltar and looking for Stone Age sites in Iraq in the 1920s and early 1930s, she traveled to the eastern Mediterranean coast, where she found promising caves at Mount Carmel in what is now Israel. These, she realized, were the sites that would yield a sequence of changing Stone Age cultures potentially as rich as that from southwestern France. Between 1929 and 1934, she excavated the **Mount Carmel** caves with the assistance of American biological anthropologist Theodore McCown, an expert on human remains. Garrod and McCown excavated three caves, one of which, appropriately dug by McCown, contained Neanderthal skeletons. The excavations at Mugharet el-Wad, et-Tabun, and es-Skhul rank among the most important archaeological investigations of the twentieth century.

Garrod worked miracles with a small team of colleagues and local workers. She uncovered deep layers of human occupation, extending far back into the Ice Age. The finds were very different from those in western European caves, where tools made on fine blades followed simpler, Neanderthal artifacts. Everything was more complicated at Mount Carmel. Instead of a simple progression from crude spear points and scraping tools to fine blade artifacts, the Neanderthal levels also contained levels of fine blades and scrapers. These artifacts were virtually identical to those made by Cro-Magnons in Europe many thousands of years later. Most archaeologists had assumed that modern people and their fine stone technology had first evolved in Europe, then spread elsewhere. The Mount Carmel discoveries turned everything on its head. Now the earliest blade technology, thought to be the work of modern humans, appeared in southwestern Asia, as if *Homo sapiens sapiens* had first evolved there, then spread into Europe.

The European Neanderthals were short people, with receding foreheads, prominent jaws, flat noses, and massive bone brow ridges over their eye sockets. When Garrod excavated es-Skhul cave at Mount Carmel, she found a series of burials, where the dead showed a remarkable mix of thick Neanderthal bones and compact limbs combined with such traits as high foreheads and reduced brow ridges that are more typical of modern humans. The Mount Carmel Neanderthals were anatomically more advanced than their European contemporaries.

In 1936, Dorothy Garrod gave an address to the British Association for the Advancement of Science, in which she proclaimed that the distinctive culture of the Cro-Magnons had originated not in Europe, but in southwestern Asia, whence modern humans had spread north and westward. At the time, her address caused a stir, especially among those who believed that modern humans had originated in western Europe. Garrod was one of the first prehistoric archaeologists to look at human prehistory from a global perspective— to argue that the story of early humanity could not be understood from Europe alone.

The publication of the first volume of *The Stone Age of Mount Carmel* in 1937 established Garrod as a prehistorian of the first rank. Unfortunately, World War II broke her tenure at Cambridge. She served in the Royal Air Force aerial photography interpretation unit. After the war, she devoted much energy to expanding degree programs in prehistoric archaeology at Cambridge, insisting that a course on world prehistory be introduced into what had previously been a somewhat narrow curriculum. But her heart was not in the administrative and committee work expected of a university professor. Nor was she comfortable in a predominantly male academic environment. She took early retirement in 1952 and moved to France, where she resumed fieldwork on Stone Age caves. Garrod's legacy was not only Mount Carmel, but the first stirrings of a truly global prehistory.

Grahame Clark's *World Prehistory*

Grahame Clark of Star Carr fame joined the Cambridge department in 1936 and remained there for his entire career. He was elected to the Disney Professorship in 1953, just as radiocarbon dates were becoming more commonplace. Clark also assumed the chair at a time when archaeology was beginning to expand from the size of a mere family into a large international community. He himself was an ardent internationalist, partly because he was editor of the *Proceedings of the Prehistoric Society*, a journal in which he insisted on publishing archaeological research from as far afield as Australia. He also trained a small number of students who worked in Africa before World War II.

Archaeology was expanding, but mainly outside the narrow confines of Britain. From the mid-1950s, Clark encouraged a steady stream of young Cambridge graduates to pursue archaeological careers overseas, among them the Australian archaeologist John Mulvaney and the African prehistorian Ray Inskeep. At the same time, his own intellectual interests widened to encompass the broad ebbs and flows of human prehistory. Just over a decade after the first announcement of radiocarbon dating, Grahame Clark wrote the first synthesis of human prehistory based on radiocarbon chronologies, and also on potassium-argon dates for early hominid evolution.

Clark's book, *World Prehistory*, published in 1961, was a descriptive work, based on culture histories and radiocarbon dates from all parts of the world. The book was very incomplete, biased heavily in favor of Europe and the eastern Mediterranean, along with the better-known parts of the Americas, but it was a first attempt at a truly global synthesis. Grahame Clark was to produce two later editions, which benefited greatly from his extensive travels, especially in Asia, North America, Australia, and New Zealand, but he never attempted much explanation of the past. This was very much Clark's style, for he was, above all, an environmental archaeologist. But the book had a great influence on contemporary archaeological thinking about prehistory and was widely used as a basic textbook, especially by Clark's own students, who worked in many parts of the world.

By the mid-1960s, Cambridge-trained archaeologists were working in Australia and New Zealand, in tropical Africa, in India, and in other parts of the world, bringing ecological approaches and other then-cutting-edge perspectives to archaeologically unknown parts of the world. By the time Clark retired from the Disney chair in 1974, he had ensured that world prehistory was a truly global enterprise. Of course, he did not do this by himself; but his broad, often magisterial perspective encouraged young archaeologists to take risks, to work in areas where no one had been in the field before, and to carve out unusual careers far from the familiar enclaves of Cambridge, Oxford, London, or Edinburgh. One of Clark's most prized possessions is said to have been a map adorned with colored pins marking the locations where his former students worked, which he published in a semiautobiographical work, *Archaeology at Cambridge and Beyond*, in 1979.

At the same time that Clark was fostering international research and training archaeologists who became professionals without obtaining doctorates, American prehistoric archaeologists were beginning to look overseas, following the lead of Harvard University's Peabody Museum in the 1930s. Robert Braidwood of the University of Chicago's Oriental Institute was one of the pioneers, working at Jarmo and on the hilly flanks of the Fertile Crescent with a multidisciplinary team in the late 1950s. The federal government's National Science Foundation actively encouraged overseas research with its expanded grant programs, so an increasing number of young American archaeologists became involved with research in distant lands, often including early hominid sites in eastern Africa and in eastern Mediterranean lands. What began as a trickle has now become a flood, especially in well-trodden areas like the Maya lowlands and the Andes, where American scholars have worked steadily since before World War II.

By 1960, world prehistory was a well-established idea, fostered not only by Grahame Clark and other internationally minded scholars, but also by a rapid expansion of job opportunities both in North America and Europe, as well as in the non-Western world. But for the most part, archaeology was still largely an increasingly sophisticated form of culture history, concerned, nay obsessed, with the description of a well-ordered past defined by artifacts and cultural sequences. Despite the pioneering work of Grahame Clark, Julian Steward, Gordon Willey, and others, both ecological and settlement archaeology on any scale lay in the future. Before the new approaches took hold, new theoretical paradigms were needed, which duly appeared in the ferment of the 1960s and are described in Chapter 12.

Salvage Archaeology

Many diverse strands of archaeology came together in the late 1950s, among them a growing concern over the destruction of archaeological sites by highway construction, hydroelectric schemes, deep plowing, and urban expansion. This concern slowly evolved into what was called "salvage archaeology," the ancestor of today's cultural resource management. The same concerns generated a jigsaw pattern of complicated legislation that was the foundation for the even more complex cultural resource management laws of today. All post–World War II legislation built on the Historic Sites Act of 1935, which gave the National Park Service a broad mandate to identify, protect, and preserve cultural properties of all kinds, including archaeological sites. It also meant that the federal government acknowledged broad responsibility for archaeological and historic sites on and off federally owned land.

The Reservoir Salvage Act of 1960 authorized archaeologists to dig at salvage sites that were in danger of destruction. It was a last-minute measure passed as major dams threatened western sites in particular, but it did make possible some important surveys, among them the Navajo Reservoir Survey in New Mexico, which flooded 88 square kilometers (34 square miles). The area was surveyed before flooding by jeep and on foot. The archaeologists inventoried as many sites as possible, but were never asked to recommend ways of saving sites. Nor were they consulted about the siting of the water project, so that archaeological factors could be taken into account.

The Glen Canyon Survey spanned the Upper Colorado River in Utah and Arizona, covering the vast area that was eventually flooded by Lake Powell. Here the archaeologists had more time. They made a total sampling of all cultures and periods in the area their first priority. The research team placed great emphasis on accurate records and publication of their results, for no one would be able to check their results in the field later. The project was a success archaeologically, but here again the archaeologists were not expected to make recommendations about the management of threatened archaeological sites.

More comprehensive legislation took effect during the mid-1960s, which set up a national framework for historic preservation and took the first steps toward integrating archaeological sites into government land use planning. Numerous state, local, and tribal laws also came into effect, which further protected archaeological sites in the United States. Broadly similar legislation came into being in many other countries after 1960, as global consciousness of the rapid destruction of the archaeological record came into sharper focus.

Crude as it often was, salvage archaeology laid the foundations for the highly professional, elaborate cultural resource management (CRM) of today. Cultural resource management under various labels now represents most archaeological fieldwork in many parts of the world. Mandated by antiquities legislation, CRM involves the conservation and management of artifacts and archaeological sites as a means of protecting the finite record of the past. As such, it can involve survey, excavation, and especially recommendations to mitigate the potential destruction of the archaeological record by industrial and other activity.

Summary

Chapter 11 describes developments in archaeology during the 1940s and 1950s. There was widespread dissatisfaction with the narrow perspective of culture history that was widespread in archaeology before 1960. Walter Taylor's *A Study of Archaeology* (1948) argued for a "conjunctive approach," which involved more scientific excavation and artifact analysis, as well as ethnographic analogy and environmental reconstruction. Taylor, like Julian Steward, called for multidisciplinary field research, such as was practiced by Robert Braidwood at Jarmo in Iraq; by Kathleen Kenyon at Jericho, Jordan; and by Richard MacNeish in Mexico's Tehuacán Valley. At the same time, radiocarbon dating, announced by J. R. Arnold and Willard Libby in 1949, began to revolutionize the chronology of later prehistory. The new dating method made possible the first truly global archaeological chronologies, permitting studies of the rate of cultural change in different parts of the world.

Meanwhile, major advances in the study of human origins culminated in the Leakeys' discovery of *Zinjanthropus boisei* at Olduvai Gorge, Tanzania, in 1959, followed by the Laetoli footprints, also from Tanzania. These discoveries, and potassium-argon dating, extended the date of human origins back to at least 2 million years. The 1940s and 1950s witnessed many other important discoveries, among them the spectacular burials of the horsemen of Pazyryk, Siberia; Tollund Man and other bog bodies in Denmark; and the Olsen-Chubbock Paleo-Indian bison kill.

Radiocarbon dating, and a steady stream of archaeologists working in remote parts of the world, allowed the development of a truly global prehistory of humankind. Dorothy Garrod was one of the first archaeologists to teach world prehistory, and she introduced a course of that title at Cambridge University after World War II. The first synthesis came in Grahame Clark's *World Prehistory,* published in 1961. At the same time, Clark trained an entire generation of archaeologists who left Europe to work in distant parts of the world, including tropical Africa, Australia, and New Zealand.

The years after World War II saw accelerating destruction of archaeological sites by deep-plow agriculture, hydroelectric dams, and other industrial activities. A patchwork of federal legislation tried to define the problem. The Reservoir Salvage Act of 1960 saw the first attempts at large archaeological surveys in threatened areas, notably the Glen Canyon project in the Colorado River region. These early attempts at salvage archaeology were the precursors of the cultural resource management of today.

Guide to Further Reading

Clark, Grahame. 1961. *World Prehistory.* Cambridge: Cambridge University Press.

The first synthesis of its kind. Compare this with a contemporary world prehistory volume and you will get some idea of how much archaeology has changed (for the better).

———. 1979. *Archaeology at Cambridge and Beyond.* Cambridge: Cambridge University Press.

Clark describes the evolution of the Cambridge department and the great diaspora of archaeologists he trained.

Glob, Peter. 1969. *The Bog People.* London: Faber and Faber.

A nicely written account of the discovery of the Tollund corpse and other bog bodies.

Libby, Willard F. 1955. *Radiocarbon Dating.* Chicago: University of Chicago Press.

Libby's own account of the revolutionary new dating method.

Rudenko, Sergei. 1970. *Frozen Tombs of Siberia: The Pazyryk Burials of Iron Age Horsemen.* Trans. by M. W. Thompson. Berkeley: University of California Press.

The classic account of the Pazyryk finds. Lavishly illustrated.

Taylor, W. W. 1948. *A Study of Archaeology.* Menasha, WI: American Anthropological Association.

The book that everyone, or almost everyone, hated. A fascinating insight into the archaeology of a half century ago.

Wheat, Joe Ben. 1972. *The Olsen-Chubbock Site: A Paleo-Indian Bison Kill.* Washington, D.C.: Smithsonian Institution and the Society for American Archaeology.

An exemplary monograph, one of the best of its day.

chapter 12

The "New Archaeology"?

The ultimate in cultural resource management. The excavation that preceded the restoration of King Henry VIII's Privy Garden at Hampton Court, England, showed the outlines of flower beds and other features.

As I was riding on the bus not long ago, an elderly gentleman asked me what I did. I told him I was an archaeologist. He replied: "That must be wonderful, for the only thing you have to be to succeed is lucky." It took some time to convince him that his view of archaeology was not mine.

Lewis R. Binford, *In Pursuit of the Past*, 1983 (p. 19)

chapter outline

Cultural evolution had long been out of favor in archaeological circles, until there was a revival of interest in the subject during the 1950s and 1960s. The new evolutionary theories exercised a profound influence on a new wave of archaeological theory that developed during the 1960s and 1970s. The new interest in evolution was part of an intense theoretical ferment, a seeming change in archaeological direction that became known, erroneously, as the "new archaeology." Today, it is more commonly known as "processual archaeology," the subject of this chapter.

Multilinear Evolution

In Chapter 4, we described the unilinear evolution theories of nineteenth-century anthropologists, which had humanity passing through several universal stages. We showed how this simplistic perspective on the past soon collapsed in the face of more comprehensive anthropological data, to the point where evolutionary thinking was discredited for several generations.

Multilinear evolution, often called neo-evolution, was largely developed by two influential ethnologists, Leslie White (1900–1975) and Julian Steward, the father of cultural ecology, whose work was described in Chapter 10. White, an anthropologist at the University of Michigan, was an ardent foe of Boas's historical particularism and offered instead a concept he called "general evolution," an assumption that progress was characteristic of human cultures in general.

To White, a culture was an elaborate thermodynamic system, which evolved to serve its own needs. Cultural systems included many components, some of them technological and economic, others social and ideological. "Social systems are determined by technological systems," he wrote.

"Philosophies and the arts express experience as it is defined by technology and refracted by social systems" (White 1949:390–391). White paid little or no attention to environmental factors. Nor did he consider the impact of one culture on another. He was interested in the most advanced cultures of each successive period of the past, arguing that, in the long term, cultures that failed to keep abreast of developments were superseded or absorbed by more progressive ones.

Leslie White can be called a "technological determinist," for he gave primacy to the relationship between technology and society, at the expense of other relationships. In the context of a world where technological advances and space travel were dominant themes in daily life, this is hardly surprising. White's favored treatment of technology reminded some observers of the European prehistorian Oscar Montelius, who had argued that technology changed because of a human desire to control nature more effectively (see Chapter 7).

Julian Steward championed a much more sophisticated formulation, in which the environment was a major factor in culture change. He assumed that there were significant regularities in cultural development. Ecological adaptation fashioned the limits of variation in cultural systems. Steward believed in comparative studies on a global basis as a way of studying the different ways in which human cultures had developed in different kinds of environments—on the assumption that they would assume much the same forms and follow similar paths of development in broadly similar environments. This was Steward's "cultural core," already described in Chapter 10—economic, political, and religious patterns that were most closely tied to subsistence activities and could be assumed to have major adaptive significance. Steward argued that multilinear evolution should be used to explain the common features of human cultures at similar levels of development. These stood in contrast to unique features that were the result of historical accident.

There were profound differences between Steward and White's approaches to cultural evolution, which were mediated by anthropologists Marshall Sahlins and Elman Service, also faculty members at the University of Michigan. They distinguished between general evolution concerned with progress, and specific evolution that was a product of environmental adaptation. For all their efforts to disassociate cultural evolution from notions of human progress, both of them used ethnographic data to develop speculative general stages of human cultural evolution, as did another anthropologist, Morton Fried. They proposed a generalized scheme of bands, tribes, chiefdoms, and states—a four-part subdivision of human societies, ancient and modern, that assumed that technologically more advanced societies were endowed with greater selective fitness. Thus, progress was a distinctive characteristic of culture change and a general feature of human history. Still another anthropologist, Marvin Harris, argued that cultural systems were shaped by a variety of material factors, among them technology, economic relations, and the relative costs of different strategies for survival. Harris's materialist approach tried to explain such phenomena as food taboos, religious beliefs, and so on in terms of their relationships to basic economic realities.

All of this seems like a throwback to the evolutionary schemes of yesteryear, except that the protagonists espoused very different causes. White placed technology at the center of evolutionary theory. Steward stressed ecological factors, Harris broader economic causes. All of them considered human behavior to be shaped almost entirely by nonhuman constraints. Such perspectives contrasted sharply with Marxist approaches, in which humanly arranged relations of production in the economic base determine social change.

Multilinear evolution attracted many American archaeologists because of its emphasis on general regularities in human culture. Furthermore, many of these regularities were easily reconstructed from archaeological data— information on technology and subsistence, for example. Only a few archaeologists criticized the new approach as encouraging simplistic explanations of the past and inhibiting alternative approaches.

By 1960, a growing interest in ecology and settlement archaeology was finally permeating archaeological circles on both sides of the Atlantic. At last, archaeology was moving away from a concern, nay obsession, with archaeological cultures as merely collections of different artifact types, each of which had profound significance. A paper by the midwestern archaeologist Joseph Caldwell, "The New American Archaeology," appeared in the influential pages of the journal *Science* in 1959. Caldwell pointed out that archaeological cultures should be thought of as cultural systems, and that the primary goal of archaeology was not to describe cultures made up of artifacts, but to explain changes in archaeological cultures in terms of processes of culture change. His paper stemmed not only from the new interest in ecology and subsistence, but also from the interest in multilinear evolution, which provided a conceptual framework for examining cultural regularities through time.

Caldwell's article was symptomatic of emerging changes in American archaeology that resulted not only from anthropological researches, but also from fine examples of ecological archaeology like Star Carr, the multidisciplinary work of Robert Braidwood and others in southwestern Asia, and Gordon Willey's Virú Valley research in coastal Peru. All of this came together in a powerful new synthesis, popularized in large part by a young University of Michigan archaeologist, Lewis Binford, who, more than anyone else, was responsible for the intellectual ferment that swept archaeology in the 1960s.

Processual Archaeology: Cultural Systems and Cultural Process

The 1960s were a decade of controversy and social unrest, of sweeping changes in Western society as well as controversies over the Vietnam War. The heady feeling of change and unease also swept over an archaeology that had long been enmired in conservative ways. There was already disillusionment and discontent, already some questioning of the status quo. What was needed was a prophet, an eloquent advocate for a new generation of research. The articulate and charismatic Lewis Binford (1929–) was the anointed.

Binford was (and still is) a persuasive speaker, with a gift for polemic. He had a remarkable training. At the University of Michigan, he came under the influence of Leslie White; Albert Spaulding, an expert in the emerging field of statistical analysis in archaeology; and James Griffin, a leading culture historian and an expert in a modified form of the Midwest Taxonomic System. Griffin taught Binford basic artifact and descriptive archaeology. Spaulding introduced him to statistical techniques for handling specific problems, relationships between different sites, artifact clusters, and cultures. Leslie White exposed Binford to logic and explicit assumptions, and urged him to steep himself in the philosophy of science. As a result, Binford read the works of the influential philosopher of science Carl Hempel, who dealt with epistemological issues (how we know and how we know what happened). Hempel argued that statements of explanation in science are closely related to statements of prediction. Thus, if archaeologists seek to explain the past, set up their discipline as a science, and produce lawful generalizations, they will be able to use their scientific explanations both to explain contemporary events and to predict future ones. Hempel's deducto-nomological approach involved the science of general laws (nomology), and working from the general to the particular (deduction).

All this background had a powerful effect on the young archaeologist. Binford himself later wrote, in a highly personal account of his intellectual development: "Theory became a meaningful word. Culture was not some ethereal force, it was a material system of interrelated parts understandable as an organization that could be recovered from the past, given the language to be learned from Spaulding. We were searching for laws. Laws are timeless and spaceless; they must be equally valid for the ethnographic data as well as the archaeological data. Ethnology and archaeology were not separated by a wide, unbridgeable gap" (Binford 1972:8). During his graduate years, Binford realized that Walter Taylor's critique of archaeology a decade earlier had been fundamentally sound. For their part, White and Spaulding had developed limited approaches that, combined, might provide some meaning for the descriptive monographs of hundreds of archaeological sites. It remained for someone to pull all this together. "I was going to be the Huxley, the mouthpiece," declared Binford (1972:25) with characteristic zest.

A "New" Approach

A mouthpiece Binford became. He outlined the program for a "new" archaeology in two now-classic papers: "Archaeology as Anthropology" (1962) and "Archaeological Systematics and the Study of Culture Process" (1965), both published in *American Antiquity*. He advocated more rigorous scientific testing in archaeology, arguing that statements about the historical or functional significance of the archaeological record or about culture change had previously been evaluated by according to how far back our knowledge of contemporary peoples could be projected onto prehistoric contexts and according to our judgment of the professional competence and honesty of the archaeologists interpreting the past. Simple induction had been used for inferences about the archaeological record, with guidance from ethnographic data and experiments with ancient technologies. Binford argued that, although induction and inference are perfectly sound methods for understanding the past, independent methods of testing propositions about the past must be developed and must be far more rigorous than time-honored value judgments arrived at by assessing professional competence.

Binford was also emphatic that archaeology's goal was the same as that of anthropology—to explain the full range of, and differences in, cultural behavior. Archaeological data was useful for studying cultural changes over long periods of time. He agreed with Leslie White that there were strong regularities in human behavior, so there was little difference between explaining a single example of social change and a whole group of such changes. In other words, one's main concern was to account for cultural similarities rather than differences.

Like Grahame Clark, Binford thought of human cultures as humanity's extrasomatic (external to the body) means of adaptation. Changes in cultural systems and their subsystems were adaptive responses either to shifts in the natural environment or to alterations in competing or neighboring cultural systems. Under this approach, cultural systems tended toward equilibrium, changes in them being induced by external, often noncultural factors.

Binford and his rapidly increasing numbers of supporters also challenged the assumption that the archaeological record's incompleteness precluded reliable interpretation of the nonmaterial, and perishable, components of ancient cultures and societies. All artifacts found in an archaeological site had functioned within a culture and society at the mercy of such transient factors as fashion or decorative style, each of which had, in itself, a history of acceptance, use, and rejection within the society. The artifacts found in sites were far more than material items that functioned in the society without reference to the many often intangible variables determining the form of the surviving objects. "Data relevant to most, if not all, the components of past sociocultural systems *are* preserved in the archaeological record," Binford wrote (1968:22). Thus, the archaeologist's task was to devise methods for extracting information that deals with *all* determinants operating within the culture or society under study.

Using this type of scientific approach, involving interaction among previous data, new ideas, and new data, a research problem was approached from a collection of observable data that enabled one to pose research hypotheses about the reasons for the observations made from the data. The general problems could be concerned with changes like the shift from hunting and gathering to farming in southwestern Asia, or with cultural relationships between neighboring, and quite different, cultures.

Working hypotheses were nothing new in science, and had been used unconsciously in archaeology for years. Now Binford proposed the use of explicit research strategies based on verifying propositions by testing hypotheses. These propositions in turn raised others, also subject to proof or disproof. Once an accepted and tested proposition was confirmed, it joined a body of reliable knowledge upon which further hypotheses could be erected, and so on.

More rigor, a greater focus on explaining processes of culture change, the notion of cultural systems as part of much larger systems: Binford's "new" archaeology caused immediate controversy and discussion in the staid and comfortable world of North American archaeology. The theoretical furor that erupted pitched culture historians against a new generation of mostly younger archaeologists, who felt that many previous archaeological interpretations were unscientific. A whole new generation of graduate students began efforts to develop a more scientific approach to the past that would employ normal scientific procedures in analyzing archaeological data with the objective of attempting explanation as well as description. They were trying their hardest to explain culture change by testing hypotheses generated by evolutionary theory, tested by the logical procedures of scientific method.

Middle-Range Theory and Ethnoarchaeology

Binford wrote about "decoding the past," bridging the relationship between present and ancient times. In one of his notebooks, he wrote: "The archaeological record is contemporary; it exists with me today and any observation I make about it is a contemporary observation" (1983:111). How could one make inferences about the past without knowing the "necessary and determinant linkages between dynamic causes and static consequences"? The dynamic elements of the past were long gone. He coined the term *middle-range theory,* a label already used in sociology, to characterize this search for accurate means of identifying and measuring specified properties in past cultural systems. "We are looking for 'Rosetta stones' that permit the accurate conversion from observation on statics to statement on dynamics" (1981:3).

Middle-range theory assumed that the archaeological record is a static contemporary phenomenon preserved in structured arrangements of matter. This static condition was achieved once energy ceased to power a cultural system preserved in the archaeological record. Thus, the contents of the archaeological record are a complex mechanical system, created both by long-dead human interaction and by subsequent mechanical forces, what are often called *site formation processes.* The new body of theory was developed to comprehend the relationship between the static, material properties common to both past and present, and the long-extinct dynamic properties of the past.

This new body of theory was often described as "actualistic," because it studied the coincidence of both the static and the dynamic in cultural systems in the only time frame in which it can be achieved—in the present. Middle-range theory was designed to be tested with living cultural systems, and to provide the conceptual tools for explaining artifact patterns and other material phenomena from the archaeological record.

Middle-range theory attracted considerable debate. For instance, another archaeologist, Michael Schiffer, argued that far from studying a static and material archaeological record, archaeology examines the relationship between human behavior and material culture in all times and places. Three decades after Binford formulated it, middle-range theory has become a useful way of mediating between the past and the present, largely because of ethnoarchaeology—the study of living societies as a way of understanding and interpreting the archaeological record. Again, Binford was a leader. He pointed out that explanations of variability among preindustrial peoples would, increasingly, have to be generated from archaeological research, for archaeology would be the only form of anthropology to seek such explanations. For this reason, he himself embarked on a major study of the Nunamiut caribou hunters of Alaska, designed specifically to study butchering practices and other material aspects of the hunt as a basis for study of ancient animal bones and subsistence practices. *Nunamiut Ethnoarchaeology* (1978) has become a fundamental source on the subject.

Binford's evangelical style attracted many younger archaeologists, who came to believe that archaeologists could study any problem that ethnologists could, and furthermore could do so over long periods of time in the past. This was a far more exciting goal than the artifact-centered culture history that they encountered on every side. Binford was not alone in his thinking. Early in the 1960s, British archaeologist David Clarke wrote a monumental critique of prehistoric archaeology, arguing for more explicit scientific methods, greater rigor, and a body of theory to replace "the murky exhalation that represents theory in archaeology." Clarke's *Analytical Archaeology*, published in 1968, greatly influenced European archaeologists, but unfortunately its author died before reaching the peak of his career.

Reaction and Legacy

The emphasis on systems theory, scientific method, and new approaches to ecology changed archaeological research profoundly in the 1960s and 1970s. The result was a state of theoretical meltdown, in which practically every familiar theory in archaeology was challenged and challenged again. Much of the debate was about archaeology's goals; some argued that it was a science, whose objective was to study basic laws of human behavior. But most archaeologists viewed archaeology as examining the activities of past human beings—as less a science than a historical discipline with its own limitations, resources, and explanatory methods. This general viewpoint has prevailed.

The fervor of debate and controversy abated somewhat during the 1970s, by which time many basic tenets put forward by Lewis Binford were widely accepted. This was not necessarily because Binford's ideas were revolutionary; many of them were foreshadowed in the two decades before he wrote his seminal papers. The scientific method came into widespread use; research designs were much more sophisticated and explicit than a generation earlier; notions of cultural and environmental systems were commonplace. The much heralded "new archaeology" was not new at all, but it was a significant advance on the largely descriptive science of the 1930s to 1950s. As the basic principles enumerated by Binford took hold, they coincided with the introduction of complex mathematical models, statistical approaches, and the digital computer, capable of handling and manipulating enormous quantities of raw data. These developments coincided with the emergence of cultural resource management as a major factor in archaeological research in North America and elsewhere. The taut, scientific approach of the "new" archaeology, with its insistence on research design and hypothesis testing, made a good fit with the compliance with legal requirements of CRM projects. Several major ventures such as the Cache River Project in Arkansas, a large scale survey program that used formal sampling methods, reflected the close interplay between the principles of processual archaeology and CRM, an interplay that continues to this day.

The 1960s and 1970s also witnessed a move away from site-oriented archaeology to a much greater concern with regional surveys and settlement archaeology. The shift was due in part to an increasing interest in relationships between ancient societies and the natural environment, and also in trade and exchange and other aspects of ancient society that had often been neglected in earlier generations. Aerial photography, satellite imagery, and rudimentary ground-penetrating radar came into quite widespread use. The growing importance of cultural resource management also contributed to a change in emphasis from destructive excavation to nonintrusive archaeology—archaeology that did not disturb the archaeological record.

Despite all these advances, there was also frustration, for many of the rich theoretical expectations of the 1960s remained unfulfilled. The achievements of archaeology during the 1960s and 1970s were impressive—among them an explosion in raw data and widespread use of statistical methods and computers to manipulate it, and a new emphasis on regional surveys. For example, the large-scale Basin of Mexico Survey carried out by William Sanders and others from Pennsylvania State University during the 1970s chronicled thousands of sites from Aztec times more than a thousand years into the past. Ecological theory and human ecology themselves became fundamental parts of archaeology, as more archaeologists became specialists in ancient animal bones and in ethnobotany—the study of plant remains. Ethnobotany received a strong boost from the development, in the Midwest during the late 1960s, of flotation as a way of recovering even tiny seeds.

Research by Kent Flannery and Joyce Marcus in the Valley of Oaxaca, Mexico, was a classic example of the intelligent application of systems, and especially of ecological approaches to archaeology. During these researches, Flannery excavated Guilá Naquitz cave, which provided a portrait of hunter-gatherers and, later, cultivators living in a semiarid environment, where scheduling of seasonal activities was all-important. Marcus, Flannery, and their students carried out important surveys and excavations in the Valley, in which they studied the increasing complexity of local society and the emergence of large communities and settlement hierarchies. Flannery, who is a gifted writer, immortalized some of the approaches used by his researchers in his edited volume, *The Early Mesoamerican Village* (1976), which featured not only serious papers on the fieldwork, but also a fictional dialogue between archaeologists of various persuasions, which put the theoretical furor of the day in a much broader perspective. Few publications better epitomize the atmosphere of archaeological research in the early days of the "new archaeology."

The legacy of these advances, and of an explosion in the number of professional archaeologists after 1960, was an increasing specialization within archaeology. The new technologies applied to the past required, and still require, researchers with the expertise to develop and use them. A proliferation of doctoral programs also contributed to the specialization, for those who taught in them tended to train people within their own already narrow specialties. For instance, the 1960s and 1970s saw a quantum jump in the number of Maya archaeologists and people working in the Southwest, to the point that graduate schools were soon training more students than could ever be employed in academia. Historical archaeology also expanded greatly during this period as a result of an increasing tempo of CRM activity as well as cultural tourism that attracted visitors to **Colonial Williamsburg** and **Martin's Hundred,** Virginia. At both locations, historical archaeologists played leading roles in studying the history of artifacts and structure, a process that continues at places like Jamestown, Virginia.

By 1970, archaeologists divided into several very general groups, all of them with specialized focus. There were those, a small minority, who concerned themselves with theoretical issues—with concepts, methods, and techniques that were occasionally applied to a body of data. Even today, the number of archaeologists who contribute seriously to archaeological theory is very small. Most archaeologists belong in the other two camps. Most of us carry out empirical studies of the same type that have been carried out for generations, many of them as part of cultural resource management projects. More "scientific" methods may be used, it is true, but the effect is often superficial. A third, and increasingly large, group of archaeologists specialize in different methods and techniques, often involving various forms of technology—to the point that some of them are little more than sophisticated technicians. There is some integration between the last two groups, and, regrettably, precious little between the theoreticians and the rest, although some scholars make vigorous efforts to bridge the gap.

The "new archaeology" was enormously important, for it sharpened the discipline's science and encouraged imaginative, out-of-the-box thinking in a very conservative academic environment. The conservatism still lingers, but there is now a much greater acceptance of the notion that theory is important, and is something that should be an integral part of archaeology. The theoretical debates ebb and flow. At present we are in a quieter phase; but the important point is that a debate is taking place. No serious archaeologist now believes that archaeology is an atheoretical discipline, a viewpoint that was commonplace a quarter century ago. In many respects, what is happening in archaeology is a transformation that occurred in biology a generation ago— a serious attempt to assemble a body of theory for archaeology as distinctive as that for physics and other established sciences. Those who started the theoretical ferment in the 1960s had no idea that the task they were undertaking was so enormous. As we shall see in Chapters 13 and 14, we have hardly begun.

Underwater Archaeology

Ever since people ventured onto the oceans, there have been shipwrecks— and attempts made to salvage their cargoes. Such efforts were at best haphazard. Even the heavy diving suit perfected during the nineteenth century was too clumsy to allow precise excavation of ancient ships. The breakthrough came in 1943, when French diver Jacques-Yves Cousteau developed the Aqua-Lung—a self-contained underwater breathing apparatus now better known by its acronym, *scuba*. Cousteau recovered amphorae (storage jars) from sunken Roman ships and realized the potential of archaeology underwater, but the major advances came from the 1950s to the 1970s, when today's sophisticated underwater excavation methods were developed. Now archaeologists work in the water almost as easily as they do on land, with scuba gear, advanced electronics, even mini-submarines. Underwater archaeology has exactly the same objectives as archaeology on land—to reconstruct ancient societies and to better understand the past. The first really systematic shipwreck excavation came with the discovery of a late Bronze Age ship that had sunk near **Cape Geledonya** in southwestern Turkey in about 1200 B.C. University of Pennsylvania Mycenaean archaeologist George Bass learned diving at the local YMCA and excavated the shipwreck with great care. The vessel had carried large numbers of copper ingots from Cyprus, along with tin to fabricate bronze tools, and bronze scrap in wicker baskets. Since most of the artifacts on board came from Syria and Palestine, Bass assumed that the ship had sailed from the eastern Mediterranean coast to Cyprus and then toward the Aegean Sea. Bass insisted that his excavations were as rigorous as those on land, the only difference being the watery environment. He also pointed out that shipwrecks were important sites, because they were sealed capsules that literally froze a moment in time when they sank.

As Bass worked at Cape Geledonya, Swedish archaeologists raised the warship *Vasa* from the bottom of Stockholm harbor. Thanks to design flaws, *Vasa* sank on her maiden voyage in 1628. Meanwhile, other archaeologists from Texas A&M University excavated the sunken buccaneer's haven at **Port Royal,** Jamaica. Between 1655 and 1675, the roistering town was the "wickedest city on earth." Then an earthquake and tidal waves on June 7, 1692, sank about two-thirds of Port Royal in water up to 12 meters (40 feet) deep. More than two thousand people perished in the disaster; disease and other aftereffects claimed at least that number, probably more. The first underwater excavations began in the 1950s and 1960s. Don L. Hamilton carried out systematic work clearing the sunken buildings with a water dredge, then digging them with conventional archaeological tools using an accurate measurement grid.

During the 1960s and 1970s, underwater archaeology became increasingly sophisticated. After the Cape Gelodonya wreck, Bass excavated a Byzantine vessel of the early seventh century A.D. near **Yassi Ada,** an island off western Turkey. This time the wreck lay in 37 meters (120 feet) of water—a pile of amphorae and corroded anchors. With meticulous care and 3,575 dives, Bass and his colleagues dissected the wreck, then recorded the position of every timber, even nails and nail holes, from which they could draw the lines of the 21-meter (70-foot) vessel. They also recovered the contents of the tile-roofed galley area.

By 1980, underwater archaeology had achieved a high level of sophistication, the only difference from research on land being in the survey methods.

At first Bass and others relied on sponge divers, who knew the seabed intimately. Once they had been trained in what to look for, they proved to be invaluable detectives. New wrecks in less than 50 meters (171 feet) of water are now scarce, so archaeologists are now turning to sophisticated sonar systems and other methods to locate deep-water wrecks.

Underwater archaeologists now work all over the world on wrecks as varied as Korean warships, East Indiamen, Elizabethan galleons, and even fur traders' canoes capsized in the rapids of Minnesota rivers.

New Chapters in Human Evolution

In 1974, biological anthropologist Don Johanson discovered the skeleton of a small, upright-walking female *Australopithecus* in the desolate **Hadar** region of northwestern Ethiopia's Afar desert. Johanson recovered about 40 percent of the diminutive hominid, which stood about 1.1 meters (3 feet 7 inches) tall. "Lucy," named after the famous Beatles song *Lucy in the Sky with Diamonds,* was potassium-argon dated to about 3.2 million years ago, far earlier than Olduvai's *Zinjanthropus.* The following year, Johanson and his team found the remains of at least 13 more individuals. Johanson and biological anthropologist Tim White named Lucy *Australopithecus afarensis.* She was proof that hominids with small, apelike brains had walked on two legs at least a million years before humans made the first stone tools.

Meanwhile, the Leakeys' son Richard began surveying a vast area of fossil-bearing deposits east of Lake Turkana in northern Kenya, where he soon located a rich array of Australopithecines, along with more specimens of a more humanlike hominid akin to Louis Leakey's *Homo habilis* from Olduvai Gorge. An international team of scientists excavated small scatters of stones and animal bones in dry water courses and established with potassium-argon dates that toolmaking began at least 2.5 million years ago.

Major Archaeological Discoveries of the 1960s and 1970s

It would be impossible to describe even a small fraction of the major archaeological discoveries of the 1960s and 1970s. The pace of archaeological research accelerated dramatically in all parts of the world—a product, in part, of a much larger population of professional archaeologists. Here are a few highlights:

Mammoth Bone Houses in the Ukraine.   Ukrainian and American archaeologists collaborated in the excavation of semisubterranean houses with

Figure 12.1   An artist's reconstruction of mammoth-bone huts at Mezhirich, Ukraine.

elaborate mammoth bone frameworks, built by late Ice Age hunters at **Mezhirich** in the Ukraine around 16,000 B.P., when eastern Europe was treeless steppe (Figure 12.1).

Lepenski Vir, Serbia.   This site, found in 1960 by a group of archaeologists from Belgrade, lies on a bend in the Danube River that forms a whirlpool where fish feed on trapped algae. For more than a thousand years after 6000 B.C., a series of communities settled on a terrace along the river, subsisting on fish and, later, agriculture. Large-scale excavations in 1966–1968 revealed a community of about 25 trapezoid-shaped houses, with central hearths and simple thatched roofs. Inside lay carved limestone boulders with humanlike faces with fishlike mouths, whose significance eludes us. **Lepenski Vir** was one of a number of complex fishing communities that took up agriculture in about 5000 B.C.

Çatalhöyük, Turkey.   British archaeologist James Mellaart excavated this large farming village, perhaps a town, dating to about 6000 B.C. that lay on the central Turkish plateau. **Çatalhöyük** was remarkable for a series of richly decorated shrines with ancestor figures and bull's heads, as well as vivid friezes, built into its houses. The settlement itself prospered off the obsidian trade. (Obsidian is a volcanic glass that was much favored for toolmaking and ornaments throughout the eastern Mediterranean.) Çatalhöyük is currently being reexcavated by an international team of researchers and has yielded occupation going back to at least 7000 B.C.

Chinese Royal Burials and the Terra-Cotta Regiment of Emperor Shihuangdi.   In 1968, Chinese soldiers discovered the undisturbed, rock-cut sepulchers of Han Dynasty prince Liu Sheng and his wife at Mancheng in Hebei province. (The Han Dynasty lasted from 206 B.C. to A.D. 9.) The prince

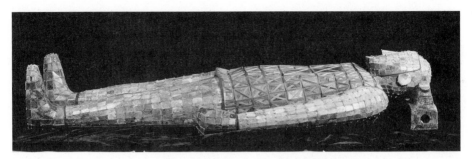

Figure 12.2   The jade burial suit of Han prince Liu Sheng, China.

and his wife were buried in magnificent jade suits, made of small jade plaques sewn together with gold thread (Figure 12.2). Jade was the symbol of immortality, but the bodies had crumbled to dust. The sepulcher contained an extraordinary range of lavish grave furniture, including lamps, fine lacquer ware, and at least six carriages with their horses.

When the first emperor of China, Shihuangdi, died in 210 B.C., he was interred in a richly adorned burial mound that lies near the city of Xi'an in Shaanxi Province. The tumulus is like an artificial mountain and has yet to be excavated. Chinese authorities believe that they lack the resources and technological abilities to do justice to it. Contemporary writings record that the burial chamber includes a map of China, with the rivers wrought in mercury. In 1974, local peasants digging a well found a complete regiment of more than seven thousand terra-cotta soldiers standing in serried rows in a pit close to the tomb. The soldiers, sculpted with individual expressions and uniforms, stood in their ranks in a complex of pits roofed with huge timbers (Figure 12.3). Other pits house the headquarters staff and cavalry units, complete with wooden chariots. Shihuangdi's regiment is one of the world's major archaeological tourist attractions.

Koster, Illinois.   This important stratified site in the Midwest's Illinois Valley, excavated by James Brown and Stuart Struever, provided a unique portrait of Archaic hunter-gatherers over more than seven thousand years. Each **Koster** occupation was stratified apart from the others, providing a wonderful opportunity for studying the increasing complexity of the food quest over many centuries, and the ways in which local communities became more permanent (Figure 12.4).

Somerset Levels, England.   Wet-site archaeology made major strides in the 1960s and 1970s. For instance, British archaeologists John and Bryony Coles spent many field seasons investigating ancient trackways in the marshy country of Somerset in southwestern England. They found sophisticated paths fabricated from tree trunks, saplings, and woven vegetation

Figure 12.3   The terra-cotta regiment of Chinese emperor Shihuangdi.

Figure 12.4   Excavations at Koster, Illinois.

dating back to before 3000 B.C. This research triggered a new emphasis on wet sites throughout Europe, and also in the United States, with the discovery and excavation by Richard Daugherty of the Makah Indian village at Ozette, Washington, buried by a mudslide nearly a thousand years ago. Even basketry was preserved at this site. Another notable find, discovered in the 1950s, was the large Boylston Street fish weir in Boston. One of the earliest multidisciplinary research teams in American archaeology showed how brush and flexible branches were placed between vertical stakes to form the weir. Brush "leaders" diverted the fish into the traps.

These are but a handful of the major archaeological discoveries that transformed our knowledge of the past during the 1960s and 1970s. However, they were often overshadowed by the passionate theoretical debates and methodological advances that transformed archaeology into a rapidly changing multidisciplinary science.

Summary

Chapter 12 describes the theoretical advances of the 1960s and 1970s that led to the formulation of what is now called processual archaeology. We discuss the development of multilinear evolution as a new perspective on culture change, which was strongly influenced by the doctrines of cultural ecology proposed by Julian Steward. Anthropologist Leslie White developed the notion of cultures as cultural systems; Steward added the ecological component. Later, anthropologists like Marshall Sahlins, Elman Service, and Morton Fried developed new schemes for subdividing the development of human societies in the past that were widely adopted but soon modified.

The 1960s saw the development of the so-called "new archaeology," a synthesis put forward by Lewis Binford, who was trained at the University of Michigan, came under the influence of White and others, and was strongly influenced by systems approaches and philosophers of science like Carl Hempel. Binford saw archaeology as anthropology, cultures as cultural systems interacting with their environments, and an explicitly scientific approach as key concepts for a new form of archaeology concerned as much with explaining the past as describing it. Binford was also concerned with the relationship between the dynamic living world and the static archaeological record—a gap that he bridged with ethnoarchaeology, the study of living peoples, and what he called middle-range theory.

The basic principles of processual archaeology were widely accepted by the 1970s, with widespread use of research designs and scientific methods, and with a new concern with ecology and subsistence. The 1960s and 1970s also saw a shift away from site-oriented research to regional surveys, more refined versions of the settlement archaeology of the 1940s and 1950s, as well as new statistical methods fostered by great inroads made by the digital computer. While the theoretical debates continued, major discoveries added new chapters to early human evolution, with underwater archeology coming of age and with spectacular finds like the terra-cotta regiment of the Chinese emperor Shihuangdi.

Guide to Further Reading

Bass, George, ed. 1970. *A History of Seafaring from Underwater Archaeology.* London and New York: Thames and Hudson.

This edited volume describes some of the major discoveries of early underwater archaeology.

Binford, Lewis R. 2000. *In Pursuit of the Past.* Rev. ed. Berkeley: University of California Press.

Binford explains his thinking and ideas in a more popular format. The revised edition has an update chapter.

Flannery, Kent V., ed. 1976. *The Early Mesoamerican Village.* New York: Academic Press.

This classic monograph is worth reading for the dialogues alone, but the studies are of lasting importance as well.

Struever, Stuart, and Felicia Holton. 1979. *Koster.* New York: Anchor/Doubleday.

A popular account of the Koster dig that is strong on reconstructions and descriptions of the methodology.

chapter 13

After Processualism

Artist's reconstruction of the Avebury archer,
Avebury, England.

*There may be rigorous ways to approach cognitive questions about
archaeology. At the same time . . . such cognitive approaches can only be used
when conditions are appropriate; that is when the body of supporting data is
sufficiently rich. When it is not so rich, cognitive archaeology becomes little
more than speculation, a kind of bungee jump into the Land of Fantasy.*

Kent Flannery and Joyce Marcus, *Cambridge Archaeological Journal,*
1993 (p. 261)

chapter outline

Ötzi the Ice Man

In September 1991, German mountaineers Helmut and Erika Simon were making their way around a narrow gully at 3,210 meters (10,530 feet) on the Similaun glacier near Hauslabjoch in the Italian Alps. Erika suddenly noticed a brown object projecting from the ice and glacial meltwater in the bottom of the gully. At first she thought it was merely a doll, but she soon identified the skull, back, and shoulders of a man with his face lying in water. She had stumbled across a corpse more than five thousand years old.

The first police on the scene assumed that the man was a climbing victim. A unique archaeological find became corpse number 91/619 on the local coroner's dissection table. Within days, however, the authorities realized that the body was very old. They called in archaeologist Konrad Spindler of the University of Innsbruck. Local archaeologists organized an excavation at the site, which was already under 0.6 meters (2 feet) of fresh snow. They used a steam blower and a hair dryer to recover parts of a grass cloak, leaves, tufts of grass, and wood fragments. By the end of the excavation, they had established that the man, now nicknamed "Ötzi the Ice Man," had deposited his ax, bow, and backpack on a sheltered ledge. He lay on his left side, his head on a boulder, perhaps taking shelter from rapidly deteriorating weather high in the mountains. A combination of high winds and extreme cold had dried out and preserved his body after he died. The **Similaun** corpse was subsequently radiocarbon-dated to between 3350 and 3150 B.C.

The Innsbruck University research team called on the latest archaeological and medical science to conserve and study Ötzi. As a result, we know more about his medical condition than he did himself. He was in his early forties. Judging from a fire-starting ember that he carried with him that came from a tree species that grows to the south of the mountains, he traveled from that direction, perhaps from the fertile Venosta Valley in northern Italy. A single grain of wheat adhering to his clothing suggests that he had been in contact with the valley within a few days of his death. The man carried a copper ax with a wooden shaft, a leather quiver with 14 bone- and wood-pointed arrows, and replacement heads and a puttylike substance for mounting them. He wore leather boots lined with hay for warmth, a stone necklace, and leather and fur garments, as well as a grass cloak of a type that was still worn by some peasants in the Alps a century ago (Figure 13.1). His knees and back bore small tattoos.

The latest techniques of medical science have established that Ötzi's stomach was empty and that he had not eaten within eight hours of his death. The Ice Man had not been in perfect health. His lungs were black with soot, perhaps from living in smoke-filled huts. His bones carried 17 Harris lines—layers of bony material that form at times of stunted growth due to malnutrition. Experts estimate that he suffered such episodes in his ninth, fifteenth,

Figure 13.1
Artist's reconstruction of the Ice Man, Similaun, Italy.

and sixteenth years, perhaps as a result of winter hunger. The dead man's hair yielded large amounts of copper dust, and there were high arsenic concentrations in his system, as if he had been involved in processing malachite, a copper carbonate commonplace in the Alps.

We do not know why the Ice Man was so high in the mountains. Perhaps he was hunting or looking for minerals like copper, which are plentiful in the Alps. Maybe he was a shepherd on his way to summer pasture, or had fled to higher elevations to escape some adversaries who caught up with him. Ötzi had been involved in a desperate fight before his death. He was wounded by an arrow, whose head lies deep in his left shoulder. DNA analysis of his wounds shows that at least four assailants attacked him, at least one of them with a dagger that left a severe laceration on one of his hands. Maybe he was killed where he fell, or perhaps he ran away seriously wounded, then collapsed helpless and died of hypothermia. We will never know.

The Ice Man discovery epitomizes the formidable multidisciplinary tools that late-twentieth-century archaeologists could bring to bear on any important find—a major innovation of the past quarter century. He is the earliest European to survive as an identifiable individual.

Ötzi's discovery caused an international sensation, at a time when archaeology was transforming itself from a purely academic discipline into an expanding profession. Cultural resource management became the dominant archaeological activity throughout most of the world between the 1970s and 1990s. In many countries, virtually all archaeological fieldwork now took place in the context of managing the past, or at least recovering archaeological data before it was destroyed. At the same time, archaeologists everywhere realized that the public at large was ignorant of the importance of their work, and of the significance of archaeology as a way of reconstructing the human past. Public outreach, or public archaeology, became a rapidly expanding part of archaeology in the 1980s and 1990s, focusing both on school curricula and on more general audiences, as well as on the persistent problem of looters and pot hunters.

Meanwhile, another major theoretical ferment, this time a reaction to processual archaeology, developed in scholarly circles.

Postprocessual Archaeology

Archaeology is based on the optimistic, modernist belief that knowledge about human societies has accumulated gradually through rational inquiry modeled on the hard sciences and mathematics. This notion of cumulative science and knowledge is vital to understanding the convoluted history of archaeological theory since the 1960s.

During the 1960s and 1970s, many archaeologists were talking about a "new archaeology," a revolutionary approach to the past that promised to overcome the many limitations of the archaeological record. In fact, this "new archaeology," today more commonly called "processual archaeology," failed to deliver on many of its promises. Processual archaeology has emphasized, and still does emphasize, subsistence and settlement patterns, animal bones, plant remains, and ancient settlement patterns. Its many practitioners embraced methodological rigor and interpreted the past in terms of cultural systems, with a strong focus on material objects. Many of its once "new" tenets are part of today's mainstream archaeology. One should not be surprised at this, for the history of archaeology shows how many important concepts and ideas persist and become part of the archaeological canon, while numerous others fall by the wayside and become part of the discipline's rich past.

In 1873, Victorian biologist Thomas Huxley wrote in his research notes of four stages of opinion surrounding major theoretical advances, starting with assumptions that the propounder was "fool and knave," followed by widespread acceptance. Next came serious doubts, and finally realization that "The Novelty [is] a mixture of truth and error. Explains as much as could reasonably be expected. The propounder worthy of all honour in spite of his share of human frailties, as one who has added to the permanent possessions of science" (Huxley, research notes, 1873). His remarks coincide remarkably closely with the history of processual archaeology from the 1960s to the 1990s.

Back in the 1960s, Lewis Binford and others believed that processual archaeology would allow researchers to investigate all aspects of human experience, including the intangible. But very soon, the focus shifted toward ecology and subsistence, to the point that some processualists referred to investigations of the intangible as "palaeopsychology."

Inevitably, there was a healthy reaction against this materialist approach, which seemed to dehumanize the past in a quest for the processes of cultural change. Many processual archaeologists dismissed religion, ideology, and human ideas as marginal to the central enterprise of studying subsistence and settlement. But, from the late 1970s to the 1990s, more researchers began thinking about the entire spectrum of human behavior—the development and expression of human consciousness, religion and belief, symbolism and iconography, as part of a more holistic archaeology. Thus was born what is often loosely called *postprocessual archaeology,* a sometimes violent antidote to its predecessor—in general terms a reaction against the relatively anonymous, processual approach, which emphasized general cultural processes over people and individuals.

Postprocessual archaeology was, and still is, a product of a rapidly changing world, as well as an evolving and increasingly specialized study of the past. Since the 1970s, we have lived in fractious times, in societies riven by factional disputes, competing interest groups, accusations of racism, and an atmosphere of political correctness. Postprocessualism was born of developments fostered by earlier processual approaches—by an insistence on scientific methods and a concern with culture change in the context of anonymous processes, where the process tended to ignore the contribution of people as small groups and individuals.

Postprocessual archaeology has always been a loosely defined term that covers several often aggressively expressed intellectual developments. They often parallel the "postmodernist" schools of thought in literature and anthropology. Postprocessual theory ebbs and flows through constantly shifting paradigms, to the point where archaeological theory has almost become a subdiscipline of archaeology itself. These changing paradigms are far from cumulative, and often result from total processes of renewal. In a way, postprocessualism represented a long period of theoretical instability, which continues to this day. This instability saw some scholars, notably British archaeologist Ian Hodder, turn to spatial analysis, then structuralism and postmodernism.

Three approaches to archaeology have played important parts in the development of archaeological theory—functionalism, structural archaeology, and critical archaeology.

Functionalism

Functionalism, the notion that a social institution within a society has a function in fulfilling all the needs of a social organism, is a concept that has been integral to archaeological thinking since the late nineteenth century. Functionalists assess any aspect of a society according to its contribution to the total working of the society. It is inextricable from the notions of systems and cultural systems, concepts that are fundamental parts of processual archaeology. To examine connections among cultural systems is to look at ancient society through a functionalist perspective. Archaeologists of this persuasion assume that people were rational in dealing with their environments, and see cultural systems as being in equilibrium or disequilibrium, with people as individuals playing a minimal role. It was in these contexts that ethnoarchaeology and middle-range theory became fashionable approaches (see Chapter 12).

Structural Archaeology

Critics of processual archaeology argued that there was a structure and context to all cultures that must be at least partially understood on their own terms, with their own logic and coherence. Ian Hodder described structure in an archaeological context not as a set of relationships between components of a cultural system, but as the codes and rules according to which observed systems of interrelations are observed. He argued that many studies of areas like the Peruvian coast or the American Southwest have explained the structure of human societies in terms of social functions and adaptive values.

But there was more to culture than observable relationships and functional utility. He wrote of a set of rules—a code, as it were—followed as people go about the business of survival, adaptation, and making a living.

Structural archaeology developed out of this concern, as an attempt to get at the active, social manipulation of symbol, at objects as they are perceived by their owners—not merely at their use. Structural archaeologists believe that, although functionalist analysis can yield information on the underlying codes, explanations for them must be based not on function but on the logic behind them. All of this revolves around what archaeologist Mark Leone has called "the idea of complex dimensions." Ritual life, shrines, temple structures, and other such phenomena helped shape people's lives. The notion of structural archaeology developed from a frustration with settlement research, which encountered head-on the difficulties of interpreting changing settlement patterns across a landscape except in strictly environmental terms.

This approach, which is reflected in some recent researches on Maya civilization, is part of a fundamental, long-term shift in archaeology, as it becomes a cultural and historical discipline that has the potential not only to contribute to our understanding of the past but also to contribute some highly original ideas to humanity's thinking about itself. As Ian Hodder has remarked on many occasions, there are many "voices" of the past, and the archaeologist's researches must reflect this.

Critical Archaeology

Critical archaeology assumes that people are like actors, interacting with their culture. This approach concerns itself with the patterns behind material culture. What were the links between large and diverse series of apparently unrelated artifacts? These artifacts manifested the changes in peoples' minds as time went on. The historical archaeologist James Deetz confronted this issue in a classic study of New England tombstones in which he showed how tombstone styles changed as society became more individualist and the face-to-face community of earlier times withered. Deetz's studies of this general type drew on research into folk housing and have proved a highly effective method on historic sites.

This approach assumes that since archaeologists are actors in contemporary culture, they must have some active impact on our society. Archaeologists' reconstructions of the past have a social function, just as astronomy did in Maya civilization, for example. Thus, argue Michael Shanks and others, archaeology may be more than a neutral, objective science. By engaging in critical analysis, an archaeologist can explore the relationship between a reconstruction of the past and the ideology that created that relationship. One extreme is the Marxist view of archaeology, which states that all knowledge is class-based, so archaeology composes history for class purposes. Much critical archaeology now focuses on understanding the pasts of people who have been "denied" a history—women, African Americans, societies in the developing world—the archaeology of inequality. In a sense, this approach demands that archaeologists be socially and politically responsible in their work. Many archaeologists have objected to this thesis because of its strong critical and moral undertones, which, they feel, undermine basic method and theory in the discipline.

Critical archaeology, like much other postprocessual thinking, developed as a reaction to a sense that archaeology had become too dehumanized, too divorced from its "proper role" in modern society—that it had no cultural context. Archaeologists were thought of as mediators between the past and the present, as part of a process in which they became more critical of their own place in the unfolding intellectual development of Western scholarship.

Almost without exception, variations on the postprocessual theme arrive in archaeology from other disciplines, in what a British prehistorian, John Bintcliff, once called "a novel bibliography of intellectual traditions likely to be esoteric and unpalatable to their predecessors—who 'write themselves out' of the debate by failing to read the new sacred texts" (Bintcliff 1991:211). Very often, the originators of the theory, in, say, sociology, have never thought about archaeology in their lives! With such constant renewal going on, there is often very little debate or even dialogue among people who adhere to or have developed new theoretical approaches. Much of the new theory is not durable enough to be tested against basic data in the field.

This theoretical debate is mainly in the hands of a minority of archaeologists, many of them based in Europe, and is of great importance to the long-term vitality of archaeology, even if much of it falls by the wayside in the short term. In the long term, borrowing from other disciplines will assume lesser importance, as archaeology develops its own body of original theory—something that still lies, at least partially, in the future.

The Contributions of Postprocessual Archaeology

For all its constantly shifting paradigms, postprocessual archaeology has contributed three positive and important principles that will endure into the future:

First, meaning is more important than materialism. No longer can archaeologists interpret the past in terms of purely ecological, technological, and other material considerations. Culture is interactive. In other words, people are actors who create, manipulate, and remake the world they live in.

Second, archaeologists must critically examine their social responsibilities, looking beyond their specialties to the broader aims of the discipline and to issues of moral and emotional involvement with the past in contemporary society. How does the public interact with the past?

Third, there are many perspectives on ancient society that have been neglected, among them those of women, ethnic minorities, and those who are often called "the people without history"—anonymous, often illiterate commoners.

Postprocessual archaeology has been described, somewhat extravagantly, as a "rampant monster," best understood by reading the original authors in other disciplines, who started the postmodernist movement, and the perceptive and often powerful critiques their works evoked. But for all its extravagant and often passionate debate, some of postprocessualism's approaches offer promise when combined with the best of processual archaeology, with its empirical data collection, rigorous description, and meticulous analyses of archaeological sites and their ecological contexts.

In the final analysis, all archaeological research, including theory, is a cumulative process that continues to unfold from one generation to the next. Postprocessualism ultimately stemmed not only from a dissatisfaction with processualism, but also from a growing concern on the part of some very fine archaeologists that their discipline engage more closely with society as a whole, as well as with the wider academic community.

When the debate over postprocessual archaeology was at its height, a spectacular discovery from Peru showed the importance of factoring in ideology in the interpretation of ancient society.

The Lords of Sipán

Coastal Peru's Moche state flourished during the early to middle first millennium A.D. The discovery of the undisturbed Moche burials at Sipán, on Peru's northern coast, in 1989 ranks as one of the greatest archaeological discoveries of all time. Peruvian archaeologist Walter Alva spent months painstakingly excavating the royal tombs, using conservation laboratories in Peru and Europe. The result is a triumph of scientific archaeology and an excellent example of how rigorous science can help interpret the meaning of ancient burials.

Tomb I held the body of a man in his late thirties or early forties buried in about A.D. 400. The mourners had built a brick burial chamber deep in the pyramid, building the sepulcher like a room, with solid mudbrick benches along the sides and at the head end (Figure 13.2). They set hundreds of clay pots in small niches in the benches. Priests dressed the dead lord in his full regalia, including a golden mask, and wrapped his corpse and regalia in textile shrouds. Then they placed him in a plank coffin and set it in the center of the burial chamber, the lid secured with copper straps. They laid out more ceramics, mainly fine spouted bottles, at the foot and head of the coffin. Next, someone sacrificed two llamas and placed them on either side of the foot of the coffin. At some point, the priests also sat the body of a nine- or ten-year-old child in poor health at the head of the deceased.

Figure 13.2   Reconstruction of a burial of a Lord of Sipán, Peru.

Five cane coffins were then lowered into the grave, each containing the body of an adult. The two male dead, perhaps bodyguards or members of the lord's entourage, were each laid on top of one of the llamas. One was a strongly built male, more than 35 years old, adorned with copper ornaments and laid out with a war club. The other bore a beaded pectoral and was between 35 and 45 years old. Two of the three women's coffins lay at the head of the royal casket; in the third, at the foot of the coffin, the woman had been turned on her side. Interestingly, the women's disarticulated and jumbled bones suggest they were not sacrificial victims, for they had died long before the lord, and were partly decomposed at the time of their burial. Perhaps they had been wives, concubines, or servants. Once the coffins had been positioned, a low beam roof was set in place, too low for anyone to stand inside the chamber. Then the tomb was covered, a footless male victim being laid out in the fill. Finally, a seated body with crossed legs watched over the burial chamber from a small niche in the south wall, about 1 meter (3 feet) above the roof.

The other lordly graves contained men adorned with identical regalia. They wore gold nose and ear ornaments, gold and turquoise bead bracelets, and copper sandals. Ceremonial rattles, crescent-shaped knives, scepters, spears, and exotic seashells surrounded their bodies. When they appeared in public, the lords in their full regalia would glitter like flamboyant gods in the sun's rays (see Figure 1.1).

But who were these important men? UCLA archaeologist Christopher Donnan has spent his career studying thousands of painted pots made by Moche potters. He examines the scenes adorning such vessels by "unrolling" them photographically, rotating the pot as it is photographed in the laboratory. Comparing the objects found in the Sipán tombs with people depicted in Moche art, Donnan identified the men as "warrior-priests." Such individuals are depicted on Moche pots presiding over sacrifices of prisoners of war (Figure 13.3). Apparently, Moche warriors went to war specifically to take captives. They would strip them of their armor and weapons and lead them in front of the warrior-priest. Then the prisoner's throat was cut, the warrior-priest and others drinking the blood of the slain victim while the corpse was dismembered. On pot after pot, the warrior-priest wears a crescent-shaped headdress atop a conical helmet, exactly the regalia found in the Sipán tombs. Such men were a priesthood of nobles living in different parts of the kingdom who enacted the sacrifice ceremony at prescribed times.

When warrior-priests died, they were buried at the place where they had performed the ritual, wearing the formal regalia and the objects they had used in the ceremony. Their successors assumed their roles, wearing new sets of the same costumes and artifacts, not only perpetuating the official religion but also ensuring work for the dozens of skilled artisans who manufactured precious artifacts for the nobility.

The Sipán graves offer vital insights into the lives of prominent Moche families, and into the rituals that surrounded their rule. Such discoveries are the meat and drink of archaeology in the popular mind, but they often

Figure 13.3   A Moche warrior-priest presides over a parade of prisoners who are being sacrificed. A frieze from a painted pot "unrolled" photographically.

overshadow a major development of the 1970s to 1990s—an increasing concern with the lives of individuals and groups.

The Archaeology of Individuals, Groups, and Gender

Archaeology is the study of the material remains of ancient human behavior. By its very nature, it tends to be anonymous, concerned more with society as a whole than with individuals or groups within it. The 1970s to 1990s saw a shift in emphasis toward people as decision makers, as members of society both by themselves or in small groups.

Individuals

Human burials are relatively commonplace in archaeological sites, but the archaeology of death is such that a scholar normally studies generalized populations rather than recognizable individuals. To a great extent, this is a product of preservation. During the late twentieth century, remarkable advances in biological anthropology gave insights into the skeletal pathologies of ancient populations. For instance, Phillip Walker and Patricia Lambert examined skeletons from ancient Chumash Indian cemeteries on the shores of the Santa Barbara Channel. They were able to record instances of chronic disease and incidents of malnutrition, as well as data on combat wounds, which showed that the people were under severe environmental and social stress during the late first millennium A.D., a time of rising populations and serious drought. But such studies, while using the bones of individuals, are necessarily generalized in what they can tell us.

The situation is very different when the archaeologist encounters a well-preserved individual like the Ice Man, or a known historic figure like the Egyptian pharaoh Rameses II. As we saw with the Ice Man, the full apparatus of modern medical science can be brought to bear on a well-preserved corpse. For instance, Rameses II's mummy tells us that the pharaoh stood 1.4 meters (5 feet 8 inches) tall. He suffered from arthritis, dental abscesses, and poor circulation.

Gender

Until the 1980s, few archaeologists concerned themselves with gender roles in the past. Archaeology lagged behind sociology, history, and other disciplines in examining sexual division of labor and changing gender roles. During the 1980s and early 1990s, a new generation of feminist scholars urged an engendered archaeology, epitomized by a series of essays edited by

Joan Gero and Margaret Conkey in *Engendering Archaeology,* published in 1991, which took advantage of feminist theory in other disciplines. Conkey, Gero, and others wrote of "engendering" archaeology—attempting to reclaim men and women from the past in nonsexist ways. Such an approach went much further than merely demonstrating that pots were made by women and stone projectile points by men or trying to identify womens' activities in the archaeological record. It was an attempt to initiate research to find out how gender "worked" in ancient societies, to unravel its cultural meaning. This meant focusing not only on major material achievements such as metallurgy or pot making, or on ancient environments, but also on interpersonal relations and the social dynamics of everyday activity.

The most important gender research focused on people as individuals and on their contributions to society. For example, the British biological anthropologist Theya Molleson studied the skeletons found at the early farming village at **Abu Hureyra** in Syria. She found that the women's bones bore telltale signs of pathological conditions resulting from hours on their knees grinding wild seeds and cereal grains, with gross arthritic injuries caused by curling their toes forward. The repetitive stress injuries at Abu Hureyra incurred during food preparation were one of the first evidences of the division of labor to be found in the archaeological record.

Gender research advanced in other directions, too, with, for example, a study of Aztec weaving combining archaeological and historical sources to show that the roles of women in Aztec society were much more varied than hitherto suspected. Elizabeth Brumfiel argued that cooking and weaving were important political tools—ways for women to maintain considerable social and political control in the wider society. Art representations, ornaments, even food remains, provided fresh insights into the functioning of ancient societies. In some cases, archaeology could be linked with ethnohistorical data, among such societies as the ancient Maya, pre-Columbian maize farmers in the Andes, and Stone Age farming villages in southeastern Europe. One scholar, Ruth Tringham, has envisaged the archaeologist as "an active mediator" who encourages the reader (or spectator) to view, visualize, and imagine the past.

The engendering of archaeology was one of the most promising approaches to the past to emerge from the theoretical ferment of the 1970s and 1980s, and continues to generate exciting new research.

Ethnicity and Inequality

Feminist archaeology concerned itself with male and female roles and social inequality. The archaeology of social inequality came into prominence during the 1970s and 1980s—a departure from archaeologists' traditional preoccupations with culture history, "origins" problems like that of the first Americans, and adaptations to changing ancient environments. A number of scholars reacted against these preoccupations, which tended to minimize the importance of social power and assumed that ancient societies enjoyed a high degree of cultural uniformity. They used archaeology's unique perspective to study ethnic diversity and the ways in which people exercised economic and social power over others.

Archaeology of this persuasion was, and is, based on the assumption that elites used many tactics to exercise power over others, everything from gentle persuasion to divine kingship, precedent, economic monopolies, and naked force. A great deal of effort was put into studies of the ideologies of domination, especially among societies like the ancient Maya, whose lords built great ceremonial centers with towering pyramids and vast plazas that were symbolic models of the sacred landscape of the Maya universe. The Khmer rulers of Cambodia erected Angkor Wat and other stupendous temples and palaces that were statements of power and replicas in stone of the Hindu cosmos (Figure 13.4). In Khmer society, everything flowed to the center, to the service of the divine king.

Many scholars, especially historical archaeologists, realized that artifacts offered a unique way of examining the history of the many communities that kept no written records but expressed their diverse feelings and cultures through specific artifacts that they purchased and used. Fascinating pioneer studies of peoples' resistance to the submerging of their culture came from the American South, where the earliest Africans to reach North America brought their own notions of religion, ritual, and supernatural power to their new homes. Some of them even maintained small shrines in their living

Figure 13.4   Angkor Wat, Cambodia.

quarters. Slave plantations were parts of complex, much wider networks that linked planters to other planters, planters to slaves, and slaves to slaves on other plantations. Within these harsh and repressive environments, slaves were able to keep important elements of their own culture alive, revealed by finds of the tools of an African curer (medicine man) in southern Texas. The historical archaeologist Leland Ferguson undertook a study of African American clay vessels from the southeastern United States, found them remarkably standardized, and concluded that this pottery, which he named Colono ware, reflected African American eating habits that were radically different from those of Europeans and were an unconscious resistance to slavery and the plantation system (Figure 13.5).

Another fascinating example of ethnic resistance came from the archaeological investigation of the route taken by the Northern Cheyenne Indians when they broke out of Fort Robinson, Nebraska, on January 9, 1879. They fought a running battle with the garrison, and it was 11 days before the military captured the runaways. Controversy surrounded the route, until a group of historical archaeologists and local Cheyenne investigated potential routes over exposed ridges and hidden drainages, searching for bullets. They duly found them not on the higher ground, but along the strategically wiser lower paths. This may seem like a minor footnote to history, but it was important, for it validated native oral tradition of a classic story of the American West, and showed the conventional story, that the Indians went along the bluffs, to be a fable concocted by the victors.

The archaeology of inequality showed that artifacts could tell powerful stories about the lowly and anonymous, the men and women who labored in the shadow of great states and mighty rulers. The artifacts of ordinary folk

Figure 13.5
A Colono vessel.

tell tales as compelling as those recorded on clay tablets, in government archives, or on Egyptian papyri.

From the 1970s to the 1990s, archaeology came into its own as a potential source of information on the mundane and the trivial—the minutest details of daily life. Thanks in considerable part to the researches of historical archaeologists, it became an unrivaled tool for the study of social inequality and ethnicity, as well as studying broader interactions among people and groups, through artifacts passed along exchange and trade routes.

Cognitive Archaeology

Cognitive archaeology emerged in the 1980s and 1990s as a form of middle ground, when some of the best minds in archaeology attempted to create a "cognitive-processual" approach—a study of what has sometimes been called the "archaeology of mind," of human cognition.

This approach was based on the assumption that one can never establish *what* people thought, but it was possible to give insights into *how* they thought. Cognitive archaeology has developed in two broad areas. The first is the study of the cognitive faculties of early hominids and archaic humans, such as, for example, the relationship between toolmaking and cognitive abilities, the origins of language, and the social contexts of early human behavior. The other area covers the past forty thousand years and the cognitive aspects of such developments as the origins of food production and civilization. The challenge is to establish how the formation of symbolic systems in, say, early Mesopotamia or predynastic Egypt molded and conditioned later cultural developments, such as pharaonic civilization along the Nile.

Until the 1980s and 1990s, the methodologies for such research were in their infancy. They still are, but the convergence of such diverse fields as cognitive psychology, artificial intelligence, computer simulation, and a cognitive archaeology with a rigorous and explicit methodology may one day replace many of the simplistic generalizations that masqueraded under the rubric of postprocessual archaeology.

Kent Flannery and Joyce Marcus of the University of Michigan were among those who experimented with cognitive archaeology. In an early attempt to understand ancient Zapotec subsistence behavior in Mexico's Valley of Oaxaca, they took into account what Spanish writings told of Indian cosmology. They considered cognitive archaeology to be the study of "all those aspects of ancient culture that are the product of the ancient mind," but only feasible when research methods were rigorous and the supporting data was rich. Flannery and Marcus reconstructed models from ethnohistoric sources, then isolated temples, artifact styles, and other cultural elements that could be identified archaeologically. They studied them in their cultural contexts, comparing the observed archaeological remains with the model from ethnohistoric documents. In the Valley of Oaxaca, many village farming communities functioned without any apparent social ranking between 1400 and 1150 B.C. Between 1150 and 850 B.C., the first artistic depictions of supernatural lineage ancestors appear; some represent the earth, others the sky, in the form of lightning or a fire serpent. Some forms of hereditary social ranking seem to accompany the new art. Then the Zapotec state came into being, with a powerful elite ruling from Monte Alban. A tiny minority became associated with depictions of sky and lightning, while earth and earthquake symbols faded into obscurity. It is as if those who rose to prominence were associated with lightning's descendants, in an ideological shift in which hereditary social inequality was condoned for the first time.

Cognitive archaeology has developed as an approach to cosmology, religion, ideology, and iconography based on rigorous analysis and data from many sources. This theoretical approach still offers enormous promise for the future, but falls far short of reconstructing entire ideologies from the orientation of a building or a single carving.

High-Technology Archaeology

The 1970s to 1990s saw archaeology become truly hi-tech, as researchers everywhere drew heavily on technologies developed for medicine and other sciences. Many of them were refinements of earlier methods, especially techniques for remote sensing and for sourcing exotic materials. Whereas such innovations had been exotic in earlier decades, they now became routine, especially such methods as spectrographic analysis of obsidian, which resulted in major studies of the trade in volcanic glass in such widely separated areas as California, the eastern Mediterranean, and Mesoamerica. As a result of such analyses, at least 50 obsidian sources are known from California alone.

Accelerator mass spectrometry (AMS) radiocarbon dating, neutron activation analysis, ground-penetrating radar, and bone strontium chemistry: these are but a handful of the many scientific methods that became routine during the 1990s. Much of this technological innovation came to archaeology from cultural resource management projects, which rely heavily on technology, as they operate under very tight deadlines.

Few finds show the difference such methods have made better than the recent discovery of the Avebury archer in southern England.

The Avebury Archer

The so-called Avebury archer epitomizes the best of scientific archaeology at the beginning of a new millennium. He was buried in about 2470 B.C., 4.8 kilometers (3 miles) from Stonehenge in southern England at the very time that the great sarsen stones that form Stonehenge's circles were brought from the nearby Marlborough Downs and the smaller bluestones 380 kilometers (240 miles) from Preseli in western Wales. The strongly built 35-to-45-year-old man lay on his left side with his legs bent and his head facing north. He had suffered from an abscess in his jaw and had sustained a serious accident a few years before his death that ripped off his left kneecap. As a result, he walked with a straight foot, which swung out to his left. He also suffered from a bone infection that caused him constant pain. The large, rectangular grave was probably timber-lined and perhaps once covered with a wooden roof now plowed away, also by a circular burial mound, such as was commonly built at the time for prominent people.

All the organic materials like bow staves and clothing had long vanished, but we can make intelligent guesses as to his clothing and possessions on the basis of what survives. The man wore a leather cloak or mantle fastened with a bone pin (see chapter opener). A copper knife lay partially under his torso, as if he had once worn it on his chest. Two pots known to archaeologists as beakers, perhaps made especially for his funeral, lay near his head, together with a deer bone spatula for making stone tools. A copper dagger and various flint tools as well as some boar's tusks also lay close by, perhaps once stored in a leather bag. Behind his back were more boar's tusks, a cache of stone tools, and other beakers. Sixteen flint arrowheads had been scattered across the body before it was covered. More belongings, including two more beakers and two gold earrings, were scattered by his feet, as if they had been placed there separately. The archer went to the afterlife with everything he needed to survive—clothing, tools, and spare flint to make more arrowheads.

Another grave lay close by, dug at the same time as the archer's, containing the skeleton of a man between 25 and 30 years old. He wore two golden hair tresses identical to those buried with the archer—a rare find, here present in two graves dug side by side. The date of these two important burials, and their proximity to Stonehenge, hints that both men may have been involved in the building of the stone circles. Or perhaps they were drawn to the site by its ritual importance. We will never know. But modern archaeological science, some of it unimaginable even a generation ago, tells us much more about the two men. A detailed study of their bones displayed the same unusual bone structure in the foot—a heel bone joined with one of the upper tarsal bones in the foot itself. This strongly suggests that they were relatives.

Oxygen isotope analysis of the archer's teeth provided a startling clue as to his homeland. The oxygen isotope ratio of the water a person drinks depends on the source of the water, the distance from the coast, and the altitude, latitude, and local temperature of the rainfall. Drinking water in warmer climates has more heavy isotopes than that from colder environments. Thus, the scientist can compare the isotope ratios of ancient teeth with those from modern drinking water samples and find out where the ancient people lived. When Carol Chenery of the British Geological Survey analyzed the oxygen isotope record of the Avebury archer's teeth, she found that he had spent his youth in a colder climate than southern Britain—in central Europe. More recent tests have shown that he came from the Swiss Alps, probably Switzerland, Austria, or Germany.

In contrast, the younger man in the second grave had a lighter oxygen isotope ratio in his wisdom teeth, as if he had spent his late teens in central England or northeast Scotland. Sourcing tests using trace elements in the metal showed that his copper knives came from what is now Spain and Portugal, evidence for exceptionally wide trade networks during Europe's Early Bronze Age.

The Avebury archer is an extremely important find, because both his body chemistry and the artifacts found with him testify to regular contacts between Britain and the Continent at an early stage in the Bronze Age. He is also proof that people traveled long distances at this early time far more often than was hitherto suspected.

The Role of the Human Mind

The ecological–evolutionary approach gave us a better understanding of what archaeologists know, but clearly this was useless without a better comprehension of the kind of human behavior that produced the archaeological record. During the 1990s, many archaeologists came to think that human behavior was less orderly than many cultural evolutionists would like us to believe, yet not entirely random, as some historical materialist scholars assumed. There were sufficient regularities in cultural developments in different regions, such as, for example, in the development of agriculture and village life in the Near East and Mesoamerica, to suggest that recurrent operations of cause and effect did result in the evolution of similar forms of behavior in widely separated areas. But there was much we did not know about the nature of cultural and social systems. Did a change in one subsystem affect all others, as many archaeologists assumed? It was by no means certain that this was the case.

Humans never adjust to the physical world as it really is, but to this same world as they perceive it through their own cultural conditioning. Thus the human ability to reason and adjust cultural perceptions plays an essential role in the ways in which people interact with one another and with the environment. In other words, the human mind plays an important role in all aspects of human behavior. As the Canadian archaeologist Bruce Trigger has said (1991:567), we should view human behavior as "the product of interaction between the ability of individual human beings to foresee at least some of the consequences of what they do and the sorts of constraints on human behavior, both physical and imagined, that such calculations must take into account." Understanding the part played by individuals and groups, and their interactions, is one of the great challenges for future archaeologists.

By the early years of the twenty-first century, archaeology had come into its own as a sophisticated, multidisciplinary science, deeply involved in the contemporary world. Gone were the days of uncontrolled searches for spectacular treasure, replaced by an era of ever-increasing specialization and remarkably detailed archaeological detective work. Such narrow perspectives on the past have not necessarily been good for archaeology, for we have tended not to see the forest for the trees—to forget that our primary concern is to understand the history of human society over an immensely long period of time, in order to achieve a better understanding of humanity; that is, of ourselves. There are signs that this will change in the new millennium, when archaeology becomes an international, multivocal science, fully engaged in society and a vital tool for helping us plan for a self-sustaining future. In Chapter 14, we briefly discuss some of the directions that lie ahead.

Summary

The past three decades of the twentieth century saw a reaction against processualism, its materialist approach, and the somewhat anonymous cultural processes that it produced. The reaction was part of the cumulative history of archaeological theory over the past half century. Postprocessual approaches to archaeology were a product of a rapidly changing world, and of an increasingly specialized archaeology. Postprocessualism represents a period of theoretical instability that endures to its day, with many archaeologists still using the basic principles of processualism in their research. Three approaches played an important part in the development of processualism: functionalism, structural archaeology, and critical archaeology. Postprocessual archaeology contributed three important principles to the discipline: the idea that meaning is more important than materialism; the belief that archaeologists should examine their social responsibilities; and the reality that there are many perspectives on ancient society that are often neglected. As postprocessualism developed, archaeologists played increasing attention to the people of the past as decision makers, as individuals and in groups, and also to ethnic minorities. An engendered archaeology also assumed increasing importance in late-twentieth-century archaeology. So did issues of social inequality, for archaeology could tell powerful stories of the lowly and anonymous, not merely great lords and rulers. Cognitive archaeology developed as a meld of processual and postprocessual approaches to studying emerging symbolic systems in ancient societies, epitomized by Kent Flannery and Joyce Marcus's study of emerging Zapotec civilization in Mexico's Valley of Oaxaca.

As these theoretical developments unfolded, archaeology became increasingly hi-tech, calling on a wide variety of methods from the sciences that resulted in remarkably detailed reconstructions of ancient life. The impact of science on archaeology is epitomized by the discovery of the Avebury archer in southern England, a man who, bone and tooth chemistry tells us, came from Switzerland.

Guide to Further Reading

Gero, Joan, and Margaret Conkey, eds. *Engendering Archaeology: Women and Prehistory.* Oxford: Blackwell.

>The pioneer source on gender in archaeology, with a series of articulate essays from different parts of the world.

Hodder, Ian. 1999. *The Archaeological Process: An Introduction.* Oxford: Blackwell.

>Ian Hodder's short summary, based on his evolving thinking and fieldwork, is eloquent and to the point.

Johnson, Matthew. 1999. *Archaeological Theory.* Oxford: Blackwell.

>An excellent introduction to theory, which is good on postprocessual issues.

Mithen, Steven. 1989. "Evolutionary Theory and Postprocessual Archaeology." *Antiquity* 63:483–494.

>An eloquent essay on evolutionary archaeology.

Trigger, Bruce G. 1989. *A History of Archaeological Interpretation.* Cambridge: Cambridge University Press.

>Trigger's intellectual analysis is of great use for this chapter.

chapter 14

The Future

CRM (cultural resource management) excavation on the center median of Interstate 10, Tucson, Arizona.

Archaeology is the latest born of the sciences. It has but scarcely struggled into freedom, out of the swaddling clothes of dilettante speculations. It is still attracted by pretty things rather than by real knowledge.

Flinders Petrie, *Methods and Aims in Archaeology*, 1904

The past is always around us, offering encouragement and inspiration, precedent and cause for apprehension. We archaeologists study ancient times over a very long chronological span, and are unique in our ability to look back over thousands of years of human experience. The history of archaeology is *our* past, for we cannot hope to advance knowledge of ancient societies without a clear comprehension of how our predecessors thought about their discoveries and of their ways of studying human behavior over two and a half million years. In previous chapters, we have described the transformation of archaeology from little more than a glorified treasure hunt into a highly sophisticated scientific discipline. We have rejected simplistic diffusionist and evolutionary interpretations of culture change, examined the potential of ecological archaeology, moved beyond processualism into the uncertain smorgasbord of contemporary archaeological theory. One question remains. Can we distill a sense of where archaeology's future lies from this tangled web of historical strands? This chapter briefly examines some of the trends that lie ahead. This is no academic exercise, for the decisions that we make about the past in the next few generations will help determine whether archaeology has a future at all.

Discoveries

No one can predict what sensational archaeological discoveries lie ahead, beyond a certainty that many exciting finds will transform our knowledge of the human past over the next century. Such discoveries are inevitable, given the growing population of archaeologists in different parts of the world and the increasing industrial activity that disturbs more and more of the earth's surface every year.

Some general trends in archaeological discovery are easily predictable:

The late twentieth century saw an enormous international investment in palaeoanthropology—the study of human origins. This investment will continue in the new millennium. We can expect numerous fossil discoveries, which will further complicate the diffuse portrait of human evolution. New finds in northeast Africa and the Sahara will fill the enormous 3.5-million-year time gap between *Ardipithecus ramidus* and the Chad hominid, *Sahelanthropus tchadensis,* found in 2002 and said to be 7 million years old. Within a few years, fresh light will also be thrown on the immediate ancestry of *Homo* and on the evolutionary relationships between *Homo* and *Homo erectus* during that critical period of human evolution in Africa at 2 million years before the present.

Genetics will have a profound impact on the study of major population movements in prehistoric times; witness recent important advances in MtDNA (mitochondrial DNA) research into the ancestry of modern humans and the first Americans. Genetic research will also throw important light on the prehistory of the archaic world before 200,000 years ago, the least known period of our past, as well as providing insights into such issues as the first settlement of Australia and Europe's first farmers.

Much intensified archaeological research in Siberia will probably confirm what we already suspect—that the first settlement of the Americas took hold at the end of the late Ice Age, probably no earlier than about 15,000 B.P.

An ongoing revolution in paleoclimatology through ice cores, tree-rings, and other methodologies will transform our understanding of the origins of food production and early civilization. The new climatology will reveal the impact that short- and long-term climate change exercised on economic, social, and political institutions. A resumption of excavations and surveys in politically sensitive regions of southwestern Asia, including Iraq, will provide a great deal of new, fine-grained data to flesh out a new body of sophisticated theory.

The greatest potential for spectacular discoveries lies not in well-trodden regions like Europe, North America, Mesoamerica, the Andes, or the eastern Mediterranean, but in areas where the footprint of the archaeologist is still a rarity. There is no question that new finds will refine, and sometimes even transform, our knowledge of, say, Moche civilization in Peru; but the pace of truly important discovery will probably be slow, partly because of the large number of researchers in the field and also because of the damage done by looters. The looting problem is also endemic in parts of Africa and Asia, but the potential for major discovery is far higher.

The possibilities are endless. Without question, the excavation of the royal sepulcher of the first Chinese emperor Qin Shihuangdi, he of terra-cotta regiment fame, will provide the most dramatic discovery story of the twenty-first century—if and when the Chinese authorities decide that they have the expertise and resources to open the burial mound. China and the deserts of

Central Asia offer unique opportunities for major city excavations, for studies of desiccated mummies and of long-distance trade. Southeast and southern Asia are virtually unexplored archaeologically. New research in Cambodia and Thailand is already providing fresh perspectives on the origins of social complexity and states in this historically critical region. The Harappan and Mauryan civilizations of southern Asia are only slightly known and offer many opportunities for fascinating discoveries. Sub-Saharan Africa enjoyed a brief spurt of archaeological popularity in the 1960s, but research has languished since then, in part because of unsettled political conditions. The present century will see important finds at the southern margins of the Sahara Desert, where long-distance trade transformed African history. The kingdom of Mali in West Africa alone offers rich historical potential for the archaeologist: we forget that ancient Mali provided two-thirds of Europe's gold in the year that Christopher Columbus landed in the Bahamas. And our knowledge of early African states generally is still in its infancy.

Unfortunately, a great deal of archaeological training prepares young archaeologists to work on ever-more-specialized projects in already familiar regions rather than encouraging them to venture boldly into unexplored areas, where the greatest potential for many advances lies. The leaders in twenty-first-century archaeology will be those who work deliberately to fill the still-looming gaps in our knowledge of world prehistory.

Archaeological Method and Theory

An archaeologist of 1900 would feel completely lost in today's research environment, so great are the scientific advances of the past century. We can be sure that we would feel just as lost in the complex archaeological world of 2100.

Method

The twentieth century saw archaeologists develop, or make use of, an impressive array of often highly specialized methods for reconstructing the past, often drawing on other disciplines. These included aerial photography and other remote sensing techniques, including satellite imagery; pollen analysis; radiocarbon dating; trace element analysis for artifact sourcing; and flotation—to mention only a few. The new millennium will witness equally spectacular advances in high-technology archaeology, many of them developing in the crucible of cultural resource management, where the use of such approaches is both commonplace and economic.

It is difficult to predict long-term trends in archaeological method, for the advances are cumulative rather than dramatic. Without question, however, the greatest changes will come in the ways in which archaeologists investigate sites without resorting to destructive excavation. Quantum jumps in the efficiency and accuracy of subsurface radar and other sensing devices may well make much excavation unnecessary, especially on large sites like cities and towns, where remote sensing will allow the reconstruction of street plans and even individual structures with much greater definition than we can imagine today. Such research combined with GIS (Geographic Information Systems) approaches and new survey methods will revolutionize the study of settlement patterns and ancient landscapes.

For all the major scientific developments that lie ahead, the basic processes of archaeological method will always remain the same, including establishing context in time and space, precise recording, and full publication of the results.

Theory

Archaeological theory hardly existed before 1960, and we have come a long way since then, through the turbulent years of processual archaeology and claims of an archaeological revolution, to the confused, often murky but fascinating era of postprocessual archaeology. We are currently in a period of relative theoretical tranquillity compared with ten years ago, as we await the next threshold of theoretical discussion. It's well to remember that only a handful of practicing archaeologists are innovative theoreticians, with the best of us being content to make use of their refined formulations. An expertise in archaeological theory requires a specific kind of mind-set, with a sound grounding in the philosophy of science and in the thinking of many disciplines, including evolutionary psychology. Few of us enjoy the unusual gifts of a truly expert theoretician.

Currently, most American archaeologists, and many others around the world, subscribe to a variety of evolutionary schools, among them evolutionary ecology, behavioral and Darwinian approaches, as well as a variety of what archaeologist Michelle Hegmon has called "processual plus." The prophets of new theoretical approaches come and go, and no one can predict which direction the major advances will take. We can, however, take note of some long-term trends.

Cognitive Processual Archaeology. The most firmly established paradigm is that of processual archaeology, which, with its preoccupation with systems, ecology, and subsistence, as well as settlement patterns, remains the dominant theoretical approach. As we saw in Chapter 13, processual approaches have been much criticized for their anonymity and emphasis on processes of culture change. A few archaeologists have attempted to meld the scientific approach of processualists with carefully formulated inquiries into the role of individuals and groups, or into ancient ideologies, with careful use of ethnographic or historical records. Such work is still in its infancy, and requires the greatest of care. Controlled approaches are likely to become commonplace in the archaeology of the future, combining cultural systems theory, settlement archaeology, environmental reconstruction, close studies of such topics as households (archaeological context), and the carefully controlled use of written records or ethnographic analogy.

The Archaeology of Individuals and Groups. In future years, we can expect more attention to be paid to perspectives on ancient societies that have been much ignored in the past. This includes attention to women, children, ethnic minorities, and anonymous, often illiterate commoners, often called "people without history." We can also anticipate more research into the role of individuals in shaping events of the past, which will mean working with known historic figures like ancient Egyptian pharaohs and Maya lords. It will also require careful examination of the constraints that shape human cultures, for the human ability to use our imaginations, to make calculated decisions, plays a significant part in streamlining any form of innovation. We have tended to ignore the reality that cultural traditions play a major role in constraining and shaping social change.

The Archaeology of Landscape. The current fashion for studying cultural landscapes is likely to evolve into a major theoretical perspective aimed at understanding the ways in which ancient peoples looked at their world, their cosmos. Again, this will be a multidisciplinary approach, closely tied to settlement archaeology and to an increasing involvement of archaeologists in long-term environmental issues.

Self-Sustainability. Many people still dismiss archaeology as a self-indulgent academic discipline of no use or interest to anyone but those who practice it. Unfortunately, in many instances they are right. But in the twenty-first century, we are likely to see archaeology assume a much wider role in research relating to contemporary environmental problems, especially those of self-sustainability. This may seem like a surprising role for archaeology, but we are the only science that has the ability to study changes in human societies and their adaptations to changing environments over long periods of time. The environmental lessons that the modern world has to learn from the past are of fundamental importance. One cannot, for example, understand the contemporary crisis over the deforestation of the earth without a perspective on ancient forest clearance, which goes back well before the beginnings of agriculture ten thousand years ago. With our sophisticated and fine-grained methods for studying ancient adaptations and subsistence, to say nothing of settlement patterns, we have a great deal to offer ecologists and others concerned with long-term problems of sustainability, especially in the developing world. The initiative will have to come from archaeologists, for many of our colleagues in other disciplines are only dimly aware of the potential of archaeology for investigating sustainability problems. For instance, when archaeologists reconstructed raised potato fields near Tiwanaku by Lake Titicaca in Bolivia, they revived a form of self-sustaining agriculture that had been largely ignored for more than a thousand years.

An Original Body of Archaeological Theory. Almost all significant archaeological theory has drawn from theoretical formulations in other disciplines—from the natural sciences, physics, sociology, and philosophy. Even after a half century of experimentation and debate, there is almost no original archaeological theory that is truly unique to the study of the past. Given the much larger bodies of data now available, the awesome power of computers, and our much greater experience with theory, I would predict that a unique body of archaeological theory will emerge in this century, much of it stemming from the bold and often highly theoretical thinking of scholars who belong loosely in the postprocessual way of thinking.

External Influences on Academic Archaeology. Cultural resource management, public archaeology, conservation, issues of heritage and tourism—these and many other realities crowd on the consciousness of academic archaeologists. I believe that valuable new theoretical ideas will feed into archaeological thinking from these and other areas of archaeology as a synthesis of activity reflecting the realities of a very changed twenty-first-century archaeological world and will change the way we do business (see below).

Evolutionary Archaeology and Genetics. Archaeology is about the study of people, concerned with human behavior over 2.5 million years. As archaeologists have studied the material remains of the past, evolutionary psychology has made startling advances. *Homo sapiens sapiens* is a cultural animal, and our capacity for culture is a product of evolution in which natural selection played an important part. What is crucial for archaeologists is whether these same evolutionary processes had any consequences for the nature of human behavior. In other words, is culture independent of its biological roots and thus irrelevant to the study of human behavior? A fierce debate, which shows no sign of subsiding, surrounds this issue. Evolutionary approaches in archaeology will be most concerned with active individuals endowed with common psychological propensities. Research will revolve around people who think and act in certain ways rather than others. They make unique decisions in ecological, social, and historical contexts.

The important findings of molecular biologists have cast important new light not only on the origins of humankind, but also on later prehistory. In recent years, mitochondrial DNA (mtDNA) inherited through the female line has assumed great importance for the study of major population movements and the study of the ancestry of modern humans, the first Americans, and the first Australians. Such research is likely to transform the broad sweep of human prehistory dramatically in future generations.

Ian Hodder has argued cogently that both archaeological research and fieldwork are fluid processes of interpretation, where theory begins with "the edge of the trowel." We live in an increasingly diverse yet homogeneous and networked world, where the sensitivities and rights of a wide diversity of groups make it impossible to police the boundaries of archaeology or to cut off any fieldwork, however limited, from the realities of the wider world. Hodder makes a case for a "multivocal" archaeology, for "flows of the past, continua of interpretation." He thinks that archaeology is a way of breaking established patterns of thought and domination in the twenty-first century. Herein lies the challenge for archaeological theory in the future—not to dominate interpretations of the past with sterile reporting and standardization, but to encourage what Hodder (1999) calls "an open and diverse engagement of the past, a participation from multiple perspectives and interests." This engagement has hardly begun, and it represents the promising future of basic archaeological research.

Archaeology as a Profession

The archaeological record is under siege in all parts of the world. Since the 1960s, archaeologists have responded both by supporting legislation and by what was once called "salvage archaeology" and is now known as "cultural resource management" (CRM) or "cultural heritage management." This mushrooming concern with saving and managing the finite archives of the past is now the dominant form of archaeology in many nations, to the point where archaeology is becoming as much a profession as an academic discipline. Some of the most important advances in archaeology are unfolding not in the academic core, but at the periphery, where such concerns as looting, legislative compliance, mass tourism, and reburial or repatriation of ancient skeletal remains are assuming center stage. Increasingly, too, CRM and heritage are a concern of private-sector companies as much as government agencies, as nations everywhere grapple with a tidal wave of destruction, much of it in the hands of professional looters, and with a quantum jump in international and local tourism.

In some countries, like Britain, Egypt, and Mexico, cultural tourism and archaeology are major segments of the economy—with potentially devastating long-term effects on such well-known archaeological sites as the pyramids of Giza, Egypt, and the pueblos of Chaco Canyon, New Mexico. In one of the ironies of the popular appeal of archaeology, they are being loved to death, and archaeologists are often little involved in working out strategies for their long-term survival. Conservation and management of the archaeological record will be the dominant and overwhelming theme of the archaeology of the future. It cannot be otherwise, simply because the record is vanishing before our eyes like rapidly melting snow.

Conservation and Public Outreach

Until recently, archaeological conservation all too often has been thought of as little more than stabilizing a fragile basket or reconstructing broken pots, or the stabilization of an ancient structure. In fact, conservation of the archaeological record has to begin from the moment a site is identified and disturbed in any way. We are moving into an era when all archaeologists will have to receive training in conservation as an integral part of their graduate curricula, and when conservation concerns will lie at the very center of all research, indeed will become its first priority. This may slow down the pace of acquiring new knowledge about the past, but the stakes for the long-term future are simply too high for priorities to be ordered any other way.

Conservation means far more than cultural resource management, legislation, and management of archaeological sites impacted by tourism. It also means inculcating into human societies everywhere the notion that archaeology has an important role to play in the contemporary world, as a way of understanding our biological and cultural differences, our origins, and our identities. We are concerned here with the ethics of living in a world surrounded by unique and irreplaceable archives of the past—ethics that outlaw collecting for personal profit, respect the cultural traditions of others, and insist that the past be preserved for future generations, sometimes at high cost to society. Only recently have archaeologists become aware of the critical importance of reaching out to the wider audience—of general archaeological education, often called "public archaeology." Public archaeology depends on what Ian Hodder called an "engaged archaeology," where the past interfaces with and informs the present and the future, and has diverse voices. We are still a long way from achieving this ideal, but a start has been made. Public outreach, or public archaeology, will grow by leaps and bounds in the future.

We have come a long way from the days of William Stukeley or Austen Henry Layard, from an archaeological world of high adventure and treasure hunting. By the year 2000, archaeology had become a highly sophisticated multidisciplinary science. Now we stand at a significant watershed, where archaeology is under a potential death sentence, unless its practitioners concentrate almost single-mindedly not on archaeological discovery, but on preserving what is left of the past for the future. This is the greatest challenge of the future, and a challenge we have barely begun to address. Whatever the responses to this challenge, we can be certain of one thing. The archaeologist of A.D. 2200 will be as distant from us as we are from Victorian gentlemen in top hats shoveling their way into burial mounds.

Summary

Chapter 14 briefly summarizes some of the major developments that are likely in the archaeology of the future, beginning with the potential for archaeological discovery. The most spectacular and important discoveries of the next century are likely to be made outside familiar archaeological territory, in regions like China, central Asia, southern and southeast Asia, and sub-Saharan Africa, where much major work remains to be carried out. Methodologically, we are likely to see increasingly fine-grained methods and techniques for reconstructing even minute details of the past. Nonintrusive archaeology and remote sensing are likely to become increasingly important as the archaeological record is destroyed.

Theoretical advances are likely to come from many directions, among them more refined processualism, cognitive-processual archaeology, and an increasing concern with individuals and groups and their roles in decision making in the past. We will also see evolutionary archaeology, genetics, and cultural resource management making major contributions to archaeological theory. And, for the first time, we may witness the emergence of an original body of archaeological theory, which borrows but little from other disciplines, as has been the case in the past.

Some of the greatest advances in archaeology will come from its increasing transformation from an academic discipline into a profession, to the point where conservation and management of the past will become the dominant activity of the archaeological community. The future of the past, and of archaeology, depends on our developing an archaeology that is fully engaged with society as a whole.

Guide to Further Reading

Hegmon, Michelle. 2003. "Setting Theoretical Egos Aside: Issues and Theory in North American Archaeology." *American Antiquity* 68(2):213–243.

An excellent summary of the current state of archaeological theory in North American archaeology.

Hodder, Ian. 1999. *An Archaeological Perspective.* Oxford: Blackwell.

Hodder provides a short, closely argued essay on the current state of archaeology.

glossary

Archaeological Sites and Cultural Terms

Sites in this Glossary are in **bold** in the main text. By no means are all sites mentioned in the text described here. Those referred to in passing are usually placed in context as part of the narrative and no further mention is required.

Abu Hureyra, Syria Early farming village near the Euphrates River, which dates to before 11,700 B.P. and was finally abandoned in about 6000 B.C.

Abu Simbel, Egypt Temple of Pharaoh Rameses II with a magnificent façade overlooking the Nile in Lower Nubia. Completed in 1244 B.C.

Acheulian An early Stone Age cultural complex widely used by archaic humans in Africa, Asia, and Europe, c. 1.9 million to 200,000 years ago.

Agade, Iraq A major Sumerian city and city-state, third millennium B.C.

Altar de Sacrificios, Guatemala Maya center conquered by non-Classic Maya neighbors in the ninth century A.D.

Anau, Turkestan An oasis city dating back to as early as 3000 B.C. and an important Bronze Age trade center.

Andean A generic term used to describe the area of South America where state-organized societies (civilizations) arose.

Assur, Iraq Capital of the Assyrian civilization c. 1200 B.C.

Aurignacian culture Upper Palaeolithic culture named after the Aurignac site in southwestern France, dating to c. 30,000 B.P.

Avebury, England A stone circle and earthwork complex that was part of a long-lived sacred landscape in southern Britain. Built by Stone Age farmers, c. 2500 B.C.

Baalbek, Syria Phoenician city famous for its spectacular Roman ruins, whose golden age began in 15 B.C.

Barton Ramie, Belize Maya center of the late first millennium A.D.

Behistun, Iran Polished rock face bearing a trilingual inscription commemorating King Darius's victory over rebels in 522 B.C. The inscription helped in the decipherment of cuneiform script.

Biskupin, Poland Late Bronze Age–Iron Age fortified village of the seventh and eighth-centuries B.C. remarkable for its well-preserved material culture.

Canyon de Chelly, New Mexico Location of a group of important Ancestral Pueblo settlements. Late first to early second millennium A.D. and later.

Cape Geledonya, Turkey Site of a Bronze Age shipwreck that contained copper and tin ingots, also bronze tolls and pottery. Thirteenth century B.C.

Carchemish, Syria   Important Hittite city of the second millennium B.C., strategically located near a ford across the Euphrates River. Carchemish was later an important Roman frontier city.

Çatalhöyük, Turkey   Stone Age farming village dating to c. 6000 B.C. and earlier, remarkable for its richly decorated shrines, which prospered from the obsidian trade.

Chaco Canyon, New Mexico   A major Ancestral Pueblo cultural focus in the late first and early second millennium A.D. Famous for its "great houses."

Chavín Horizon, Peru   A widespread iconography and art style that spread widely through highland and lowland Peru after 900 B.C.

Chichén Itzá, Mexico   Maya ceremonial center in the Central Yucatán whose apogee was after A.D. 1100.

Chimu state, Peru   A major North Coast state, which flourished c. A.D. 1200 and was conquered by the Inca in 1476.

Colonial Williamsburg, Virginia   Seventeenth-century colonial settlement in Virginia reconstructed with the aid of archaeological research.

Copán, Honduras   Major Maya city dating from before A.D. 435 to the ninth century.

Cranborne Chase, England   A vast tract of southern England, famous for its many Neolithic, Bronze Age, and Iron Age monuments, also for Roman sites, many excavated by General Augustus Lane Fox Pitt Rivers in the 1880s. Fourth millennium B.C. and later.

Cro-Magnon, France   Rock shelter near Les Eyzies in southwestern France where the first modern human burials from the late Ice Age were found. The people of the late Ice Age were named after the site. Burials date from c. 20,000 B.P.

Dunhuang, China   Buddhist shrines founded by Chinese monks after A.D. 366.

el-Amarna, Egypt   Capital of the heretic pharaoh Akhenaten, 1350–1334 B.C.

el-Kahun, Egypt   Middle Kingdom worker's town dating to the nineteenth century B.C. Associated with the mortuary complex of Pharaoh Senusret II (1897–1878 B.C.).

Emeryville mound, California   Shell midden in the San Francisco Bay area first occupied about three thousand years ago and into the second millennium A.D.

Fort Ancient culture, Ohio   An earthwork-building culture contemporary with the Mississippian. Early second millennium A.D.

Gallehus, Denmark   A Danish village where a golden horn was discovered in 1639, a second in 1734. Fifth century A.D.

Gamble's Cave, Kenya   Stone Age cave excavated by Louis Leakey containing well-documented Late Stone Age occupation, dating to as early as 3000 B.C.

Ghurab, Egypt   Eighteenth Dynasty community of the New Kingdom, dating to 1570–1293 B.C. Famous for the discovery of Mycenaean painted vessels in its deposits.

Giza, Egypt   The location of the three greatest Old Kingdom Pyramids, c. 2550 B.C.

Gournia, Crete   A Minoan town of the second millennium B.C.

Great Zimbabwe, Zimbabwe   A shrine and chieftain center in South Central Africa with an economy based on cattle herding and long-distance trade in gold and ivory, c. A.D. 1100 to 1450.

Hadar, Ethiopia   Desert region in northeast Africa famous for its fossil-bearing beds, which have yielded *Australopithecus afarensis* and *Ardipithecus ramidus*. Hominid occupation dates to before 2.5 million years ago.

Hadrian's Wall, England   Great Roman frontier fortification built right across northern England to keep out the Scots on the orders of Emperor Hadrian, A.D. 122 to 130.

Harappa, Pakistan   City of the Harappan civilization in the Indus Valley in its heyday, c. 2000 B.C.

Harappan civilization   A preindustrial civilization based in the Indus and Saraswati Valleys in south Asia, c. 2600 to 1800 B.C.

Hawara, Egypt   Egypto-Roman cemetery of A.D. 100 to 250, remarkable for the portraits painted on the sarcophagi.

Herculaneum, Italy   Roman town buried by an eruption of Mount Vesuvius, A.D. 79.

Hissarlik, Turkey   Important Bronze and Iron Age city in northeastern Turkey, which was once Homeric Troy. First to second millennium B.C.

Hittite civilization   A major eastern Mediterranean civilization of the second millennium B.C. and an important competitor of ancient Egypt.

Hopewell complex   An extensive set of shared religious beliefs, reflected in distinctive mortuary customs and earthworks throughout the Midwest. Early first millennium A.D.

Hoxne, England   A village in eastern England famous for the discovery of Acheulian hand axes and the bones of extinct animals by John Frere, 1797. c. 250,000 years old.

Hvidegaard, Denmark   Bronze Age burial mound dating to c. 2100 B.C. excavated by Christian Jurgensen Thomsen.

Jarmo, Iraq   An early farming village in the Zagros foothills dating to c. 6000 B.C.

Jericho, Jordan   An ancient city with extensive Stone Age farming towns and villages dating back to c. 9000 B.C., as well as prolonged Bronze and Iron Age occupation.

Karnak, Egypt   Major temple of the ancient Egyptian sun god Amun at the city of Was-et (now Luxor), especially after 1500 B.C.

Key Marco, Florida   Ancient Calusa Indian settlement over shell mounds, remarkable for its finely preserved artifacts. A.D. 500 to 900.

Khorsabad, Iraq   Palace city of Assyrian King Sargon (721–705 B.C.).

Khotan Empire, China   An important kingdom on the Silk Road between China and the west, conquered by Islam in the eighth century A.D.

Knossos, Crete   Palace of the legendary kingdom of King Minos, a site first occupied as early as 6100 B.C. and finally abandoned in about 1400 B.C.

Koster, Illinois   Important stratified site in the Midwest's Illinois Valley, which documents hunter-gather occupation before 8000 B.C. until about three thousand years ago.

Kuyunjik (Nineveh), Iraq   The palace city of Assyrian King Sennacherib (704–681 B.C.).

Labná, Mexico   Late Classic Maya center, ninth to tenth centuries A.D.

La Chapelle-aux-Saints, France   A cave in France's Dordogne that yielded a Neanderthal burial in 1908, dating about 50,000 B.P. The arthritic skeleton led to misinterpretations of Neanderthals as shambling humans.

Laetoli, Tanzania   Site where hominid footprints were discovered, dating to 3.6 million years ago, probably those of *Australopithecus afarensis.*

Lagash, Iraq   A major Sumerian city and city-state of the third millennium B.C.

La Madeleine, France   Upper Palaeolithic rock shelter, famous as the type site of the Magdalenian culture, c. 17,000 B.P.

Lepenski Vir, Serbia   Mesolithic and early farming settlements in the Iron Gorge region of the Danube River Valley, dating to between 6000 and 5000 B.C.

Little Woodbury, England   Iron Age village in southern England occupied from the fourth to second centuries B.C., at which a single round house lay inside an oval ditched enclosure.

Luxor, Egypt   Temple of the sun god Amun in Was-et, now Luxor. In its heyday after 1500 B.C.

Machu Picchu, Peru   An important Inca town high in the Andes, c. A.D. 1300 to 1450.

Magdalenian culture, western Europe   A late Ice Age culture that reached its climax in southwestern France and northern Spain, c. 17,000 B.P.

Maiden Castle, England   Iron Age hill fort with elaborate fortifications that were attacked and overthrown by the Romans in A.D. 43.

Makapansgat, South Africa   A bone cave containing fractured animal bones and hominid fragments, c. 1 million years ago, which formed part of a predator den.

Martin's Hundred, Virginia   Colonial settlement and plantation established in 1619 and destroyed by Indians in 1622. The center of the plantation was known as Wolstenholme Towne.

Meilgaard, Denmark   Shell mound of the Mesolithic Maglemose culture, c. 6000 B.C.

Mesa Verde, Colorado   A major center of Ancestral Pueblo culture, A.D. 1000 to 1250. The largest pueblo is the Cliff Palace.

Mesoamerica   That area of highland and lowland Central America where state-organized societies (civilizations) came into being.

Mesolithic   From the Greek, *mesos* and *lithos,* "middle" and "stone," whence *Middle Stone Age,* a term applied to Stone Age hunter-gatherer cultures dating to after the late Ice Age. Mainly used in Europe.

Mezhirich, Ukraine   A settlement of mammoth bone houses erected by Late Ice Age people, c. 14,000 years ago.

Minoan civilization, Crete   Bronze Age civilization centered on Knossos, Crete, that reached its heyday in the second millennium B.C., collapsing c. 1450 B.C.

Moche state, Peru   Major Andean state that controlled major river valleys on Peru's North Coast, c. 200 B.C. to A.D. 650.

Mohenjodaro, Pakistan   City of the Harappan civilization at its apogee, c. 2000 B.C.

Mount Carmel caves, Israel   Stone Age caves with a long sequence of Neanderthal and later occupation dating back to c. 75,000 years ago. A crucial location for the study of the origins of modern humans.

Mycenae, Greece   Citadel and burial place of important Mycenaean lords, c. 1400 B.C.

Mycenaean civilization   Bronze Age civilization on mainland Greece, late second millennium B.C.

Naqada, Egypt   Predynastic kingdom and important trading town in Upper Egypt, c. 3400–3100 B.C.

Neander Valley, Germany   Location of the first discovery of remains of *Homo sapiens neanderthalis* in 1856, c. 75,000 B.P.

Neolithic,   or New Stone Age, from the Greek—*neos*, "new," and *lithos*, "stone." Refers to Stone Age farming cultures.

Newark, Ohio   Extensive Hopewell earthwork complex of the early first millennium A.D.

Nimrud, Iraq   Assyrian city, with the palaces of kings Assurbanipal (883–859 B.C.), Esarhaddon (680–669 B.C.), and Tiglath-Pileser (774–727 B.C.).

Nippur, Iraq   Sumerian city famous for its temple archives. Third millennium B.C.

Obermeilen, Switzerland   Farming village dating to c. 4000 B.C., famous for its waterlogged artifacts and other organic remains.

Olduvai Gorge, Tanzania   A deep gorge in Tanzania's Serengeti Plains that cuts through deep lake beds. Hominids lived along its shores from about two million to 100,000 years ago.

Olorgesaillie, Kenya   Lakeside settlement in Kenya's Rift Valley occupied by Stone Age hunters 300,000 years ago.

Olsen-Chubbock, Colorado   A Paleo-Indian bison kill site of c. 6500 B.C.

Olympia, Greece   Site of the Olympic games in southern Greece from the fifth century B.C. onward.

Pachacamac, Peru   An important shrine on Peru's South Coast, which was revered by the Inca and their predecessors.

Palaeolithic   Old Stone Age, after the Greek *paleos*, "old," and *lithos*, "stone." A term used to describe human cultures from the earliest times up to the end of the Ice Age.

Palenque, Mexico   Major Maya city and ceremonial center of the first millennium A.D. associated with an important dynasty of Maya lords, A.D. 421 to 799.

Palmyra, Syria   A prosperous Roman caravan city, celebrated for the Temple of Bel and other fine ruins during the early first millennium A.D.

Pazyryk, Siberia   Burial mounds dating to 400 B.C. in the Altai Mountains containing richly adorned burials of horsemen.

Peacock's Farm, England   A Mesolithic site in peat deposits, c. 6000 B.C.

Pecos Pueblo, New Mexico Major pueblo complex, which provided an archaeological sequence from historic times back to the first millennium A.D. Site of Alfred Kidder's pioneer excavations.

Persepolis, Iran Residence of the Achaemenid kings captured by Alexander the Great in 331 B.C.

Petra, Jordan A Nabatean and Roman caravan city of the first millennium A.D.

Philae, Egypt An island in the middle of the Nile by the First Cataract, famed for its magnificent Temple of Isis, dating to the late first millennium B.C. and finally abandoned only in A.D. 550.

Pompeii, Italy Roman town buried by an eruption of Mount Vesuvius A.D. 79.

Port Royal, Jamaica Caribbean town that was a buccaneers' haven between A.D. 1655 and 1675. Two-thirds of the town was destroyed and submerged by an earthquake and tidal waves on June 7, 1692.

Pueblo Bonito, New Mexico Ancestral Pueblo "great house" dating to after A.D. 650 to 1150.

Quirigua, Guatemala A small but important Maya city, founded more than two thousand years ago and occupied until the tenth century A.D.

Rusinga Island, Kenya Location where a 20-million-year-old specimen of *Proconsul africanus* came to light in 1951.

Samothrace, Greece Northern Aegean island settled as early as 700 B.C., famous into Hellenic times for its shrine of the Cabiri deities.

Saqqara, Egypt Site of Pharaoh Djoser's Step Pyramid and the burial places of other Egyptian kings. Third millennium B.C.

Seibal, Guatemala Classic Maya center at the height of its power A.D. 770 to 900, as other Maya centers were declining.

Signal Butte, Nebraska A stratified site in western Nebraska that had sporadic occupation from about 2500 B.C. to the historic period.

Silchester, England Romano-British town of the second century A.D.

Silk Road Ancient caravan routes that connected China with the west through Central Asia.

Similaun, Italy Site of a burial of a Bronze Age man high in the Alps, dating to c. 3200 B.C.

Sipán, Peru Major center of the Moche state on Peru's North Coast that yielded three burials of warrior-priests, c. A.D. 400.

Skara Brae, Scotland A Stone Age farming village dating to between 3100 and 2500 B.C., remarkable for its stone-built houses and interior stone furniture.

Star Carr, England A Mesolithic hunting camp in northeastern England famous for its organic finds, located in a birch-forested environment and dating to 8700 to 8400 B.C.

Stonehenge, England A stone circle complex in southern England associated with solar alignments. Its heyday was in about 1800 B.C.

Sumerian civilization, Iraq The first major civilization in southern Mesopotamia, which appeared c. 3100 B.C.

Sutton Hoo, England   An Anglo-Saxon ship burial, thought to be that of King Raedwald, who died in A.D. 625.

Taung, South Africa   Site of the original discovery of *Australopithecus africanus* in 1924.

Taxila, Pakistan   A trading city in northwestern Pakistan occupied as early as 2000 B.C. and settled more or less continuously until A.D. 200.

Tehuacán Valley, Mexico   A highland Mexican valley celebrated for its dry caves and evidence of early maize agriculture, c. 2500 B.C.

Telloh, Iraq   Sumerian city and city-state of the third millennium B.C.

Teotihuacán, Mexico   A major city and state on the edge of the Valley of Mexico that enjoyed extensive trade relations with Maya civilization c. 200 B.C. to A.D. 750.

Tiwanaku, Bolivia   Important Andean state and ceremonial center around Lake Titicaca that flourished during the first millennium A.D.

Tollund, Denmark   Site of a bog body dating to c. 2000 years ago.

Ukhaidir, Iraq   Abbassid palace built A.D. 774–775 by Isa ibn Musa remarkable for its innovative architecture using brick vaulting.

Ur, Iraq   The biblical city of Calah, also a major Sumerian city, at the height of its powers c. 2300 B.C. Ur was uncovered by Leonard Woolley in classic excavations before World War II.

Uxmal, Mexico   Late Classic Puuc Maya center whose heyday was A.D. 800 to 1000.

Valley of the Kings, Egypt   An arid valley on the west bank of the Nile River at Luxor, which was the burial place of Egypt's New Kingdom pharaohs, 1500 to 1070 B.C.

Verulamium, England   Romano-British city (modern St. Albans), founded soon after the Roman conquest of A.D. 43.

Virú Valley, Peru   A heavily settled valley on Peru's North Coast occupied for more than 3,000 years. Well known because of Gordon Willey's pioneer settlement research there.

Yassi Ada, Turkey   Site of a Byzantine shipwreck of the seventh century A.D.

Zhoukoudian, China   A deep cave containing numerous animal bones, stone artifacts, and fossils of *Homo erectus,* dating to c. 400,000 to 250,000 B.P.

references

Belzoni, Giovanni. 1822. *Narrative of the Operations and Recent Discoveries within the Pyramids, Temples, Tombs, and Excavations in Egypt and Nubia.* London: John Murray.

Binford, Lewis R. 1968. "Archaeological Perspectives." In *New Perspectives in Archaeology.* S. R. Binford and L. R. Binford, eds. Pp. 5–32. Hawthorne, NY: Aldine.

_____. 1972. *An Archaeological Perspective.* New York: Seminar Press.

_____. 1981. "Behavioral Archaeology and the Pompeii Promise." *Journal of Anthropological Research* 37:195–198.

_____. 1983. *In Pursuit of the Past.* London and New York: Thames and Hudson.

Bintcliff, John. 1991. "Post-modernism, Rhetoric, and Scholasticism at TAG: The Current State of British Archeological Theory." *Antiquity* 65(247):274–278.

Clark, Grahame. 1989. *Prehistory at Cambridge and Beyond.* Cambridge: Cambridge University Press.

Daniel, Glyn. 1981. *A Short History of Archaeology.* London and New York: Thames and Hudson.

Dart, Raymond. 1925. "*Australopithecus africanus:* The Man-Ape of Southern Africa." *Nature* 115:195.

Darwin, Charles. 1871. *The Descent of Man, and selection in relation to sex.* London: John Murray.

Droop, J. P. 1915. *Archaeological Excavation.* Cambridge: Cambridge University Press.

Fagan, Brian. 1979. *Return to Babylon.* Boston: Little, Brown.

Flannery, Kent V., and Joyce Marcus. 1993. "Cognitive Archaeology." *Cambridge Archaeological Journal* 3(2):260–267.

Green, Charles. 1963. *Sutton Hoo: The Excavations of a Royal Ship Burial.* London: Merlin Press.

Haven, Samuel. 1856. *The Archaeology of the United States.* Washington, D.C.: Smithsonian Institution.

Jefferson, Thomas. 1788. *Notes on the State of Virginia.* Philadelphia: Pritchard and Hall.

Kroeber, Alfred. 1909. "The Archaeology of California." In *Anthropological Essays Presented to Frederic Ward Putnam in Honor of His Seventieth Birthday, April 16, 1909, by His Friends and Associates.* Editorial Committee, eds. New York: Stechert.

Layard, A. H. 1849. *Nineveh and Its Remains.* London: John Murray.

Leakey, M. D., and Harris, J. D. 1990. *Laetoli: A Pliocene Site in Northern Tanzania.* Oxford: Oxford University Press.

Lynch, Barbara D., and Thomas F. Lynch. 1968. "The Beginnings of a Scientific Approach to Prehistoric Archaeology in Seventeenth- and Eighteenth-Century Britain." *Southwestern Journal of Anthropology* 24(1):33–65.

Mallowan, Max. 1977. *Mallowan's Memoirs.* New York: Dodd, Mead.

Martin, Paul S., George I. Quimby, and Donald Collier. 1947. *Indians before Columbus.* Chicago: University of Chicago Press.

Mirsky, Jeannette. 1977. *Sir Aurel Stein: Archaeological Explorer.* Chicago: University of Chicago Press.

Montelius, Oscar. 1986. *Dating in the Bronze Age: with special reference to Scandinavia.* Stockholm: Kugl. Vitterhets Historie och Antikvitets akademie (Originally published in 1885).

Oates, Joan. 1979. *Babylon.* London and New York: Thames and Hudson.

Stein, Aurel. 1912. *The Ruins of Desert Cathay.* London: Macmillan.

Stephens, John Lloyd. 1841. *Incidents of Travel in Central America, Chiapas, and Yucatan.* New York: Harpers.

Tedlock, Dennis. 1996. *Popol Vuh.* New York: Simon and Schuster.

Thomas, Cyrus. 1894. *Report on the Mound Explorations of the Bureau of Ethnology.* Washington, D.C.: Smithsonian Institution.

Trigger, Bruce G. 1991. "Distinguished Lecture in Archaeology: Constraint and Freedom." *American Anthropologist* 9(93):551–569.

White, Leslie. 1949. *The Evolution of Culture.* New York: McGraw-Hill.

Woolley, Leonard. 1929. *Ur of the Chaldees.* London: Edward Benn.

credits

Phillip V. Tobias; page 185: John Reader/Science Photo Library/Photo Researchers, Inc.; page 187: © Silkeborg Museum, Denmark; page 189: Joe Ben Wheat/University of Colorado Museum—Boulder.

Chapter 12

Page 196: Historical Royal Palaces Enterprises Ltd.; page 209: Jack Unruh/NGS Image Collection; page 210: Robert Harding World Imagery; page 211 (top): The Bridgeman Art Library International Ltd.; page 211 (bottom): D. Baston, Center for American Archaeology, Kampsville.

Chapter 13

Page 214: Wessex Archaeology; page 216: Wieslav Smetek/Stern/Black Star; page 223: Painting by Percy Fiestas. Courtesy Bruning Archaeological Museum, Lambayeque; page 224: Drawing by Donna McClelland; page 227: Tim Hall/Getty Images, Inc.—Photodisc; page 228: South Carolina Institute of Archaeology and Anthropology, University of South Carolina, Columbia.

Chapter 14

Page 235: © Copyright: All rights reserved. Adriel Heisey Photography.

Page 279: University of California at Santa Barbara.

index

Note: Page numbers for figures are followed by *f*.

about the author

Brian Fagan is one of the leading archaeological writers in the world and an internationally recognized authority on world prehistory. He studied archaeology and anthropology at Pembroke College, Cambridge University, and then spent seven years in sub-Saharan Africa working in museums and in monuments conservation and excavating early farming sites in Zambia and East Africa. He was one of the pioneers of multidisciplinary African history in the 1960s. Since 1967, he has been Professor (now Emeritus Professor) of Anthropology at the University of California, Santa Barbara, where he has specialized in lecturing and writing about archaeology to wide audiences.

Professor Fagan has written six best-selling textbooks: *Ancient Lives: An Introduction to Archaeology; In the Beginning; Archaeology: A Brief Introduction; People of the Earth; World Prehistory;* and *Ancient Civilizations* with Chris Scarre—all published by Prentice Hall—which are used around the world. His general books include *The Rape of the Nile,* a classic history of Egyptology; *The Adventure of Archaeology; Time Detectives; Floods, Famines, and Emperors: El Niño and the Fate of Civilizations; Ancient North America; The Little Ice Age;* and *The Long Summer.* He is General Editor of the *Oxford Companion to Archaeology.* In addition, he has published several scholarly monographs on African archaeology and numerous specialized articles in national and international journals. He is also an expert on multimedia teaching and received the Society for American Archaeology's first Public Education Award for his indefatigable efforts on behalf of archaeology and education.

Brian Fagan's others interests include bicycling, sailing, kayaking, and good food. He is married and lives in Santa Barbara with his wife and daughter, four cats (who supervise his writing), and last but not least, a minimum of five rabbits.